Teaching Secondary Geography
as if the Planet Matters

Young people are growing up in a culture where they are increasing
and warnings of environmental 'crisis'. In recent years, climate change, loss
destruction of biomes, natural disasters and the challenges of a rapidly urbanising world has
all become significant issues. More recently, the economic crisis has raised questions about the
viability of the high-mobility, high-consumption lifestyles associated with advanced capitalist
societies.

Schools are important places where young people can learn about and begin to understand
these complex questions, and school geography is a subject that focuses on all of the above
issues. However, this thought-provoking text argues that, in its present form, the simple
models of people and environment found in school geography serve to inhibit understanding
of the causes of environmental problems, and that there is an urgent need to promote
approaches to curriculum development that, drawing from advances in human and
environmental geography, can help students understand the nature of the contemporary
world.

Features include:

- examples of suggested teaching activities;
- questions and activities for further study;
- detailed case studies;
- sources of further reading and information.

The true worth of a school subject is revealed in how far it can account for and address
the major issues of the time. The issue of the environment cuts across subject boundaries
and requires an interdisciplinary response. Geography teachers are part of that response,
and they have a crucial role in helping students to react to environmental issues and
representations.

John Morgan is Reader in Geography Education at the Graduate School of Education,
University of Bristol and at the Institute of Education, University of London.

Teaching School Subjects as if the Planet Matters

Series Editors: John Morgan (University of Bristol and Institute of Education, London) and Sasha Matthewman (University of Bristol)

We live in a time when there are serious questions about the ability of the planet to sustain current levels of economic development. Future generations are likely to face a bleaker environmental future and will need to learn how to mitigate and adapt to the effects of climate change. However, despite the obvious importance of these issues, most schooling continues with little direct engagement with questions of environmental change.

The true worth of a school subject is revealed in how far it can account for, and respond to, the major issues of the time. This series aims to inform teachers about environmental issues and offer inspiration for teaching lessons with critical environmental awareness. It asserts that only by helping pupils to recognise and understand the multi-dimensional nature of these issues will they be able to contribute to society's attempts to deal with rapid natural and human-induced environmental change.

Teaching Secondary Geography as if the Planet Matters

John Morgan

Routledge
Taylor & Francis Group

LONDON AND NEW YORK

First published 2012
by Routledge
2 Park Square, Milton Park, Abingdon, Oxon OX14 4RN

Simultaneously published in the USA and Canada
by Routledge
711 Third Avenue, New York, NY 10017

Routledge is an imprint of the Taylor & Francis Group, an informa business

British Library Cataloguing in Publication Data
A catalogue record for this book is available from the British Library

Library of Congress Cataloging-in-Publication Data
Morgan, John.
    Teaching secondary geography as if the planet matters / by John Morgan.
    p. cm. – (Teaching ... as if the Planet Matters)
    Includes bibliographical references and index.
    1. Geography – Study and teaching (Secondary) I. Title.
    G73.M616 2011
    910.71'2 – dc22
    2010053255

ISBN: 978-0-415-56387-1 (hbk)
ISBN: 978-0-415-56388-8 (pbk)
ISBN: 978-0-203-81045-3 (ebk)

Typeset in Bembo by
Saxon Graphics Ltd, Derby

MIX
Paper from
responsible sources
FSC
www.fsc.org   FSC® C004839

Printed and bound in Great Britain by
CPI Antony Rowe, Chippenham, Wiltshire

Contents

Introduction

People can't change the way they use resources without changing their relations with one another. For example there are dozens of ways to economize energy: some would stop the rich wasting it, others would freeze the poor to death. Forests or beaches or country landscapes can be conserved to be enjoyed by many, by few, or by nobody. Rich and poor can be made to contribute very fairly or very unfairly to the costs of reducing pollution. Old city streets and neighbourhoods can be conserved for the people who live in them, or they can be conserved by methods which drive those people out, bring richer people in and make speculative fortunes for the richer still. How to conserve is usually a harder question than whether, or what, to conserve.

(Stretton, 1976: 3)

This book has its origins in the late 1980s. At that time in Britain, there was a surge in media interest in environmental issues. A range of global environmental events, including tropical rainforest deforestation, acid deposition, desertification and the greenhouse effect, all stories that had rumbled on through the decade, now seemed to come together to create a 'perfect storm'. In March 1989, *The Sunday Times* magazine had a cover that posed the question, 'The Earth is dying. What are you going to do about it?' I remember that cover because I had just started out as a geography teacher and I used it in my lessons on 'the environmental crisis' (a significant number of pupils at that time were aware of, and concerned about, environmental issues). Macnaghten and Urry (1998) confirm that during the late 1980s, 'the environment had become firmly established as a major issue of British politics and culture'. Prime Minister Margaret Thatcher's 1988 speech to the Royal Society argued that global environmental issues were an important concern; membership of environmental campaigning organisations such as Greenpeace and Friends of the Earth soared; and Elkington and Hailes' (1988) *The green consumer guide* was published (within a year it had been reprinted eleven times and sold 350,000 copies).

But there was a particular way of thinking about the environment that was problematic for geography teachers. It tended to suggest that the 'cause' (and therefore the 'solution') of these environmental issues was individuals. As *The Sunday Times* magazine article explained:

1

You damage the earth just by living on it. You burn fossil fuels – petrol, oil, coal – and huge amounts more are burnt by those who supply you with goods and services. You create waste, which has to be buried, burnt, or discharged into the sea. You accept the profits of investments which are trading on Third World poverty and putting further strain on already over-stretched resources. You buy goods from farms and factories whose ill-effects from chemical wastes range all the way from dead fish to dead people.

In those early days as a geography teacher, I was very concerned to find ways to counter this view that individuals were to blame for environmental problems, and the implication that they could just as easily solve them through better consumption choices. In developing teaching approaches, I was inspired by the work of Ron Johnston (1989), David Pepper (1984) and, especially, John Huckle (1988), whose geographical perspective insisted on the importance of understanding that environmental issues were as much about people's relations with one another as about people's relationships with the environment. As Hugh Stretton (quoted overleaf) states: 'People can't change the way they use resources without changing their relations with one another.'

It was significant that I was attempting to develop this approach to geography teaching in the days prior to the introduction of a National Curriculum; as I argue later in this book, one of the effects of that educational innovation was to shift responsibility for curriculum construction away from teachers, and instead to encourage teachers to see themselves as experts in 'learning'. While this is important, the effect has been to make it difficult for many teachers to read and think deeply about the nature of the subject – geography – they teach. That is why the emphasis in this book is on teaching – I am concerned with what geography as a discipline has to say about people–environment (or society–nature) relations, and what that means for curriculum development.

This focus on the perspectives of geography as a subject is ever more important at a time when teachers are urged to teach about climate change and sustainability. Before we rush into devising schemes of work and activities to 'deliver' these curriculum aims, surely it is important that we understand how geographers themselves conceptualise these topics?

In the past two decades, geographers working in this area have continued to develop understanding of the relations between society and nature. However, while in the 1980s human geographers were strongly influenced by models of political economy, the 1990s and 2000s were characterised by a 'cultural turn', and it became less common to think of the existence of a pre-existing and pristine nature capable of objective and detached study by geographers. Since the publication of Neil Smith's (1984) *Uneven development*, human geographers have explored the idea that nature is a social production. For those working from a political economy perspective, this 'second nature' is produced in the process of accumulation of wealth. For others, adopting a broadly constructionist approach, nature is a 'text' that is produced and interpreted in different ways. In general, geographers are nowadays ready to recognise that there is no single 'nature', but rather multiple 'natures'.

It will be helpful to offer a few caveats before introducing the chapters that make up the book. First, rather than adopting an approach that focuses on geography, it might be thought better to make use of the broader terms 'education for sustainable development' or 'environmental education', or the emerging field of 'ecopedagogy'. While there is useful work emanating from these fields of study, this book responds to the fact that, in the UK, for the moment at least, teachers define themselves as geography teachers, history teachers and so on. While some may wish that teachers would be prepared to give up some attachment to their subject disciplines, this book starts from a recognition that geography teachers spend a good deal of time and energy becoming geographers, and seeks to build on that investment and enthusiasm. As readers will see, contemporary geography is a far from enclosed and insular field of study.

Second, alert readers may have already recognised a tendency to use interchangeably terms such as 'environment', 'nature', 'people' and 'society'. This reflects the fact that these terms are all used in the literature reviewed. To seek purity and consistency of terms would have limited the opportunity to make links between different parts of the literature. In any case, we are sufficiently attuned these days to the power of language, so it is significant when geography texts use words like 'society' rather than specific terms such as 'capitalist society'; or speak of 'people' rather than recognising the existence of 'social classes'. In this book, I try to be attentive to the subtle variations in how terms are used.

Third, the book does not claim to provide geography teachers with a comprehensive survey of contemporary geography's approach to 'nature' or 'environments'. Excellent treatments exist already; for starters, I would recommend Huckle and Martin (2001) *Environments in a changing world*; Castree (2005) *Nature*; Robbins *et al*. (2010) *Environment and society*. My aim has been to write a book addressed specifically to the field of geographical education. The chapters that follow are written to address the concerns of geography teachers who seek to develop approaches that help students to understand the making and remaking of society and nature.

The chapters

Section one: Contexts

Chapter one sets the scene for the book as a whole, setting about the 'battle for ideas' which, I argue, should be the concern of geography education. The chapter explains how, under successive New Labour governments from 1997 to 2010, schools were encouraged to teach pupils about issues of climate change and sustainability in order to help them to play their part in overcoming the problems associated with climate change. This 'state-sponsored' environmental education provoked a backlash from those who argued that the state's involvement in this area is anti-educational and represents a diminished view of humanity's drive to transform nature to increase wealth and well-being. The chapter then considers a recent publication by Jonathan Porritt (2005), a leading figure in the British green movement, which argues the case for a capitalist solution to environmental problems. It concludes with a discussion of those who suggest that what is needed is a transformation of capitalist societies in ways that encourage more relaxed, less consuming lifestyles. Though the arguments discussed in chapter one do not exhaust the range of positions available, they serve to make the point that any discussion of environmental issues cannot be divorced from wider questions of how economy and culture are organised, and this is where geography education can make a contribution to pupils' knowledge and understanding of environmental issues. It is these relations between society and nature that are the focus of the rest of the book.

Chapter two discusses the development of environmental perspectives in the school curriculum. It argues that, while environmental education had its origins in the pre-Second World War period, it was shaped in significant ways by the processes of modernisation that transformed the both the landscapes of Britain and the experience of living in Britain from the mid-1950s to early 1970s. These changes – with the emergence of the motor car and fast road systems, slum clearance and new forms of architecture, and the development of New Towns – were disorienting to many, and led to cultural movements to make sense of (and sometimes resist) the changes. In this period, a distinctive form of 'environmental geography' appeared, one that encouraged pupils to develop 'an eye for the urban country'. Chapter two argues that, while environmental geography was concerned to develop responses to pupils' own localities and environments, in the 1980s there emerged a form of environmental education that adopted a more holistic, global perspective. This came to influence how environmental education was understood, and at times was based on a critique of the school subjects and curriculum, which it viewed as part of a mechanistic worldview. Finally, the chapter notes the way in which education for sustainable development was seen as an intrinsic part of the broader project of 'environmental modernisation' from the mid-1990s.

Chapter three serves as an introduction to the variety of ways in which geography as an academic discipline has conceptualised the relationship between society and nature. The chapter provides some important background to the types of approach – largely based on political ecology and the social construction of nature – that inform the analysis of geographical themes in the middle chapters of the book.

Taken together, the three chapters that make up section one of *Teaching Geography as if the Planet Matters* provide an argument about the importance of the subject as an intellectual resource for helping students understand the relationship between society and nature.

Section two: Themes

This section comprises of five chapters, each of which deals with a theme or themes that are commonly taught in school geography. The aim of the chapters is quite simple: to discuss how each topic might be reviewed to develop more theoretically informed approaches that allow for greater understanding of the processes that shape society–nature relations. This does not mean that the chapters share a common format. Each one attempts to develop an argument that, it is hoped, will be recognisable to school geography teachers. They are starting points for further study and analysis. In this sense, the chapters in this section have a clear pedagogical intent. The references cited will, it is hoped, provide the impetus for further study and reflection. This, in my experience, is how teachers develop intellectually robust approaches to teaching geography.

Chapter four takes the form of an analysis of recent GCSE and AS level specifications, and examines the way they represent the topics of natural hazards and consuming resources. The chapter starts with reference to some earlier critiques of school geography, and asks whether the criticisms that were made in the 1980s about the perspectives offered still hold true.

Chapter five is concerned with the food question. It starts with a discussion of how earlier teaching of the 'geography of agriculture' changed in the light of the shift from a productivist to post-productivist agricultural system from the mid-1980s onwards. The chapter suggests that this opened up the space for a broader discussion of the cultural politics of food, and provides examples of this type of approach. The chapter contains a discussion of recent moves to change the food culture of schools, and suggests how a geographical approach can offer a wider perspective on these issues. The chapter thus points to ways in which geographical knowledge can be applied outside the classroom.

Chapter six recognises that the world is increasingly urbanised, yet the teaching of urban geography in schools tends to focus on social rather than environmental concerns. The chapter is intended as an introduction to work in urban studies, which recognise the way in which urban nature is produced as part of the political economy of cities.

Chapter seven is concerned with the teaching of economic geography in schools. Too often, it suggests, school geography offers pupils simplistic and ideological representations of economic processes. In addition, many geography teachers feel ill equipped to address questions of economic theory. The chapter provides an account of the changing nature of economic geography, paying particular attention to shifts in the nature of capitalism. This approach, it is hoped, will allow teachers to contextualise their teaching of economic geography. The chapter ends on a note of speculation, since it is clear that the financial crisis of 2008 has resulted in the end of one dominant way of producing economic space – neoliberalism – yet it is unclear what comes next. The chapter invites teachers to explore alternatives with their students.

The final chapter in section two discusses the issue of how to teach about climate change to ensure pupils have a strong sense of how it is linked to global economic systems, based on the notion of climate capitalism. This is supported by a short discussion of how systems of mobility might be transformed in the face of climate change and the need for reduced carbon consumption. This leads into a final section on the implications of teaching 'Anthropocene geographies', where humans play a crucial role in shaping Earth systems.

Section three: Practices

This section contains one chapter and a short conclusion, which situate the arguments in this book within the wider context of the development of school geography teaching. Together, these provide an account of how, over time, geography teachers have come to lose control of the curriculum, and assess the prospects for teachers to develop the type of disciplined geography teaching discussed in this book. Though the signs are not always promising, a realistic understanding of the relationship between society and schooling suggests that the advent of a 'post-progress' world offers significant space for geographers to engage pupils with the battle for ideas with which we started this book.

Section one:
Contexts

CHAPTER

1

Geography teaching and the battle for ideas

Introduction

This chapter is concerned with what I term the 'battle for ideas' in geography education. It argues that geography teachers in schools are faced with the challenge of helping young people to make sense of important arguments at a time when the politics of nature are coming to take centre stage in economic, political and cultural life in the affluent world. It is tempting to seek to justify the focus of this chapter, but I think it is beyond doubt that 'environment', 'nature' and 'sustainable development' are already firmly embedded in the language of education and curriculum. For example, the QCDA's (2009) publication *Sustainable development in action* indicates how the environmental challenges society is facing are reflected in official curriculum discussion:

> We need to find a way to live on earth that enables all people to satisfy their basic needs and enjoy quality of life, without compromising the ability of future generations to meet their own needs.
> Most experts agree that our current mode and rate of development on earth is not sustainable. The way we are living is over-taxing the planet's supply of natural resources – from fresh water supplies to fish stocks, from fertile land to clean air. In addition, the inequalities between peoples, both within countries and across the world, are growing.
>
> (QCDA, 2009: 4)

These quotations demonstrate the extent to which the arguments of environmentalists have come to occupy the mainstream of informed educational thinking. Sustainable living is enshrined as a key element in children's educational entitlement:

> Learning about sustainable development can help young people to understand the needs and rights of present and future generations, and to consider the best ways to tackle interrelated challenges such as climate change, inequality and poverty. It can

also motivate learners to want to change things for the better – whether that's on their doorstep or on the other side of the world – equipping them with the skills, knowledge, understanding and values that are crucial to envisaging and creating a sustainable society and future.

(QCDA, 2009: 2)

The QCDA publication makes special mention of the issue of climate change, echoing the New Labour government's view that this represents 'one of the greatest challenges facing our generation'.[1] It argues that cutting the levels of greenhouse gases we produce is one of the most important steps necessary to slow climate change:

Learning about climate change at school has inspired many children and young people to take their messages to the wider community to try and bring about change. They believe that the key to success lies in working as a community and that we can all be part of the solution.

(QCDA, 2009: 5)

This statement makes it clear that learning about sustainable development requires making the link between theory and practice, and appears to encourage forms of 'environmental citizenship' (Dobson and Bell, 2005).

A further indication of government concern for learning about sustainable development was the decision of the Department for Environment, Food and Rural Affairs (Defra) and the Department for Education and Skills (DfES) in 2007 to distribute to all schools a pack entitled *Tomorrow's Climate, Today's Challenge*, which contained a copy of former US Vice-President Al Gore's film *An Inconvenient Truth*. The guidance produced for teachers of science, geography and citizenship stated that the film has had a big impact and that it 'has a huge potential for engaging pupils on a complex subject'. It notes that the film is based on four central scientific hypotheses, all of which 'are regarded as valid by the great majority of scientific opinion worldwide'. However, the advice warns, at times Gore presents evidence that does not accord with the scientific mainstream, and the guidance is designed to help pupils assess the 'validity and credibility of different information sources'. Here, then, is an example of concern to develop forms of scientific and sustainability literacy, being able to understand, interpret and, if necessary, challenge popular representations of environmental issues.

To summarise this section: since 1997, education for sustainable development has become an integral part of the National Curriculum and an important element in school improvement, with the aim that all schools are Sustainable Schools by 2020. These developments should be seen as part of the UK government's wider attempt to bring about environmental modernisation. Advice and guidance on how to deliver these initiatives is available (see www.teachernet.gov.uk/sustainableschools).

Geographers against progress?

At this point, we should acknowledge that not everyone welcomes the moves to introduce learning for sustainable development in schools, and some argue that this state-sponsored promotion of sustainable development and action on climate change is anti-educational. For example, Austin Williams' (2008) book *The enemies of progress*[2] includes a chapter called 'The indoctrinators', which argues that 'critical thinking has been redefined, especially around the "givens" of sustainability and environmentalism':

> Now there is an automatic assumption of a prior knowledge that climate change is the problem and the only point of classroom learning is a fine-tuning exercise to work out what to do about it. From nursery to university, from science to geography, education has primarily become a route for teaching political environmentalism.
>
> (Williams, 2008: 74)

Williams provides examples of attempts to teach environmental messages in schools. These include:

- a year 6 science project exploring 'the role of the caretaker, the amount of oil used by the school, and the school's fuel and electricity bills' as part of a sustainable science project

- the Designs of the time (Dott) programme targeted at year 8 pupils, which asked them to 'redesign some aspect of their school making it more user-friendly, with less impact on the environment and the planet's natural resources'.

For Williams, these represent a 'brazen attempt to manipulate children into the new green morality'. He concludes that:

> Education has become less of an arena to learn, to be challenged, to critically analyse, to develop abstract thinking, and to lay the ground rules for a genuine sense of intellectual enquiry, and instead has become a means of winning the hearts and minds of a compliant future generation. Unfortunately, this means that any lessons that could be learned are missed in the blinkered attempt to see everything in a framework of the morally-loaded sustainability orthodoxy.
>
> (Williams, 2008: 79)

Thus *The enemies of progress* is concerned with what the author sees as society's loss of belief in the idea of progress:

> The future, today, is regularly viewed with foreboding, experimentation is frequently discouraged as unnecessarily risky, and progress itself is presented as a fallacy. Man has gone from being a solution, to becoming seen as the problem.
>
> (Williams, 2008: 2)

11

Similar arguments are made by Worldwrite, an education charity that describes itself as committed to global equality. It is critical of what it regards as an anti-modern, tentative approach to the solution of problems such as global poverty and underdevelopment. It explains that its slogan, 'Ferraris for all', means demanding the best for everyone:

> [...] this means recognising that our peers globally are not different from ourselves and should equally enjoy a great life. This requires we campaign for freedom from toil, hardship and a struggle to survive, to allow us all the freedom to learn at the highest level, to exercise our creativity, advance new knowledge and impact upon society. To make this possible, we support and promote aspirations for the best of everything for all, and campaign for global equality. We want the best of all worlds and this means standing up for unfettered growth, serious development and freedom.
>
> (Worldwrite website, www.worldwrite.org.uk)

Worldwrite's Critical Charter is called 'Time to ditch the sustainababble' and argues that there is a strong link between economic development and living standards. It argues that calls for the countries of the South to undertake 'sustainable development' will inevitably mean that people are denied the lifestyles and living standards enjoyed by those in the affluent North, which were achieved by what they call 'serious development':

> If we are serious about our intention of helping the world's poor to have decent living standards, we must ditch the absurd notion of sustainable development and put serious development on the agenda instead. Serious development means industry, infrastructure and the best possible environment to live in – just as the West itself enjoys.
>
> (Ibid.)

These concerns are expressed in a more local context in an edited book, *The future of community (reports of a death greatly exaggerated)* (Clements et al., 2008). Alastair Donald's chapter, 'A green unpleasant land', starts with a quote from the influential green spokesman Jonathan Porritt (whose arguments are discussed later in this chapter), stating that 'sustainable development and community participation must go hand in hand. You can't have one without the other.' However, Donald suggests that community participation is defined in a particular way, meaning that individuals have to demonstrate their environmental citizenship by being seen to consume ethically and recycle in public. This represents an important shift in how communities traditionally have undertaken collective tasks. In the past, Donald says, environmental problems would be resolved at the level of society:

> If we wanted to live in neighbourhoods in attractive but flood-prone riverside locations, we designed flood barriers; cars may have polluted the city air but improved engine design meant we could enhance our mobility and develop more extensive networks of friends and acquaintances.
>
> (Donald, 2008: 26)

Today, says Donald, the opposite seems to be the case. We choose to build on less attractive locations and seek to limit our freedoms to the local community. Donald is a convenor of ManTownHuman and wrote a manifesto, 'Towards a new humanism in architecture' with Austin Williams as a co-author.[3] The authors are in favour of an architecture 'that imposes its will on the planet' and against architecture that 'treads lightly on the earth'. It is in favour of building more, in the knowledge that we can, and should, rebuild later. This ambitious vision for architecture is in stark contrast to what the authors see as a 'culture of decline', which questions whether we should be building at all:

> With half the world's population living in cities, where is the sense of exhilaration in the creative urbanisation of the planet for 7, 8 or 9+ billion? Such a dynamic moment in history demands maximum engagement, but architecture has become paralysed in its growing acceptance of the Malthusian environmental orthodoxy that humanity is a problem. Rather than an opportunity for creative improvement, rapid urbanisation is frequently presented as symbolic of the problems of over-population and the dangers this creates for communities and the environment. Lacking the confidence to impose principles, ideals and a sense of purpose, architects commonly defend virgin green fields over the expansive reach of the metropolis. 'Sprawl' and 'suburbia' have become euphemisms for irresponsible expansion as opposed to a representation of a creative dynamic.
>
> (Donald *et al.*, 2008: 5)

Dick Taverne (2005) makes a similar argument in relation to science in his book *The march of unreason: science, democracy, and the new fundamentalism*. The 'new fundamentalism' is the widespread acceptance of green ideas and public mistrust of Western science. This is reflected in the vogue for organic farming and homeopathic medicine, and concerns over genetic modification. For Taverne, this contributes to a mood of anti-science (especially that funded by business corporations), and undermines faith in the scientific promise of enlightenment and wealth creation.

Finally, in his book *The moralisation of tourism*, Jim Butcher (2003) argues that even the relatively simple and innocent pleasures involved in taking a holiday are being made an object of moral concern, as Western tourists (especially those involved in mass tourism to places such as Benidorm and the Costa del Sol) are required to adopt an apologetic stance for their presence, and learn to consume environments and places in ways that are environmentally aware. As a result, he argues, our holidays 'have become a vessel into which we are encouraged to pour environmental angst and fears of globalisation'. In contrast, he regards tourism as one of the benefits of modern development:

> The growth of mass tourism has been a mark of real progress in modern society. Many can travel abroad for leisure when only a couple of generations ago foreign travel was a rarity for most people. New opportunities have opened up as the holiday companies have expanded to ever more destinations. This has not been at the expense of those hosting the growing numbers of tourists.
>
> (Butcher, 2003: 139)

Butcher concludes that the portrayal of tourists as 'rather thoughtless people who contribute to the exploitation of the places they visit, is belittling. It also trivialises any discussion of poverty and how to tackle it.'

How should we interpret these ideas? On the one hand, we have an educational establishment that is keen to promote values of good citizenship and sustainable living through the school curriculum. On the other hand, we have a set of writings that suggests that this leads to the promotion of a diminished self, part of a society that downplays the idea of progress and sets more limited aims for its current and future development. Instead, these authors argue for 'real' or 'serious' development and increased use of, and human control over, the natural world. This position is summarised by the sociologist Frank Furedi (2009), who bemoans what he sees as loss of faith in 'radical humanism' in contemporary society. He argues that human progress, once embraced as desirable, is today represented as a risk to be avoided. It is those who see themselves on the political Left who have become most risk-averse and most vociferous in denouncing the idea of progress. While in the past radical opponents of capitalism denounced the system for failing to provide people with the material possessions they needed for a decent life, today anti-capitalists believe that we have too many possessions and call for people to reject the mindless consumerism perpetuated by the market. Furedi argues that 'An anti-modernist critique of mass society often lurks behind the label of anti-capitalism'.

While all these writers are purportedly concerned with the battle of ideas, it is worth noting that these ideas translate into actual, practical stances towards environment and development. The logic of their position is for governments to pursue policies that favour large-scale urban development and the spread of towns and cities; the adoption of Western models of economic development – serious development – by all nation-states; the privileging of scientific advance often funded by large transnational corporations; and the removal of politics from education. In other words, this sounds like untrammelled *laissez-faire* capitalism. In their various arguments, these writers are rejecting the ideology of 'soft' environmental governance that is currently promoted by the state.[4]

In summary, this section has shown how commentators such as Frank Furedi, Austin Williams, Jim Butcher and Dick Taverne, and organisations such as Worldwrite and ManTownHuman, argue that arguments for environmental precaution risk falling into the trap of regarding human beings and the economic systems they have developed as the 'problem' and encouraging an over-cautious stance towards development. They argue that human progress has occurred precisely because humans were able and willing to take risks and transform the natural world. In terms of geography education, they worry that moves to teach education for sustainable development risk leaving pupils with a diminished sense of human ambition and an anti-modern/anti-development view of the world.

For further study

1. How do you react to the argument that current approaches to school geography, with their focus on teaching about climate change, sustainability and encouraging forms of environmental citizenship, are contributing to a 'diminished' view of human nature and development?

2. Make a study of the geography textbooks and schemes of work used in your school. What view do they offer pupils of the relationship between people and environment? Is there evidence of an 'anti-progress' view, or that human activity is a threat to environments? Do they support the idea that humans can 'solve' environmental problems through better management and/or technology?

A capitalist solution?

In line with the argument of this chapter that we should see the battle of ideas as having real material consequences, it is important to ask how the mainstream of educational thinking about education for sustainable development relates to broader ideas of society and social change. The QCDA's (2009) document discussed earlier in this chapter effectively condenses a series of assumptions about the purposes of environmental education. It basically accepts that the current ways of organising economy and society are sound, but that there are limits to the process of development. In the past, these limits were either not recognised, or ignored, but this can no longer happen. This means that governments and individuals (perhaps acting as part of communities) must be prepared to act to ensure that these limits are not broached, in the interest of both our own society and future generations. This position also underpins the argument in Jonathan Porritt's (2005) book *Capitalism as if the world matters*.[5] Porritt starts his book with examples of why he feels optimistic about the possibility of making progress towards a green society. These include the responses to the Indian Ocean earthquake and tsunami in December 2004, and the ongoing global campaign to Make Poverty History. He notes that in the past ten years he has been working with a large number of senior people in government and business, and that his 'overwhelming impression is that more and more of them are now intent upon seriously pushing forward on more sustainable ways of doing their jobs'. Porritt notes that these are not radical people. They would not dream of looking for change outside the system. Given that time is short, Porritt believes that 'Incremental change is the name of the game, not transformation.' As he states, 'capitalism is the only game in town', and its logic is inescapable.

Porritt argues that 'there need be no fundamental contradiction between sustainable development and capitalism', and he recognises that this assumption 'stands in stark contrast to the prevailing views of many radical academics and non-governmental organisations that there are profound (and possibly unmanageable) contradictions which demand a completely different world order'.

This is the starting point for Porritt's analysis in the rest of his book. *Capitalism as if the world matters* is made up of three sections. In the first section, Porritt provides a critique of the existing model of capitalism that prioritises economic growth above human well-being and the environment. This adds an important layer of complexity to his argument, since it is clear that Porritt is no apologist for unbridled free-market capitalism. In the middle section, Porritt introduces what he calls the 'five capitals framework'. He raises the possibility that 'there is no inherent, fixed, or non-negotiable aspect of capitalism in general (rather than today's particular form of capitalism) that renders it for all time incompatible with the pursuit of a sustainable society' (Porritt, 2005: 111). While capital is often thought of in terms of 'stocks' of capital (land, machines and money), the five capitals framework widens out these stocks to include natural, human, social, manufactured and financial capital:

> These five forms of capital, judiciously combined by entrepreneurs, are the essential ingredients of modern industrial productivity. Natural capital, despite modern sophistications, is still required to maintain a functioning biosphere, supply resources to the economy and dispose of its wastes. Human capital provides the knowledge and skills which create manufactured capital and operate it effectively. Social capital creates the institutions that provide the stable context and conditions within and through which economic activity can take place, and which enable individuals to be vastly more productive. Financial capital provides the lubricant to keep the whole system operating.
>
> (Porritt, 2005: 114)

The chapters that make up the second part of Porritt's book focus on each of these capitals, suggesting ways in which they can be produced and re-produced in ways that do not diminish them. For example, in the case of manufactured capital, there are discussions of how buildings, infrastructure and machines might be developed in ways that make them more sustainable, through ideas such as biomimicry and cradle-to-cradle wealth creation. The argument (and the hope) running through all these discussions is that it is theoretically possible to transform the workings of contemporary capitalism in order to achieve a sustainable economy. This leads on to the final section of *Capitalism as if the world matters*, which is entitled 'Better lives in a better world'. Porritt raises the question of why it is proving so difficult to address the challenge of transformation, 'bringing us back to the uncomfortable but pervasive phenomenon of *denial*'. He suggests that such denial may have been understandable twenty years ago, when environmental issues were rising to prominence, but the data amassed by official government scientists, independent academics and international agencies tell 'pretty much the same story'. The problem, for Porritt, is that people interpret these data in different ways, and for most 'the basic model of progress (achieved through unfettered growth in an increasingly global economy) still remains sound, requiring only a little bit of market-based corrective action for the environment and more concerted efforts to address poverty in the world's poorest countries' (Porritt, 2005). There is denial in terms of the scale and pace of ecological decline, a reluctance to countenance the need for redistribution on the part of even progressive politicians (Porritt notes that the past twenty-five years have been a 'fiercely anti-tax age'), and a refusal to think about the effects of dependence on oil that has led to resource conflicts and heightened expenditure on arms and security. As Porritt admits, all this does not offer a 'happy global prospect'. Confronting denial requires a different set of values and approaches, and these are discussed in the final chapters of the book, where there is an emphasis on 'changing the metrics' (finding different ways of measuring progress), pursuing business excellence in relation to sustainability, and reinvigorating the public sphere so that individuals see themselves as more than consumers and are able to exercise political choice and agency in relation to environmental and social sustainability.

In concluding *Capitalism as if the world matters*, Porritt reiterates that sustainability and capitalism do not necessarily go hand-in-hand. Sustainability is all about the long term, is about working with limits, making more from less, and re-engaging with the natural world. Contemporary capitalism is concerned with the short run, does not recognise limits or sees them as extendable, celebrates excess, and regards the natural world as a commodity. This version of capitalism has to be transformed, through a reform agenda rather than revolution (though some may see reform as revolutionary). It requires:

> [...] a different level of engagement, both as citizens and as consumers, and a much greater readiness to confront denial at every point, to challenge the slow, soul-destroying descent into displacement consumerism, and to take on today's all too dominant 'I consume therefore I am' mindsets and lifestyles.
>
> (Porritt, 2005: 309)

Capitalism as if the world matters is an important contribution from an influential voice in debates about sustainability. Porritt was a leading voice in the green movement in the early 1980s, when he wrote two election manifestos for the Ecology Party (which later became the Green Party) and an influential book called *Seeing green* (Porritt 1984). His position in that book was clear, that the idea of green economic growth was logically impossible, and that what was needed was a radical change in the culture of industrialism which is predicated on ever-greater expansion and use of natural resources. Porritt appears to have changed his mind. In the 1990s, he was co-founder of the think-tank Forum for the Future, with a mission to 'accelerate the change to a sustainable way of life, taking a positive, solutions-oriented approach in everything it does'. One way to read this shift is that it reflects the process through which the green movement has 'grown up' and become an acceptable and established part of the political mainstream. Another interpretation is offered by David Miller and William Dinan, who are less inclined to see Porritt's new-found belief in the ability of capitalism to deliver sustainable development as the outcome of decades of reflection-on-action:

> Old Etonian Porritt was a Green Party activist, but now he has also been recruited to many of the elite networks which the corporations use to co-opt their critics.
>
> (Miller and Dinan, 2008: 94)

Porritt's close links to these 'elite networks' is reflected by those providing plaudits for the dust-jacket of *Capitalism as if the world matters*, who include Lord May, President of the

Royal Society; bastion of the television establishment Jonathan Dimbleby; Lord David Puttnam; and Mark Moody-Stuart, chairman of Anglo American plc. Their comments are at pains to praise the non-revolutionary nature of Porritt's analysis, notably his argument that capitalism is the solution, that business is to play a central part, and that he is a 'realist'.

Porritt's position, and that adopted by the UK government, is based on acceptance of the discourse of ecological modernisation, which challenges the traditional view that too many environmental restrictions, taxes and costs would make industry less competitive, leading to a slowdown in economic growth rates, unemployment and capital flight. At the core of this argument is the notion that economic growth and environmental deterioration can be decoupled by pursuing 'greener growth'. Greener growth means economic growth that uses less energy and resources, produces less waste, and seeks constant technological innovation in production methods and product design. It is reflected in ideas about the next industrial revolution, which will be a 'green revolution' and will usher in an era of 'natural capital' and eco-efficiency. The report to the Club of Rome, *Factor four* (von Weizsacker *et al.*, 1997), maintained that wealth would probably double if resource use could be halved; its recent successor, *Factor five* (von Weizsacker *et al.*, 2009), continues in this vein but incorporates ideas of sustainable well-being and happiness, also a prominent feature of *Capitalism as if the world matters*.

What are the implications of Porritt's argument for geography education? From an initial concern with environmental education, geographers have become more comfortable with the idea that the subject can contribute to education for sustainable development, where this is concerned with the three pillars of sustainability – environmental, economic and social. Over the past twenty years, good practice has moved away from providing doom-laden pronouncements of environmental catastrophe and has focused on the types of practice that can promote sustainable development. There has been a concern to link the local and the global. Another way of putting this is that there is a focus on 'actually existing sustainabilities'. At the same time, there are some difficulties with the way in which education for sustainable development is being undertaken in schools, which a reading of *Capitalism as if the world matters* may exacerbate. For example, there is the idea that sustainable development is business as usual, but 'greener' and 'fairer'. An emphasis on recycling is problematic as it seems to legitimise more consumption, and there tends to be a focus on what *actions* individuals can take to become more environmentally aware. All of this may involve the injunction for students to become more critical of the way things are currently done, but this is within strict limits. The limits to critical thinking within education for sustainable development are evident in the brief discussion Porritt dedicates to the topic. Most of this section (about five pages) is concerned to make the point that the situation in the UK is much healthier than in the United States, where the teaching of science (the building blocks to understand sustainability) is being challenged by those who favour the teaching of creationism. Porritt is optimistic about the situation in the UK, where there are a lot of 'smart' NGOs providing curriculum materials and resources, and practical work in terms of eco-schools and playground regeneration. Porritt asserts that education for sustainable development competes 'for space and funds to find creative and intelligent ways of enabling young people to learn and experience what it means, *in practice*, to be a citizen of our living Earth, and in terms of making sure that all places of learning embody that heightened awareness about responsibility to the world and its people in their design, construction, management and engagement with their surrounding communities' (Porritt, 2005: 310, emphasis added). Even if we ignore for a moment that this is a fairly romantic view of the status of education for sustainable development in most schools, what is particularly worrying is the lack of reference to any critical analysis of the idea that there could be alternatives to the way things are currently organised.

It is this critical stance to sustainable development that many would see as fundamental to an educational approach, rather than mere training in being a good 'environmental citizen'. To facilitate such work in classrooms, geography teachers will need to go beyond the framework provided in *Capitalism as if the world matters* and seek out other ideas and sources.

Despite these criticisms, *Capitalism as if the world matters* is a significant achievement. One of its most important contributions is to bring to consciousness the idea that capitalism is the name for the system that is generating environmental crisis, rather than some vague notion of industrialism or our Western way of life. Capitalism is a social, historically produced system by which wealth is produced, distributed and consumed. Porritt raises the important challenge that capitalism can be organised differently, and this provides the basis for any discussion of environmentalism in education. The trouble for Porritt is that his is not the only take on this issue, and just as he has come from the political margins to the view capitalism as 'the only game in town', it is possible to find examples of individuals travelling in the other direction,[6] and there are powerful intellectual arguments that challenge the idea that capitalism as an economic system can reform itself in ways that protect and conserve natural resources, notably Joel Kovel's (2007) *The enemy of nature*.

Jonathan Porritt's book makes an important contribution to discussions of sustainable development, which has implications for geography teachers. His central focus is on the nature of the economic system – capitalism – which is responsible for the build-up of environmental problems. If we accept this argument, it is no longer viable to teach geography in schools without offering pupils some understanding of this economic system. The main question raised for geography teachers is the extent to which Porritt's optimistic assessment of the potential for reform is realistic. In developing geography lessons that require pupils to discuss solutions to environmental problems, how we represent capitalism is crucially important.

The trouble with capitalism

Joel Kovel's (2007) *The enemy of nature* is an important statement of the relationship between ecological crisis and the nature of capitalism, and can usefully be read alongside Porritt's book. Kovel's argument is that there is an inbuilt tendency for capitalism to generate the destruction of nature. This is related to the basic mechanism of accumulation in which capital is assembled and used to purchase a mix of built environments, technology and labour power – the means of production – and value is added through production in the form of surplus value or profits. The competitive nature of capitalism means that this flow of capital cannot stop; otherwise there is a crisis of accumulation (an argument made powerfully in David Harvey's 2010 book *The enigma of capital*). At the present time there is a sense in which the environmental repercussions of this 'treadmill of production' are increasingly being recognised. A useful concept in this context is James O'Connor's (1998) idea, based on a reading of Marx's *Capital*, of the second contradiction of capitalism. The first contradiction is that of overproduction. In a period of economic expansion, capitalists increase production because there are profits to be made. However, there are limits to how much of this production can be realised because of the tightly regulated wages of labour, aggressive marketing and increased competition. This leads to a crisis of realisation, in which prices and profits fall and workers are laid off. In short, capitalism has an inbuilt tendency towards crisis. The second contradiction relates to capitalism (almost literally) undermining the conditions for its own continuation. These conditions include the environment. The environment is literally used up in the drive to increase production: water courses are polluted, raw materials are extracted and consumed, and so on. The result is increased costs and the need to clean up the environment. It may be argued that the rapid expansion and rate of growth of industrial capitalism in the post-war period was considerably higher than it would have been if the true costs of using the environment were recognised. In the past four decades, there has been increased awareness of the second contradiction, even though mainstream political thought remains optimistic that the market can provide the 'fix' to environmental problems.

The writers discussed in this section (Kovel, O'Connor and Harvey) oppose Porritt's view that capitalism can be reformed in order to resolve the environmental crisis. They share with Porritt the view that the capitalist drive to accumulate profits leads to misuse of the environment, but argue that this drive (the 'capitalist imperative') is at the heart of capitalist society. If profit is not made, the system breaks down. It is this imperative to expand production in order to realise profits that leads to nature being seen as a commodity to be used to realise wealth. If there is oil in rocks beneath the ground, it will be exploited because it can be used to make profits. Many geography teachers are not used to dealing with these ideas, but they are central to many debates within geography concerned with the environment, and we will encounter them throughout this book.

For further study

1.   This section draws on writers who argue that environmental problems can be understood only in relation to the nature of a capitalist economic system. What (if anything) do pupils learn about this economic system in school geography?

2.   Look at the index of a series of school geography textbooks – do they make reference to terms such as 'capitalism', 'politics' and 'industrialisation'? What does this suggest about how school geography treats the relationship between economics and environment?

Redefining progress

One of the criticisms of Marxist analysts such as Kovel and Harvey is that they portray a capitalist system that is so dynamic, creative and flexible that it seems to offer little space ever to develop new ways of organising economic and social life so as to forge new, less exploitative relations with the environment. The final section in this chapter considers one further position that explores the relationship between capitalism, the environment and social well-being. This position is associated with writers and thinkers who are attempting to fashion an updated 'left', linked to organisations such as the New Economics Foundation, Compass, and the journal *Soundings*. All these organisations can be seen as developing out of the epochal transformations that occurred in the breakdown of the post-Second World War consensus in the 1970s and 1980s. This saw the emergence of 'new times', in which the older Fordist economy and society was gradually and partially replaced by a post-Fordist society. In the neoliberal approach that emerged out of these changes in the late 1970s, governments assumed that economies were most successful when they allowed the development of free markets, rewarded risk-taking entrepreneurs through high salaries and low taxation, and encouraged the belief that the state should provide welfare only in the case of the most needy and unfortunate. For some commentators, this has resulted in an increasingly unequal society, in which family and community life has been replaced by the need to work ever-longer hours in order to pay for higher levels of consumer goods and services. Over time, the costs of this approach to individuals, communities and the environment have become increasingly apparent. This position is encapsulated in the introduction to a collection of essays entitled *Feelbad Britain: how to make it better*:

> Three decades of neoliberalism, extended by New Labour into the heart of the welfare state, have undermined the institutions and social relations on which solidarity, trust and citizenship depend and in which they were once embedded. Our sense of social membership and our shared identity as citizens have been effaced by individualist consumerism, the dominant culture and common sense of the age.
>
> (Devine *et al.*, 2009: 8)

This analysis suggests the problems are economic – to do with the 'incorrigibly expansionist dynamic of capitalism' – but that this does not mean that 'there is no alternative'. The current phase of neoliberalism – which disembeds social relations, causes overwork and promotes individualism – is, according to these writers, a political creation, and is therefore amenable to change. The writings associated with this group focus on re-establishing the bonds of families and communities, developing a 'post-autistic' economics, and moving towards developing an 'alternative hedonism' and environmental critique. The argument is that these developments have led to a condition of 'feelbad Britain', one in which it is becoming increasingly obvious that the gains of materialism and pop culture are not enough to sustain a good life. In her contribution to the book, Kate Soper (2009) develops the idea of alternative hedonism as a new political imaginary. She argues that people are increasingly aware of the way that contemporary ways of living, working and relation to one another can serve to deny pleasure or fulfilment. She offers a series of examples of this. For instance, people who live in cities and suburbs are denied the experience of total silence, and rarely have a clear vision of the night sky. As pedestrians, they are constantly interrupted by traffic lights, and face the noise, dust and smell of motorised vehicles. Travellers by bus and train face the abuse and stress that have followed from underfunding and privatisation. But Soper suggests that, very slowly, we are witnessing the emergence of an alternative hedonism, one based on pursuing pleasures that do not rely on the excessive consumption of goods and services. Taking picnics, collecting blackberries to be baked at home in a crumble, going for a walk or cycle ride, buying locally sourced food from a village market (to give a few examples) can all serve to offer a glimpse of lives less driven by the tempo of fast capitalism. Of course, it may be suggested that these pleasures themselves are, at present, the preserve of those social classes who can afford to 'go slow', but the notion of alternative hedonism speaks to the pleasures or fulfilments of post-consumerism. Another contributor to *Feelbad Britain* is a geographer, Noel Castree (2009), who argues that although, as a political issue, the environment has been incorporated into the mainstream of society's thinking, business interests tend to resist the environmental challenge altogether, apart from those that stand to benefit from 'going green'. Meanwhile:

> the average British citizen is enjoined to spend their hard-earned income in 'ecofriendly' ways, even as they are simultaneously encouraged to holiday abroad, consume ever more imported commodities, and aspire to the lifestyles of the rich-and-famous.
>
> (Castree, 2009: 226)

He argues that the environmentalism adopted by governments is set in a 'problem-and-solution' framing which is techno-centrist and thoroughly neoliberal:

> A combination of profit-making 'clean technology' and market-disciplined human behaviour will, so our political masters believe, make 'sustainable development' a reality.
>
> (Ibid.)

Despite this, Castree suggests that there are promising signs for the development of environmental consciousness. First, there is a strong sense in which it is recognised that a range of environmental issues are real, and cannot be dismissed as the fantasies of green extremists. Second, there seems to be a growing realisation that the environment is not a special interest issue, but relates to all aspects of how people live their lives. Third, there is now a widespread recognition that environmental issues are related to distant others and future generations. Finally, recent developments in environmental awareness recognise the social justice and social welfare aspects of the environmental agenda. At the same time, Castree recognises some significant barriers to the development of environmental concern. These include the widespread belief in the notion of economic growth; the ethic of individualism, which discourages belonging and solidarity with others; a loss of faith in the political system; the dominance in everyday life of the world of info- and entertainment, which prevents engagement with political affairs; and, linked with this, a low level of political literacy. All of these suggest the need for forms of geography education that help students to understand and engage with significant political issues surrounding the relationships between economy, society and nature.

The perspective discussed in this section shares with Porritt and Kovel an analysis of the way in which, as an economic system, capitalism leads to significant social and environmental costs. The main development in this perspective is to attribute an intensification of these problems to a particular way of organising capitalism – neoliberalism – which leads to the accumulation of private wealth at the expense of the majority of people. In environmental terms, the drive to make profits through ever-higher levels of consumption and rates of turnover of goods (e.g. upgrading your mobile phone with the latest model every year, rather than using it until it does not function) has led to increased pressure on natural systems and resources. The authors of *Feelbad Britain* point to the possibilities for a less intense version of capitalism that is more tightly managed and seeks to redistribute the costs and benefits of production and consumption. Their focus on health, well-being, lifestyles and the environment has direct links with the content of geography teaching in schools.

For further study

1. To what extent does your school offer pupils the opportunity to learn about and practise an 'alternative hedonism'? How might it do this?

Conclusion

This chapter sets the scene for the rest of the book. It stakes out the battle for ideas around sustainability, which, I argue, will come to occupy schools and teaching over the coming decade. Given that there are real environmental issues to be faced, current moves to 'green' schooling will intensify in the coming years. Already, schools are being urged to go green, and school leaders are being offered courses in sustainable leadership. The culture of green consumerism and active environmental citizenship is increasingly apparent in schools (on a recent visit to a school, I was greeted by a large poster that read 'Don't be a fool – be cool: recycle'). As we have seen, at the current time much of this is framed within an approach to environmental thinking which suggests that a change in individual practices and values can make a difference. These developments will be contested by those who argue that the greening of schooling represents a moral and political agenda, and that the likelihood that the near future will require reductions in consumption and restrictions on individual freedoms will generate a backlash. Geography teachers will inevitably be involved in these developments, since, as this book seeks to demonstrate, the content of the subject is centrally concerned with the relations between society and nature.

The perspectives discussed in this chapter in no way exhaust the arguments about the relationship between environmental issues and economic and social change (indeed, we have only scratched the surface). My intention has been to highlight some positions about economy, modernity and environmental change in order to illustrate the broad terrain on which contemporary geographical education should be conducted. Too often, geography lessons study issues of climate change, deforestation, tourism, urbanisation and economic development as discrete and isolated topics. The danger in this approach is that these issues are divorced from broader questions of how societies are organised in order to create and produce geographical patterns and processes (i.e. space). The result is that many students complete courses in geography without being helped to address fundamental questions about the relationships between society and nature, and lacking realistic models of political economy.

For further study

1.   What are the 'big ideas' that are taught in geography in your classroom or department? Are there other big ideas or perspectives, not discussed in this chapter, that you think should feature in school geography?

2

From environmental geography to education for sustainable development

Introduction

This chapter explores the emergence of environmental concern in the school curriculum over the past four decades. It is important to recognise the significance of this. In *The sustainability mirage*, John Foster (2009) comments that, in historical terms, the emergence of a consensus around green issues within the space of around four decades is a major achievement. The same can be said of the growing acceptance of the importance of education for sustainable development within schools. Environmental concern, once seen as the preserve of a small number of 'green teachers', has reached the point where government education departments routinely talk about education for sustainable development and sustainable schools (even though we might doubt how much importance is attached to these compared with other educational priorities such as raising attainment). This chapter is an attempt to tell something of the story whereby environmental education came to occupy a prominent position in education policy, through a discussion of how school geography has engaged with these issues. There is a particular argument in this chapter. It is that, in the post-war period, school geography increasingly responded to important changes in the rural and urban environments in which children were growing up. There were significant changes in the built environment and localities, which many geography teachers sought to help children make sense of. This I term 'environmental geography'. However, in the 1980s this concern with the local environment gave way to more global perspectives. With the drive to environmental modernisation from the 1990s, education for sustainable development became an accepted part of curriculum thinking.

Origins

In his account of the development of environmental education in Britain, Keith Wheeler (1975) suggests that the 'founder' of environmental education was Patrick Geddes, a Scottish professor of botany, who wrote in the late nineteenth century, a time when the bourgeoning growth of towns and cities in the wake of industrialisation was leading to widespread concern about social order. Geddes was dissatisfied with school and university building methods and appalled by the overpowering growth of urban conurbations spreading throughout Britain. In 1889 he opened a unique educational establishment – the Outlook Tower on the Royal Mile in Edinburgh – to reflect his philosophy. He argued that children brought into contact with the profound realities of their environment would be likely not only to learn better, but also to develop a creative attitude towards their surroundings. According to Wheeler, Geddes believed that human life can flourish only if we come to terms with our towns and cities by making them both beautiful and functional places to live in. The environment results from an interaction between place, work and folk.

Geddes' ideas resonate with forms of progressivism that influenced educational developments in the first half of the twentieth century. Though there are many strands of progressive education, the important point is that children should be free to develop through an exploration of their environment (Doddington and Hilton, 2007). Cons and Fletcher's (1938) *Actuality in school* is cited by Wheeler as one of the founding texts of environmental education. The authors worked at Goldsmiths College, and the book was an account of an educational experiment carried out in the crowded urban district of New Cross in London. This involved exploration of the neighbourhood by young children, and could be regarded as a 'rather exciting adventure into certain practical possibilities of social education' (Cons and Fletcher, 1938). The actuality to which pupils were introduced was the roles of key people such as the postman, fireman, sewerman and dustman. The approach sought to make links between the school and the world beyond the classroom:

> When we say there is a lack of reality in our teaching, this is surely what we mean. The classroom door is shut; the windows look out on the world; in very many schools there is little relationship between what is going on in the classroom, and the busy activities of the real world.
>
> (Cons and Fletcher, 1938: 2)

An important motive for learning is the child's curiosity about the world in which they live:

> So, his social environment gives us the basis for selecting certain dynamic topics such as postal service, air transport, road transport. If these topics are followed through from the immediate environment to their associations in other parts of the homeland and in other parts of the world, and backwards in time in order to understand their evolutionary development, we have a new basis for our geographical and historical teaching in the schools.
>
> (Cons and Fletcher, 1938: 7–8)

As Roy Lowe (2007) has documented in his book *The death of progressive education*, educational policy in Britain has veered back and forth between progressive and traditional ways of teaching and learning. In practice, 'conservative' ways of thinking about and studying the environment have dominated in schools for much of the post-war period. While *Actuality in school* represented an early attempt to make use of the opportunities to learn from the urban environment, the majority of environmental studies involved rather leisurely forays into valued rural beauty spots, in order to conduct nature surveys. This tradition is reflected in the work of organisations such as the Field Studies Council, which, according to Wheeler, does 'important but uncontroversial work' in propagating fieldwork methods concerned with field biology and physical geography. Wheeler describes how, by the mid-1970s, there were developing critiques of the types of education on offer to young people growing up in an uncertain world, and this approach to environmental study appeared increasingly outmoded and conservative:

> [...] environmental teachers may have developed a sharp eye for country, but they have until recently been remarkably blind to problems of the urban and technological world in which the majority of their pupils live.
>
> (Wheeler, 1975: 5)

As Wheeler documents, from the mid-1960s, the tradition of environmental studies based on apolitical naturalist practices was increasingly challenged by the more political, committed activism of environmental education. However, as the arguments developed in the next section indicate, the politics of environmental education were multi-faceted and led to sharp breaks in philosophy and practice.

This section argues that early forms of environmental study in schools grew out of a concern to introduce children to aspects of their localities. An important element in this was to take children from their limited (generally urban) circumstances and introduce them to culturally valued physical landscapes. This tradition continues still, particularly through the Field Studies Council's Centres, set in picturesque and environmentally significant locations. From the early 1970s, this approach came to be challenged by a more politically aware version of environmental education.

The politicisation of the environment

This section traces the emergence of what (following Wheeler and Waites, 1976) I term 'environmental geography', as a response to far-reaching changes in the familiar landscapes of post-war Britain. In a society in which older forms of landscape were undergoing rapid and permanent change, geography teaching risked appearing anachronistic and lacking in relevance to pupils' lives if it did not deal with the politics of landscape change and the subjective feelings of loss and disorientation that accompanied these changes. Harrison (2009) summarises some aspects of this 'new geography':

> Whether by day or by night, the United Kingdom's surface when viewed from the air changed markedly between 1951 and 1970. Superimposed on old patterns were the new field shapes and changed watercourses stemming from intensive farming. The

new motorway system was taking shape; new towns and universities were springing up on greenfield sites; housing geography was in flux.

(Harrison, 2009: 123)

These changes brought about important shifts in what it meant to live in a rapidly modernising country, and one response was mounting concern about the environment. In the inter-war period, this concern was expressed most vocally by people wishing to preserve the amenities of the countryside against the 'encroaching fingers of urbanisation'. These groups included, in Britain, the Royal Society for the Protection of Birds and the Council for the Protection of Rural England (now Campaign to Protect Rural England, CPRE). There is a tendency to be dismissive of this type of environmental politics. For instance, David Pepper (1984) regards these groups as the result of people seeking to escape the city to live in the country. These newcomers have been in the vanguard of the environmentalist movement, 'giving their wealth, time and articulateness to groups such as the CPRE and the National Trust and the anti-airport groups'. Similarly, Wheeler caricatures the CPRE as a nostalgic aesthetic movement worried about the decline of farming and with a patronising attitude to the dying rustic ways of life, seeing them as 'a strange band of naturalists, middle class countrymen, and leftwing rustic philosophers'. Its position was represented in books such as *England and the octopus* and *Britain and the beast* (Williams-Ellis, 1928, 1937), in which Britain was the countryside and the beast was the urban intruder. There was a need to educate people about how to appreciate the countryside and behave appropriately. As C.E.M. Joad stated in his contribution to *Britain and the beast*:

What this education should be it is confessedly not easy to say. Certain steps are, however, obvious. Lessons in country lore should be given at every school and country manners taught as carefully as social.

(cited in Wheeler, 1975: 6)

In his self-importantly titled *The book of Joad* (Joad, 1935) he describes a journey from London to the south coast. It is entitled 'The horrors of the countryside' and rails against ribbon development, bungalows on cliff tops, noisy visitors and motor vehicles. If this represents a position that worried about increased urban development and the scourge of the motor car, it was also concerned that the urban working classes were more and more visible in rural Britain.

However, this form of class-based exclusivity and concern to preserve the countryside was out of step with the emergence, after 1945, of a 'New Britain'. Although Wheeler (1975) exaggerates when he says that 'an enthusiasm for socialism gripped the nation', it is true that the post-war period saw high levels of state expenditure and investment, which transformed the built environment in the form of slum clearance, the growth of New Towns, suburbanisation, new shopping centres and industrial estates. These geographies of reconstruction were underpinned by the raft of legislation that sought to provide order to these developments (for example, the Town and Country Planning Act of 1947, the establishment of the Nature Conservancy Council in 1949, and the National

Parks Act of 1947 all set the framework for the management of ordered and logically managed geographical development).

These geographies of reconstruction cannot be separated from broader developments in the British economy and culture. In *Never had it so good*, the historian Dominic Sandbrook (2005) argues that the 1950s saw the coming to fruition of long-term consumer developments that had begun in the Victorian period and that, despite widespread poverty and economic depression, continued in wealthy pockets in the 1920s and 1930s. Donnelly (2005) suggests that when Conservative Prime Minister Harold Macmillan told the British people in 1957 that they had 'never had it so good', he was describing what for many people was a reality:

> A booming economy, soaring stock market values, low unemployment, a wealth of accessible consumer choice and improved welfare services were the defining features of a new age of affluence.
>
> (Donnelly, 2005: 23)

This new age of affluence was accompanied by far-reaching changes to the physical and human environments. From the early 1960s, it was becoming apparent that the levels of consumerism and the privatised lifestyles associated with modern design and culture were causing some concerns. The planned redevelopment of city centres, the building of modern residential blocks of flats, and the new suburbs all raised a crisis of meaning about what it was to belong to a place. Though rebuilding and renovation was necessary, what was lost for many people, according to historian Robert Colls (2002), was the sense of belonging to anything:

> People sensed deep change as they experienced town-centre congestion, or decay, depending on what form of redevelopment it was, during the day, followed by dispersal to estates in the evening.
>
> (Colls, 2002: 345)

Policies of suburbanisation, spatial fragmentation and town centre redevelopment meant that 'many of the tangible facts of urban life were removed'. Colls cites *The Cambridge urban history of Britain*, which notes that in little more than thirty years was eroded 'much of the ancient palimpsest, the mixture of public and private buildings, high streets and back lanes, which has given [towns] for so long a sense of place, of physical coherence and individual community identity' (cited in Colls, 2002: 346). Colls notes:

> For a nation that swore in its constitution by community and lineage, this was a bitter pill. Older people found themselves in a land bearing little evidence that they had ever lived there. The house in which they were born, the back lane where they had pushed prams, the hall where they had danced, and the streets where they had run, were gone or were going to be gone.
>
> (Colls, 2002: 346)

There was an important set of developments prompted by a growing realisation of the impact on people's lives of the decisions made by planners in their efforts to manage the urban environment. The 1964 Buchanan Report *Traffic in towns* provided an overview of the effects on urban form of increased levels of personal mobility, and posed the question whether towns could be habitable in the face of continued traffic growth. There was also a sense that the familiar townscape was in the process of being replaced by modern buildings. It is important not to underestimate the implications of these developments for what it meant to live in a place. Historians of the built environment suggest that there was a strong strain of anti-urbanism in British society which ensured a reaction against modern buildings and environments. It was reflected in the writing of architectural commentators such as Gerald Burke:

> Do we know a good townscape when we see one? Do we admire the forms and scale of building and spaces? Do we resent the eruptions of unexpected change, the loss of familiar buildings and the gain of drab slabs, the noise, dirt and danger of traffic that drives us away from streets and lanes where once we walked in relative calm? Does the pride we have in our homes extend to our towns?
>
> (Burke, 1976: 1)

At the same time, the field of environmental psychology emerged in order to understand the ways in which humans responded to the pressures involved in living in cities (Mercer, 1975).

This section has set the context for the development of an approach to environmental education concerned to help pupils come to terms with the transition from a traditional to modern landscape. Physical changes (often rapid) in the landscape, new ways of dwelling and modern modes of transport all raised questions about how to respond to and evaluate these new geographies. As the next section indicates, education was one way of helping pupils make sense of these changes.

The educational response to development

The broader cultural responses to the upheaval associated with post-war development were also expressed in education, especially in approaches to teaching school geography. Some of these responses are considered briefly in this section.

In the early 1950s, the educationalist Denys Thompson[1] published a pamphlet called *Your England – and how to defend it*. The title is a reference to George Orwell and his essay 'England, your England', written in 1941, which begins with the words 'As I write, highly civilised human beings are flying overhead, trying to kill me'. There is a sense, too, in Thompson's pamphlet that a civilisation is in the process of being destroyed.

> At its best our countryside is the finest in the world; it combines a variety of lovely scenery with a high yield of fine crops [...] For forty years or more the towns have been pushing their tentacles into the country instead of growing in rings, like a tree. The villages have in many cases lost their character and become suburbs; the country

itself is littered with garages, advertisements, bungalows, airfields and military installations that eat up good agricultural land, as well as being eyesores. [...] A beautiful and fertile countryside with its towns and villages, all the result of centuries of hard work, is being destroyed. We should all of us do something about it.

(Thompson, 1952: 3)

The pamphlet is a pictorial guide to the evolution of the human landscape. It starts with images of the 'organic community', all before 1800, with pleasing buildings wrought out of local materials and in keeping with the landscape. Then, we see pictures of industry, rows and rows of tightly packed workers' housing. Smoky, unhealthy cities, with pretentious buildings, noisy traffic and cluttered, badly designed street furniture ('This is Edinburgh, but industrial towns like Sheffield are worse.'). The towns are spoiled by excessive advertising, and the countryside by ribbon developments and bypasses that scar the countryside. The final pages of the pamphlet are a series of uncaptioned black-and-white photographs: 'in each case the reader is invited to consider why the photograph is included, and to find reasons for his likes and dislikes'.

There is an educational intent here. The reader is invited to read the landscape, and the previous examples and captions are offered as a model to help train this critical awareness. This was part of a broader cultural formation that was influenced by W.G. Hoskins' (1955) *The making of the English landscape*. At the centre of Hoskins' work was a particular way of seeing. This way of viewing landscape was rooted in forms of English romanticism and based on an assumed empiricism, which held that the best way to learn about the land was to go out and get mud on your boots.

But Thompson's pamphlet was no simple lament for the loss of a rural organic community simply preferring an idyllic to an imperfect present. There is a more complex relationship with the modern. There is a strong preference for an ordered geography here – one shaped by the geographical fact of high-density population. Thompson is not against development, but insists that towns must be developed as towns – 'real towns that are cheerful and attractive to live in', while the country must be kept a living and healthy whole 'for agriculture and for refreshing our minds and bodies':

It must not be pocked with feeble buildings, destroyed by wire or gangrened by urban sprawl or military muck. All this can be done, if we want it.

(Thompson, 1952: 30)

The Foreword to Thompson's pamphlet was written by the architectural critic Ian Nairn. Nairn wrote:

The subject that this book illustrates so ably isn't just one more item in the curriculum, it's something that goes with you on every walk you take. You can begin to understand it simply by opening your eyes and looking at the street you are in as a scene in its own right, not just a backcloth to be used or passed through. Places will cease to be names and become living things: paradoxically, you will yourself become more alive in the process.

(in Thompson, 1952: 1)

In 1964, Nairn published *Your England revisited*. He paid tribute to Thompson. The structure and approach are similar. There is a series of black-and-white photographs with captions to explain and provoke about what is appropriate and inappropriate in the landscape. The message is that, inadvertently, the landscape is being reduced to a mess of inappropriate signage and design. The argument is that these are developing by default – 'subtopias of good intentions'.

Joe Moran (2007) has argued that attempts by writers such as Nairn to make people take notice of what was happening to ordinary landscapes were largely ignored by people who were more concerned with the availability of housing and were grateful for the opportunities for leisure afforded by the new road networks. The important thing to note is that the experience of landscape change associated with modern development was acutely felt by many, and did not go without comment or discussion. Consequently, there were attempts to develop approaches to curriculum and learning in geography which helped pupils to evaluate these changes.

One of the best examples of this approach is found in Wheeler and Waites' (1976) *Environmental geography: a handbook for teachers*. The book was an attempt to 'provide a contemporary environmental philosophy for a young generation growing up in a dangerously threatened habitat'. In a chapter on the visual approach to environmental geography, Wheeler stated:

Perhaps there has been no period in history more than our own so concerned with the preservation of the visual value of landscape, rural and urban. Yet, paradoxically, it is also a time during which the unsightly deterioration of the environment has taken place more rapidly, and on a greater scale, than ever before. The reasons for this are many, but certainly much of the harm has been caused by the effects of increasing recreational and urban–industrial needs demanded by a proliferating population during a period of considerable affluence. As a result conflict is generated between the value placed on land and buildings for their aesthetic and amenity qualities on the one hand, and the social and economic needs of people on the other.

(Wheeler and Waites, 1976: 46)

Geography has long been concerned with the study of landscape:

Indeed it is the only school subject which has striven to give youngsters an insight into the processes involved in the evolution of the natural and cultural landscape.

(Wheeler and Waites, 1976: 46)

Whereas earlier geographers, concerned largely with the physical landscapes of rural areas, had been concerned to help pupils develop an eye for the country, the task of the school geography teacher was to help pupils make sense of the environments in which they lived ('And, more importantly, today we must ensure that our pupils develop an eye for the urban–industrial scene as well.'). The book provides practical ways in which teachers can develop this visual or aesthetic approach, but most important was the contribution that such learning could make to the quality of debates about how society should deal with modern technologies and ways of living:

> In attempting to educate the young person to see and evaluate the visual standards of his surroundings the teacher is advancing into the difficult field of value judgements. Geography teaching becomes in this way a more discursive subject than hitherto in which the pupil can express opinions as well as absorb facts [...] The problems facing the future evolution of the environment are not soluble by quantitative technique alone, but in the last resort must depend upon a consensus of opinion based on the view our society takes of the kind of environment it wants. The debate about the such things as mining in national parks; the control of the motorcar; and the development of the inner city, rests entirely on deciding the worth we place on 'good environment'. The choice between private affluence and public visual squalor is one that must be posed in the classroom and on the field course, and how we choose will ultimately depend on the environmental 'literacy' of the future generation.
>
> (Wheeler and Waites, 1976: 61)

Perhaps the most significant publication in this approach to environmental studies was Colin Ward's (1978) *The child in the city*. This book pointed to the way in which cities can be more or less inhabitable for children and young people.

Geography teachers' relationships to these developments were not straightforward. There was a tendency for environmental studies to be seen as a subject for pupils deemed non-academic, while academic pupils were encouraged to concentrate on academic disciplines. As geography in universities came to be 'revolutionised' by quantitative approaches and spatial analysis, geography teachers in some schools began to discard their interest in the 'man–land' relationship, and adopt instead the techniques of spatial analysis. There were attempts to develop problem-solving exercises and issues-based enquiries, but the new geography introduced into schools 'mind-bending exercises in statistics largely irrelevant to the urgent problems confronting the environment we live in' (Wheeler, 1975). The result was to divide geography teachers. The extent to which this was an issue is reflected in the editors' preface to Michael Storm's (1973) paper on teaching an issues-based approach that explored pupils' attitudes to the local area and local community, reproduced in a reader for geography teachers:

> The approach adopted by Storm would strike many people as not being geography. Would you agree? Does it matter?
> Involvement means an emotional link between the student and the subject under study. Discuss how far this might lead to the abandonment of rationality in discussing the issues concerned.
>
> (Storm, 1973: 303)

This section has explored educational responses to the changes that took place in the physical and built environments in the period after the Second World War. It has suggested that these changes were not ignored by cultural commentators such as Denys Thompson and Ian Nairn, and that, influenced by forms of educational progressivism that sought to allow children to respond to their locality, school geography became an important site where questions of what constitutes a good landscape could be discussed.

The 1970s as the turning point

The 1970s was an important turning point in debates about the environment and education. As Whitehead (1985) noted in *The writing on the wall*:

> Quite suddenly, bigness and blandness were not enough. In the seventies size came to be a disadvantage: the size of families and populations, the spread of urban 'comprehensive development' and the motorway network, the merged molochs of industry and their green siblings, the prairie farms. For many of the new campaigners [...] the community should reassert itself against the remote bureaucracy of planning, the small-scale enterprise against the multinational, the wholesome and the natural against the synthetic and the artificial – be it a matter of bread, beer or bleached veal.
>
> (Whitehead, 1985: 239)

The 1970s saw the growth of a powerful ecology lobby. Friends of the Earth was formed in 1970, and the Ecology Party (which later became the Green Party) in 1974. This growth in concern for the environment was 'a profound revulsion to the appetites of industrial society', and it was the 'radical young' who swelled the ranks of the ecology movement. As Whitehead notes:

> They ran counter-culture bookshops and health food co-operatives, organised tenants' resistance to city-centre developers and nuclear power stations.
>
> (Whitehead, 1985: 240)

At its high point, and with the demand for natural and non-renewable resources growing year by year, the message of the ecology lobby found a wide audience among all age groups (though still predominantly the middle class). This period also saw the publication of what are now regarded as classic examples of early environmental literature: *The population bomb* (Ehrlich and Ehrlich, 1968); *The limits to growth* (Meadows *et al.*, 1972); *Blueprint for survival* (*The Ecologist*, 1972); *Small is beautiful* (Schumacher, 1973). In this context, the Department for the Environment (1972) produced a report for the UN Conference on the Human Environment in Stockholm. It was called *How do you want to live?* and was a document that captured some of the anxieties that were becoming apparent as a result of the challenge of affluence. Its tone is measured, and it looks to the planning process as the means of managing human demands on the environment. It was strongly focused on the types of environment in which Britons lived, and was full of discussions of the conflicts over traffic, amenities, leisure pressures and housing quality, as well the planning system. It was prefaced by a specially commissioned poem ('Going, going...') by Philip Larkin. While the report stands as a representative summary of a society facing the question of providing resources for the future, there was little that suggested that these issues were not outside the remit of a liberal, problem-solving democracy. It should be noted that there was perhaps less obvious and uncritical acceptance of science at this point.

This faith in science and democracy was evident in early moves to introduce environmental education to the school curriculum. At a conference at the University of Keele in 1965, it was agreed that environmental education 'should become an essential part of the education of all citizens, not only because of the importance of understanding something of their environment but because of its immense educational potential in assisting the emergence of a scientifically literate nation' (Christian, 1966).

This was a significant development, and should be seen in the context of arguments for economic and social modernisation. Scientific literacy was needed to promote economic growth and environmental awareness was one aspect of this. The Schools Council Project Environment argued for a balanced approach to environmental education. It noted that:

> We live at a time when an enormous amount of public interest is focused on the environment. It is common to speak of the environmental crisis and there is a flood of publications about it.
>
> (Project Environment, 1975: 1)

The Project noted that there is nothing new in most of the activities that are being carried out. What was new was the demand of society that schools should play their part in developing a sense of environmental concern and responsibility in the population. This demand came at a time when schools were seeking to make education more relevant and realistic for young people:

> Those who are soon to enter the adult world, in particular, demand school work that is less rooted in the past, is more forward-looking and is more likely to help them to live the sort of lives and face the sort of problems that they are likely to meet in the future. There is increasing dissatisfaction and disillusion among older pupils, and increasing awareness in schools of the need to face this situation and provide, as one head teacher said, 'an education that makes sense in the modern world'. The problems of the environment and the threats to the quality of life are matters that are likely to become critical during the lifetime of children now at school and an education that makes sense to them will have to help explain their place in the world and to help prepare them to face its future challenges.
>
> (Project Environment, 1975: 2–3)

This section has argued that the conditions of industrial and urban change associated with the modernisation of Britain in the post-war period led to an educational response that sought to go beyond rural-based locality studies to those that engaged with urban issues relevant to the lives of children growing up in a fast-changing world. This was a widening of the traditional remit of geography education. It was not well received by all in the geography education community. For some it was too political, for others it represented a loss of intellectual gravitas. However, it is possible to argue that this was a form of environmental geography that focused on people and place.

The school becomes a problem

> The emergence of environmentalism as a potent social force in the late twentieth century cannot simply be explained by reference to the extent of environmental damage, or even to the strength of our scientific understanding of such damage. There have always been what we would now call environmental problems, but they were not always seen as such at the time. They might have been seen as discrete problems, rightly addressed within the context of strictly bounded social and economic practices. They might not have been seen as problems at all, simply as the effects of human activity on nature, the inevitable and unpredictable side-effects of *techne*. Doubtless they were often not even understood as being due to human activity at all. Before they could be understood as aspects of an 'environmental crisis' the environment had to be constructed, as a coherent discourse.
>
> (Szerszynski, 2005: 84–85)

So far, this chapter has argued that school geography teachers developed a response to landscape and environmental change in pupils' localities. This was part of urban-based environmental education that sought to help pupils understand aspects of geographical change. The environment here was defined in a particular way. However, as Bronislaw Szerszynski argues, to say that 'environmental issues' exist is one thing, but to suggest that these amount to an 'environmental crisis' is another. Szerszynski suggests that, from the early 1970s, it became common to regard particular environmental events (such as flooding, or the draining of a wetland) as examples or symbols of a wider environmental crisis.

This section discusses the emergence of this global environmental consciousness, and shows how it fed into debates about environmental education. From the mid- to late 1960s to the early 1970s, Western societies experienced an explosion of cultural and political experimentation, largely among the young middle classes. Among the various elements were:

- an explosion of interest in oriental mysticism

- the widespread use of psychoactive (or mind-altering) drugs

- the creation of new social spaces in which to explore personal experiences and social relationships (pop festivals, communes, etc.)

- a growing political radicalism.

Common to all these developments was a reaction against the assumed complacency of post-war society – a society that seemed to lack any motivating ideology beyond material consumption and conformity, other than the new 'religion' of conspicuous consumption. Against the conformist, instrumental, bureaucratised world, the 1960s generation sought to develop a vague but powerful notion of liberation. This liberation was partly about oppressed minorities at home and in the 'third world', but was also about the liberation of aspects of human existence that were felt to be suppressed in contemporary industrialised societies.

There were a number of aspects to this cultural revolution. First, many young people were concerned with the mismatch between the values of the private and public realms. In the private realm, the values of intimacy, openness, self-expression and care were important, linked to changes in patterns of child rearing, in which the individual was seen as sacred and unique. This was also expressed in consumer culture, which stressed the importance of individual desire and hedonism. These values were contrasted with the norms of rational, disciplined behaviour and competitive striving in the public sphere. The result was that the post-war baby-boomer experienced a conflict between the values of the private and public realms. Second, a number of other social changes encouraged the development of these private values. For instance, post-war affluence made it possible for more individuals to expect greater fulfilment in their lives. The huge expansion of higher education led to the generalisation of critical thought and liberal values. The reduction in working hours meant that more attention was given to identity, and the rise of the 'expressive professions' (e.g. welfare professionals and university lecturers) increased the value placed on sensitivity and interpersonal relations. Finally, the development of mass media and tourism eroded particular and local understandings of identity. It led to the development of a global perspective, which allowed individuals to locate themselves in a global or cosmic sense, and encouraged a concern for universal notions of human rights.

These changes were crucial for the development of environmentalism. In organisational terms, developments such as mass demonstrations, communal decision-making processes and a regenerated idea of the rural commune provided ways of organising that were developed by the environmental movement. But the environmental movement did not begin to come onto the scene until the closing years of the 1960s, when the development of the ecological sciences from the 1950s, the rapid expansion of higher education in the 1960s and a renewed interest in nature in the mass media led to increased interest in ecological ideas among the population. Writers such as Rachel Carson (1962) and Barry Commoner (1970) wrote prophetic critiques of industrial practices, suggesting that these threatened the natural order. By the end of the 1960s, the 'movement' had fragmented into a number of distinct social movements, including the peace movement (opposed to the war in Vietnam), second-wave feminism, and environmentalism. Environmentalism was given additional resonance by dramatic media images of accidents such as the sinking of the *Torrey Canyon* oil tanker in 1967.

These issues were not self-evidently 'environmental'. It was the task of the environmental movement to develop an emerging discourse of the environment to which a growing range of issues could be linked. The model of this discourse was essentially that modern industrial society – the system – was 'sick' and needed a radical reorientation if it was to survive, let alone offer people a fulfilling future. Central to this was the growing power of the mass media as a conveyor of messages and images. Images of oil platforms or nuclear power stations, and images of particular iconic species, allowed environmental groups to make links to wider critiques of a modern technological society. The early environmental movement was apocalyptic, with messages of imminent ecological and social collapse supported by influential reports such as *The limits to growth* and *Blueprint for survival*, but it was also utopian in its articulation of a social vision based on ecological interdependence and harmony with nature.

These ideas came to influence debates within environmental education, so that the environment was increasingly constructed as a global issue. For example, the influential Global Impact project at the Centre for Global Education at the University of York reached a stark conclusion about the damaging effects of the Western mindset:

> In the West our understanding of the world has been largely shaped through science which, until this century, has sought to understand the world by dissecting it, bit by bit. But this approach leaves unanswered the question of how the parts interact to sustain life and evolve. A shift of perspective is now occurring in many disciplines towards a focus on whole systems instead of constituent parts. A system, whether it is a human family or a tropical rainforest, can only be understood by looking at the relationships between the individual elements; that is the constant flow of energy, matter or information throughout the system.
>
> (Greig, Pike and Selby, 1987: 4)

This 'new age' environmental philosophy came to influence a number of important publications in environmental education, such as *Earthrights: education as if the planet really mattered* (Greig *et al.*, 1987), which noted that in the 1980s teaching and learning about the environment was marked by:

■ a recognition that the local environment is caught up in the global ecosystem

■ an awareness that human and natural systems interact in myriad ways and that there is no part of human activity which does not have a bearing on the environment and *vice versa*

■ a dawning acknowledgement of how much we can learn from other cultures, and perhaps especially indigenous peoples, about how to relate to the environment

■ an emphasis on the development of environmentally friendly values, attitudes and skills.

(Greig, Pike and Selby, 1987: 26)

Strongly influenced by publications such as Fritjof Capra's (1982) *The turning point* and Marilyn Ferguson's (1980) *The Aquarian conspiracy*, in the 1980s and early 1990s it was not uncommon for teachers to identify themselves as 'global teachers'. Part of this teacher identity was built on the argument that the formal academic curriculum is fragmented and encourages students to see the parts, but not the connections between them. As Capra (1983) put it, in a passage cited approvingly by Pike and Selby (1988):

> The belief that all these fragments – in ourselves, in our environment and in our society – are really separate can be seen as the essential reason for the present series of social, ecological and cultural crises. It has alienated us from nature and from our fellow human beings. It has brought a grossly unjust distribution of natural resources creating economic and political disorder; an ever rising wave of violence, both spontaneous and institutionalised, and an ugly polluted environment in which life has often become physically and mentally unhealthy.
>
> (Capra, 1983: 28, in Pike and Selby, 1988: 25)

From this perspective, environmental educators were less concerned with the protection of specific bits of nature, and more likely to see the destruction of nature as symptomatic of deeper problems in modern industrial culture. Their teaching was aimed less at individual sites and species, and more at certain practices of contemporary society that were seen to systematically damage the environment.

The environmental geography described in the previous section had at its centre the idea of a rational, planned society, as a reaction against the unplanned development produced by liberal capitalism. Modern nature conservation owed much to the idea that human activities should be brought under centralised, rational control; concerns to balance the aesthetic and economic values of landscape, to balance the goals of individual mobility though motor cars with the walking quality of towns, can be seen as an extension of this aim to rationalise and plan human environments. This was reflected in geography teachers' concern with rational land-use planning and modern ordered development. In this sense, environmental education served as a corrective to tendencies within industrial modernity. An important part of this worldview was the belief in science as a means to improving the human condition.

However, as this section describes, there is another important strand of environmental thinking that represented a significant break from the type of environmental geography that developed in the 1970s. In this version, threats to specific environments were seen as symbolic of universal threats to nature itself (for example, cutting down a forest is represented as a threat to the global environment), and this was linked to cultural changes that paved the way for a growing cultural resonance of ideas of global citizenship or oneness with nature. In other words, an 'environmental crisis' was constructed, which increasingly came to influence the work of geography teachers in schools, or at least shaped the terms of debate about what it meant to teach about environmental issues.

Szerszynski's argument that environmental concern is not directly linked to the scale of environmental problems has important implications, because it requires us to examine the ways in which ideas about environmental crisis are constructed. In the 1980s, environmental educators were successful in constructing the environment as a global issue. Thus tropical rainforest deforestation in Brazil's Amazonia was no longer seen as a national or regional environmental problem, but rather as a symbol of a global environmental crisis. What is more, this form of global environmentalism offered particular ways of understanding the relationship between people and nature, one based on ideas of holism and integration of the personal and the planetary. There are, of course, other ways of representing this relationship. As we saw in the previous chapter, geographers have tended to stress the capitalist economic system as a cause of environmental problems. The global education perspective had important implications for teaching and learning about environmental problems, as it tended to see school subjects such as geography and history as too closely linked to a mechanistic division of the curriculum.

The eco-modernisers' dilemma

From its marginal position in the school curriculum, environmental education has gradually gained increasing status and recognition. The 1980s were characterised by increasing concern about the environment. In a decade that saw profound economic, social and political change there were conflicts over nuclear power; the social and environmental costs of coal mining; and the intensification of agriculture and the loss of habitats. On a global scale, there was focus on the issues of desertification and the deforestation of tropical rainforests, ozone depletion and, later, global warming. Prime Minister Margaret Thatcher raised the question of the environment at a speech to the Royal Society in 1987. The UK government published in 1990 the first ever White Paper on the environment, entitled *This common inheritance*. The Earth Summit held in Rio de Janeiro in 1992 was a significant event because it was a landmark in international cooperation about the environment. It committed each national government to the production of a sustainable development plan based on Agenda 21, the sustainability action strategy agreed at the summit. Although widely regarded as a repackaging of existing environmental measures, the summit led to the publication of *Sustainable development: the UK strategy* (1994). In some ways, this reflected a shift in the Conservative government's thinking about the environment, in that it saw a greater need for government to impose limits on development and implement environmental controls, though at the same time it argued that it was not appropriate for governments to tell citizens what they should do and how they should behave. However, it is possible to suggest that the UK's commitment to sustainable development allowed it to make some important decisions about the environment.

The election of a New Labour government in 1997 was the signal for an intensification of the project of environmental modernisation, or the wider greening of society. Although this has offered a legitimate place for environmental education in schools, many environmental educators, coming from a more radical or 'deep green' position, are concerned that it is based on weak forms of sustainability that effectively mean 'business as usual'. This is evident in Selby's chapter in *Green frontiers*, where he characterises how present models of schooling are at odds with environmental thinking:

Schools remain bastions of a mechanistic mindset. The curriculum, for the most part, continues to be divided into tidy compartments and discrete subject disciplines while most teachers make, at best, tokenistic efforts to explore the interrelationships between what the learner encounters within each classroom or subject setting. The science/humanities divide underpinning the curriculum enshrines and reinforces the human/nature divide inherited from mechanism. Grade apartheid is the norm. Individualised and competitive as opposed to collaborative learning continue to dominate the learning process. There is a drum beat insistence within the agenda of most subjects that certain knowledge and real understanding are achievable through reducing any topic or theme to its discrete component parts. Explanation is addressed in terms of contiguous cause and effect events or relationships. Most schools keep community at arm's length, more often than not disregarding the locality and environment as learning contexts of rich potential.

(Selby, 2008: 252)

This statement represents the view that the school curriculum, with its fragmented and mechanistic approach to knowledge, tends actively to prevent the type of holistic understanding required to develop 'environmental consciousness'.

In their introduction to *Green frontiers*, James Gray-Donald and David Selby similarly cast doubt on recent moves to 'mainstream' environmental education. They suggest that, in order to be accepted by the educational mainstream, many proponents shy away from embracing a 'whole person, whole planet' stance. Instead, learning materials fall short of offering real diversity in learning approaches: the cognitive, classroom-based monoculture of mainstream learning is, save on special occasions, rarely departed from.

Science remains the dominant approach, with the result that most environmental educators shy away from real engagement with social justice, peace and cultural issues. Most renditions of education for sustainable development, as signed up to by environmental educators, involve an implicit acceptance of the principle of economic growth (oftentimes couched in the language of global competitiveness), the violence that the global marketplace is doing to the biosphere not withstanding. Interpretations of education for sustainable development are also anthropocentric, describing nature in resource terms as 'natural capital' or 'natural services'.

(Gray-Donald and Selby, 2008: 4)

This section argues that significant tensions exist between the type of global environmental education favoured by some environmental educators, and the more techno-centric versions of education for sustainable development associated with the New Labour government's embrace of environmental modernisation. While the former seeks to bring about a transformation of education, the latter seeks to raise pupils' awareness and develop forms of environmental citizenship that basically accept the continuation of the current economy and society. The question of geography's contribution to these debates is the theme of chapter three.

Conclusion

This chapter charted some of the important ways in which environmental themes have been incorporated into school geography. It argued that, initially, environmental concerns were a response to changes in the nature of local environments, and that this led to the development of environmental geography. This fitted very neatly with moves to develop pupils' participation in local communities. Since the 1980s, environmental issues are more likely to be framed in terms of the global environment, with examples such as desertification or tropical deforestation standing in for broader environmental crises. An important issue is whether school subjects such as geography support or hinder understanding of ecological issues. For some commentators, the structures and mechanisms of schooling are seen as part of the problem, leading to fragmented and partial understanding. Clearly, for a book entitled *Teaching geography as if the planet matters*, it is important to be clear about the contribution geography can make to environmental understanding, and this is the focus of chapter three.

Geography, society, nature – changing perspectives

The study of geography stimulates an interest in and a sense of wonder about places. It helps young people make sense of a complex and dynamically changing world. It explains where places are, how places and landscapes are formed, how people and their environment interact, and how a diverse range of economies, societies and environments are interconnected. It builds on pupils' own experiences to investigate places at all scales, from the personal to the global.

(National Curriculum, 2008)

The starting point for this chapter is the National Curriculum statement about the purposes of geography. In particular, I am interested in the part that is concerned with 'how people and their environment interact, and how a diverse range of economies, societies and environments are interconnected'. This statement takes us back to Halford Mackinder's address to the Royal Geographical Society in 1887, in which he argued that geography can 'bridge one of the greatest of all gaps', namely that separating 'the natural sciences and the study of humanity'. Although there have been some important additions to the discipline of geography – notably in the concepts of place and space – the people–environment theme continues, and there are continued attempts to 'unify' geography (e.g. Matthews and Herbert, 2004). This focus on the relationship between people and environment, or society and nature, can be termed environmental geography. The editors of *A companion to environmental geography* (Castree *et al.*, 2009) see this as a broad field that contains many different themes and approaches, and that is linked to a range of diverse disciplines and research areas such as history, sociology, economics, politics, Earth-systems science and ecology. Despite the wide variety of topics, approaches, concepts and practices under the heading environmental geography, they all:

■ study some aspect of society and nature in relation to one another, rather than alone

- are concerned with the character, purpose, meaning and proper management of these socio-natural relations

- are produced by professionals who see it as their job to produce knowledge of society–nature interrelations

- have the hallmarks of academic discourse, which is derived from disciplined thought and inquiry, is esoteric, and commands a certain degree of authority

- claim to tell us something about the actualities of human–environment relations, and in this sense continue the idea that geography is a practical subject concerned with the materiality of the world

- are intellectually outward-looking, being prepared to make creative links with other disciplines and research fields.

This book rests on the belief that the products of environmental geography should form the basis for curriculum planning and teaching about the subject in schools. Of course, there are important decisions to be made about what aspects of environmental geography to select and teach. These decisions are based on a wide range of criteria, not least those associated with issues of pedagogy. However, it is important to acknowledge that, at the present time in schools, there are those who would seek to downplay the importance of the disciplined study of such knowledge. Following this logic, it is easy to see how a school might interpret moves to teach education for sustainable development as something outside the remit of subjects such as geography, science or history, and see it as a set of activities concerned with environmental citizenship. Against this, the argument of this book is that school subjects contain the necessary knowledge, concepts and understanding required as the basis for environmental action.

The purpose of this chapter is to provide readers with an introductory account of how geography has handled the relationship between people and environment, or society and nature. To this end, the chapter provides a short survey of the distinctive contribution geography makes to our understanding of the relationship between people and environment. The survey explains that geographers have, over time, developed more complex and nuanced understandings of this relationship, and suggest that knowledge of these developments provides the basis for making choices about what to teach in school geography. The survey is not exhaustive, and readers are directed to fuller discussions found in, for example, Phillips and Mignall (2000), Castree (2005) and Robbins *et al.* (2010). However, what is offered here is a framework that is drawn upon and developed in the rest of the book.

Early developments

The histories of school subjects such as geography are closely linked with, though not determined by, developments in the nature of society. As John Huckle (1986) argued:

Geography earned its place in the school curriculum as a subject well suited to facilitating and legitimating capital's increasing exploitation of people and nature. Its revival in the late nineteenth century and rapid growth in schools in the early decades of this century, owed much to the adoption of a form of environmentalism which stressed the unity of the nature–society relationship, and the natural region as a framework for curriculum planning.

(Huckle, 1986: 9)

Much early work in geography sought to establish the subject as an integrative study of nature and culture. An influential figure in this respect was Andrew John Herbertson (1865–1915) who was recruited to Oxford University by Halford Mackinder in 1899, the year in which Herbertson's *Man and his work, an introduction to human geography* was published, which stressed the influence of the physical environment on human societies. The first paragraph of the book gives an indication of this:

The world is the home of man. All that we learn of the physical features of the Earth, its climates, plants, and animals, is of practical importance, because these things have helped make the human race what it is – here adventurous and progressive, there indolent and backward.

(Herbertson and Herbertson, 1899: 1)

This is an example of what geographers now call 'moral climatic determinism'. Herbertson claimed that nothing has a 'greater influence on the history of different races of men than climate'. For example, the dense forests of the tropical world, with their abundant vegetation, have made life too easy; the climate is 'enervating' and there is little to stimulate 'that co-operation for common ends with which social progress begins'. In the Arctic regions, life is a grim struggle and the natives of this region have 'little to arouse hope and energy and relapse into spiritless and mechanical endurance'. In those places that enjoy a temperate climate, life is neither so hard as to sap hope, nor so easy as to encourage 'improvidence', and there is a happy combination of caution and thrift with hope and energy.

The importance of these arguments is that they sought to provide a grand, over-arching explanation of the relationship between humans and environments that was large enough to establish geography as a serious academic subject. In schools, the organisation of the mass of facts and description was made easier by the development of regional schemes that allowed for forms of curricular organisation. There was a clear link between these ideas and racial and imperialist ideologies, and geography has been implicated in this (see Marsden, 1996). However, as the twentieth century progressed, there was a move from geographical determinism to geographical possibilism. Thus, in his later writings Herbertson became convinced by the arguments of environmental possibilism associated with the French regional geography school dominated by Paul Vidal de la Blache. Intensive study of 'primitive' people had highlighted the complex relationship between people and their environment. In 1911, the American anthropologist

Franz Boas published *The mind of primitive man*, which refuted the link between the two by providing examples of different groups living in similar conditions but displaying very different characteristics. For instance, the Eskimos and the Chuchki of north-eastern Siberia share an Arctic environment, but the former live by hunting and fishing while the latter base their economy on breeding reindeer.

After the Second World War, geography as a discipline took a distinctively scientific turn, encapsulated in the well-documented exchange between Richard Hartshorne and Fred K. Schaefer. Hartshorne's (1939) *The nature of geography* was a call for geographers to return to the ways of the past. It stressed the importance of geographers studying the particular and the unique, and focusing on 'areal differentiation', as compared with other disciplines that examined general processes and patterns. Schaefer (1953) challenged this, arguing that geography should be a spatial science, arguing that: 'Geography is to be conceived as concerned with the formulation of the laws governing the spatial distribution of certain features on the earth's surface.' It is important to realise that it was the question of what is meant by 'science' that interested Schaefer. According to Schaefer, science is based on careful empirical observation, has explanation as its goal, and is concerned with the identification of general laws about the behaviour of phenomena. In the 1950s and 1960s, the idea of geography as a 'spatial science' gained influence. Geography as a spatial science was concerned with systematic approaches as different phenomena were bracketed out for study. In physical geography, there was a shift from broadly evolutionary accounts of landscape formation (associated with the work of W.M. Davis) to a focus on 'process studies'.[1] In the 1960s, human geography adopted the notion of geography as a spatial science. It was assumed that human patterns and processes could be studied using the methods of the natural sciences, with result that geography courses developed in the wake of the 'new' geography were characterised by a focus on models and theories derived from the natural sciences. The effect of geography as a spatial science on the question of nature was that the environment was defined in physical terms, and this was the province of physical geography.

The challenge to value-free science

By the late 1960s, it was apparent that population increase, economic growth and mass consumption were all having a profound effect on natural resource availability and the integrity of ecosystems. In addition, the idea that Western science operated as a value-free and non-ideological set of methods was increasingly challenged. The radical science movement sought to demonstrate how, far from being objective and neutral, science tended to support the interests of the corporate state.

The result was that by the late 1970s, many geographers came to challenge the idea that it is possible to separate environmental issues and problems from the society that shapes and creates them. For example, it became clear that the impacts of natural hazards are related to societal factors such as level of economic development and poverty; that famine and world hunger could not be explained simply as the consequence of drought; and that the process of desertification is not purely an outcome of climatic shifts. Thus the implication of society in environmental processes was widely recognised. Geographers in this period came to critique and reject a series of what Paul Robbins (2004) calls 'apolitical ecologies'. The first of the apolitical ecologies identified by Robbins is 'ecoscarcity and the limits to growth'. This holds that the central driving explanation for social/ecological crisis has been, and continues to be, the increasing human population. The second is modernisation, by which it is held that ecological problems and crises throughout the world are the result of the inadequate adoption and implementation of modern economic techniques of management, exploitation and conservation.[2] Against this, geographical thinking about the relationships between people and environment came to be shaped by perspectives from the interdisciplinary field of political ecology, which is neatly summarised by Robbins:

> As critique, political ecology seeks to expose flaws in dominant approaches to the environment favoured by corporate, state, and international authorities, working to demonstrate the undesirable impacts of policies and market conditions, especially from the point of view of local people, marginal groups, and vulnerable populations. It works to 'denaturalize' certain social and environmental conditions, showing them to be the contingent outcomes of power and not inevitable.
>
> (Robbins, 2004: 12)

Examples of this approach are found in the early work of David Harvey (1974), who challenged the scientific neutrality of neo-Malthusian ideas about the relationship between population and resources; Neil Smith's (1984) argument that nature is used as an ideology to hide the reality of social relations; and Kenneth Hewitt (1983), who sought to show how natural disasters cannot be understood simply as the consequence of a calamitous nature, but are closely related to the structures of society. In geography, these approaches are summarised by the term 'social nature', which stresses that it is impossible to separate nature from the society that shapes it. The idea of social nature challenges the claim that there is a pre-existing nature 'out there' that can be objectively defined and studied. Instead, knowledge of nature cannot be gained without reference to society. This has become the dominant position in how human geographers understand the relationship between society and nature, though it is not without contestation.

What we consume

An example of how ideas about the social production of nature can inform geography teaching is found in John Huckle's (1988–93) *What we consume*, which sought to relate environmental problems to their location in the global economy. His unit on Brazil focuses on the impact of economic development on tropical rainforest ecosystems. The starting point for these activities is that rainforests are a crucial part of the global ecosystem, provide valuable economic resources, are a unique source of biodiversity, and are home to indigenous people. The problem is one of deforestation, as the frontier is opened by small farmers and large-scale cattle ranchers. The clearance of the forest leads to ecological problems, as the valuable nutrients are contained in the biomass, and once these are removed the thin soils are prone to out-washing by heavy rain. Very quickly the soil fertility is degraded and the farmers are forced to move on. The key to a political ecological understanding is to go beyond the idea that it is human greed or stupidity that drives this process. In particular, blame cannot be attached to the activities of small farmers. A more complex understanding must be related to the economic crisis of the Brazilian state and its solution in developing an export-oriented economy. In this sense, the Amazonian rainforest became a site of investment in mines, timber and ranching for foreign multinationals. In addition, the social crisis engendered by a highly divided society and landlessness in parts of Brazil led to the idea that colonisation of the rainforest was a solution to poverty and landlessness. This was facilitated by large-scale road-building and resettlement schemes. In all of this, there are winners and losers, and what starts out as an environmental issue is more accurately understood as related to an unequal and (many would argue) unjust global economic order.

These developments were important because they demonstrated that the environment was not simply a problem for science and technology to solve, but was fundamentally and thoroughly social and political. Environmental problems should be treated as simultaneously political–economic and ecological in character.

These ideas came to influence school geography teaching in the 1970s and 1980s, as geography teachers rejected the idea that global problems can be understood as Acts of God, or that levels of economic development in less-developed countries can be explained purely as the result of their internal conditions or characteristics. In doing so, geography teachers drew upon insights from geographers studying the relationships between people and environments. One influential account was provided by Tim O'Riordan's (1976) *Environmentalism*, which summarised a wide range of writing about environmental issues. He developed a classification of environmental ideologies. Environmentalism, he suggested, was divided between two perspectives. The first perspective was technocentrism, which assumes that mounting environmental problems require greater attention to environmental management and planning, and that environmental dangers can be averted without major social and economic change, so long as insights from environmental science can be incorporated into existing decision-making processes. O'Riordan thought that technocentrism was subdivided into 'Cornucopian' ideologies, which adopt a business-as-usual approach and argue that talk of environmental limits is essentially scare-mongering; and 'accommodators', which recognise the need to use economic, legislative and technological means to reduce the environmental impacts of human activity. The second perspective was ecocentrism, which recognises the potential limits to human exploitation of the environment, and argues for alternative forms of economic development which live within these limits. Again, ecocentrism was divided into two further ideologies. The first is deep ecology or 'Gaianism', which recognises the intrinsic importance of nature for humanity and asserts that nature has its own rights, which should be respected irrespective of human needs.

The second is that of self-reliance or 'soft technology', which asserts the need to create small-scale, self-reliant communities based on alternative forms of technology. Despite their differences, ecocentric approaches share a lack of faith in modern large-scale technology and its associated requirement for elitist expertise and central state authority.

The idea that there exists a range of environmental ideologies was further developed by the geography David Pepper in the mid-1980s and early 1990s, notably in *The roots of modern environmentalism* (1984). These ideas were taken up and developed for geography teachers by John Huckle (1983), who, developing O'Riordan's classification, distinguished between three types of environmental education – education about the environment; education through the environment; and education for the environment.

Writing in the mid-1980s, Huckle noted that 'the ecology movement and the new school geography emerged at the same time', and that for the majority of geography teachers 'ideas and techniques relating to the spatial analysis were given greater attention within the curriculum than those relating to ecology or environmental politics' (Huckle, 1983). As the influence of geography as spatial science waned and environmental issues found their place in school geography, much geography teaching reflected technocentric ideologies which assumed that geographers could use environmental knowledge to reform and better manage existing economic and social systems.

School geography's attachment to technocentric approaches to society–nature relations placed it in an uneasy relationship with more openly 'radical' approaches that developed in schools in the 1970s and 1980s. This period saw the emergence of a series of 'adjectival studies', which challenged the sanctity of the existing school subjects. These new subjects – which included peace studies, global education, development education, and environmental education – were in part based on a critique of existing school subjects, which were seen as rooted in the past, as socially exclusive, and as failing to engage with important issues that faced individuals and society. Peace studies, global education, environmental education, and so on were all the educational expression of a broader set of social movements that challenged the direction of contemporary Western societies. Boris Frankel (1987), in his survey of the ideas of the 'post-industrial utopians', noted that:

> In the past 20 years there has been a significant growth in movements, parties, journals and individual campaigns focusing on humane alternatives to the ugly reality of impersonal bureaucracies, exploitation of Third World peoples, the arms race, dangerous new technology, unsafe products, irrational health, education and transport systems, economic growth which destroys the environment, and agribusiness profits in a world of starvation.
>
> (Frankel, 1987: 6–7)

From the late 1970s, geographers in schools were involved in debates about the extent to which geography teaching was based on harmful attitudes and values. This was based on the types of representations offered in textbooks, the development of alternative or 'dissident' geographies, and the production of resources that challenged the racism, sexism and ethnocentrism of the traditional geography curriculum. An example of this approach is found in John Fien and Rob Gerber's (1988) edited book *Teaching geography for a better world*. The overall aim of the book can be seen in the following statement:

> Teaching geography for a better world involves making conscious decisions to challenge the ideology of conservative approaches to education, in general, and to rethink our goals, content, resources and methods in geography teaching, in particular. It also challenges many aspects of the liberal-progressive ideology of education that sees schools as a way of improving society through the education of well-meaning individuals who will be tomorrow's skilled and active citizens.
>
> (Fien and Gerber, 1988: 7–8)

Fien and Gerber go on to explain that liberal-progressive educational ideology overemphasises the role of individuals in causing social, environmental and economic problems, and the ability of individuals to solve them.

Teaching geography for a better world is best understood as representing a form of educational discourse that emerged from, and responded to, the economic, social and environmental crises of the 1970s and 1980s. In this period an increasingly globalised economy, which led to concentration of wealth in the elites of economically developed nations, challenged the models of development proposed in school geography, which placed their faith in the free market to lead to 'trickle-down'. The advent of second-wave feminism and the growth of moves to recognise the rights of indigenous peoples led to questions of *whose geography* was being taught. And the heightened awareness of a series of environmental problems challenged the assumptions of continued economic growth through the exploitation and rational management of natural resources. In this context, the chapters in Fien and Gerber's (1988) book made it clear that what was taught in schools was not innocent of politics.

The social construction of nature

One of the most significant outcomes of the debates about the social production of nature in the 1970s and 1980s was that it was no longer possible to accept uncritically the claim that geographical knowledge about environmental issues, or people–environment relationships, is value-free or neutral. As Henderson and Waterstone (2009) summarise:

> The basic notion, which now seems quite reasonable and straightforward, is that all knowledge is produced by actors who are themselves inescapably situated in particular historical and geographic circumstances, and that these circumstances have important (if often unrecognized) effects both on the means of knowledge production and on the kinds of knowledge produced.
>
> (Henderson and Waterstone, 2009: 9)

A good example of this is the work of feminist geographers, who pointed out that geographical knowledge studied and taught in universities (and schools) was largely the product of men. Jan Monk and Susan Hanson (1982) warned of the need to avoid 'excluding half of the human in human geography'. The implications of this teaching about people and environment in school geography are important, as it was largely assumed that there was no need to differentiate between different types of people. Feminist geographers pointed to the need to attend to women's experiences of places, spaces and environments, and in 1993 the geographer Joni Seager published *Earth follies: coming to feminist terms with the global environmental crisis*. In explaining the need for a feminist geographical analysis of environmental issues, Seager raised some important questions about her geographical training:

> My training as a geographer, in both the physical and social sciences, led me to conceptualise environmental problems in their physical forms – that is, I understood environmental problems as *problems of physical systems under stress*.
>
> (Seager, 1993: 2)

Seager points out that neither popular media representations of environmental issues nor her specialist training as a geographer 'encourage us to ask questions about the actors, institutions, and processes' behind environmental problems such as oil spills, the hole in the ozone layer, or tropical deforestation. However:

> The environmental crisis is not just a crisis of physical ecosystems. The real story of the environmental crisis is a story of power and profit and political wrangling; it is a story of the institutional arrangements and settings, the bureaucratic arrangements and the cultural conventions that create conditions of environmental destruction.
>
> (Seager, 1993: 3)

From this starting point, Seager goes on to explore the ideologies, institutions and practices that underpin the drive to appropriate and overexploit physical systems. As a feminist, her concern is with the way in which patriarchy – as a structured system that protects and reproduces the interests of powerful males – is reflected in the military, business elites and the emerging ecology establishment, and how the voices and experiences of women are ignored or pushed to the side. She concludes *Earth follies* with the important insight that the environment is not a separate realm that exists

> [...] beyond the ordinariness of everyday life. Instead the relationships of power and control that shape our environmental affairs are an extension of the everyday and ordinary relationships between men and women and between them and institutions.
>
> (Seager, 1993: 282)

In terms of teaching school geography, this suggests that teaching about environmental issues should begin from the everyday experiences of students in schools. The idea that there exists a wide range of geographical knowledge and perspectives is in tune with the development, in the 1990s, of the so-called postmodern turn in human geography, which came to influence how geographers conceptualised the relationship between nature and society. At its simplest, postmodern geography challenged the very notion that there exists, out there, a 'real' environment that is capable of independent study and examination. What we see as nature is shaped by our society, and nature should be seen as a social construction.[3] The idea of representation and narrative is increasingly important in how geographers understand nature. This idea has been expressed in the work of William Cronon. His edited book *Uncommon ground* (1996) is often seen as a landmark in the development of the idea that nature is a social construction. Candace Slater's (2003) *Entangled Edens* is a study of what she calls 'Amazon-centred poetics' – the systematic examination of words and images that can help us better understand such seemingly unpoetic concerns as deforestation and species preservation. The language of environment matters. As Slater argues, something that is imagined as 'the world's lungs' will provoke a different response from 'the world's heart', something that is seen as Eden rather than a tangled jungle. She traces the history of these representations.

This is closely linked to developments in post-structural thought, which is critical of the tendency of political ecology to place primacy emphasis on an all-powerful capitalism as the explanatory force for environmental degradation, and on 'grand stories' or metanarratives of environmental change. Two examples of work that seeks to explore the ways in which environmental orthodoxies develop are Stott and Sullivan's (2003) *Political ecology: science, myth and power* and Forsyth's (2003) *Critical political ecology*. Stott and Sullivan argue that powerful ideas about the extent and causes of environmental problems develop and gain ascendancy, even though there is little scientific evidence for them, or there may be evidence that contradicts these narratives. These take the forms of 'hegemonic myths' – which appear to be Northern, middle-class, white, Anglo-Saxon and male in their origins. This leads to an important set of questions:

- Who determines environmental narratives?

- How do such narratives become currency in international relations discourse?

- What alternatives are there?

The type of approach favoured by Stott and Sullivan (2003) would challenge Huckle's analysis on the grounds that it represents an over-arching or grand narrative that rainforests are the 'biological wonder of the world', that rainforest clearance is a 'bad' thing, and that we will all suffer if the rainforests are destroyed. Indeed, Stott (2001) argues that 'tropical rainforests' are an invention, the result of a particular way of seeing and interpreting the landscape. He makes the point that 'tropical rainforests have many values', which vary from North to South, country to country, and people to people. For some, tropical rainforests are a sign of underdevelopment and a lack of progress; to others they are vital for the very ecology and survival of the whole Earth. The important question is: whose values dominate decision-making concerning rainforests in our changing world?

In answer to this question, Stott and Sullivan (2003) suggest that contemporary concern with the destruction of tropical rainforests since the mid-1980s is driven by the values and concerns of the Northern middle classes, who see the preservation of rainforest as a key item on their global stability agenda. Having agreed this agenda, they have started a process of scientific myth-making to bolster their case. These myths are the 'little green lies' of the current paradigm. The fundamental aim behind them is to make us all believe that we really do need rainforests, not just want them or like them.

- Tropical rainforests are not the most complex ecosystems on Earth. There are many competitors for this title, depending on how you define complexity.

- Tropical rainforests are not millions of years old. The fossil record clearly indicates that the majority of present-day 'rainforests' are less than 18,000 years old, having been subject to drought, fire and cold during the peak of the last ice age.

- The plant diversity beneath the canopy is actually quite low.

- The rainforests are not the lungs of the world. In fact, because of their decomposition processes, most rainforests tend to use up as much oxygen as – or even more oxygen than – they give out.

- Rainforests are portrayed as vital in preventing soil erosion. While this may be true in some cases, in others it is not, and grassland ecosystems might be more effective in preventing soil erosion.

(Moore *et al.*, 1996)

Moore *et al.* suggest that this 'cavalcade of "little green lies"' has three main purposes, all relating to the essential political ecology of rainforests:

- the desire of the North to maintain a controlling interest over the resources of the South

- the worry that changes in the South, both ecological and economic, might damage the political stability of the North

- the 'desperate drive' of scientists to obtain continued funding for research into the questions that the current paradigm place on the agenda.

Global environmental change represents one of the dominant modern green paradigms, both creating the current scientific agenda and demanding certain solutions. However, all science operates within a political context, and there is a need to deconstruct this context. This is the theme of political ecology which asks important questions such as: Who actually placed global environmental change on the agenda? Why did they do so? Is the agenda agreed and shared by all, rich and poor, North and South, scientist and lay person?

One of the responses to these arguments, which focus on the social construction of nature, is that by raising questions about the existence of 'real', actually existing nature, such arguments lend credence to the views of environmental sceptics and climate change-deniers who argue that environmental concerns are Western myths. One of the problems with the social construction of nature is that it seems to deny the possibility of reaching agreement as to what is happening to 'real' nature:

> [Social nature] arguments seem practically debilitating because they evidently prevent us from acting in and on nature in appropriate ways. For instance, if 'global warming' is simply a fabrication – a myth cooked up by atmospheric scientists keen to ensure large research grants for the work they do – then we are led to conclude that polluting the atmosphere is okay, since we can never know the 'real' effects of greenhouse gases.
>
> (Castree and Braun, 2001: 16–17).

However, this fails to do justice to the work undertaken by geographers, most of whom work within the social nature perspective but are careful to note the materiality and political nature of their analyses.

For further study

1. Are there any 'grand narratives' that underpin the teaching of environmental issues in your geography department? What would it mean to deconstruct these grand narratives?

Animal geographies

Another important strand in recent work on nature and society is the emergence of interest in animal geographies, which highlights the way in which geographical studies have tended to ignore the agency of animals and the non-human world. They are part of the development of a new politics that recognises the co-existence of species. One of the most accessible introductions to this strand of thought in geography is Jennifer Wolch and Jody Emel's (1998) *Animal geographies*. The premise is that animals have been so indispensable to the structure of human affairs, and so tied up with our visions of progress and the good life, that we have been unable to (even try to) see them fully. But human practices now threaten the animal world and the entire global environment as never before. This has created a space in which it is possible and necessary to rethink human relationships with animals. Wolch and Emel note that geography has always had a long tradition of inquiry into the relationship between nature and society, but has also developed as a response to modernity and social theory. These approaches offer to 'shed light on animals as central agents in the constitution of space and place'. They organise their volume around four areas of inquiry. The first is the way that animal subjectivities and human identities are shaped and co-reliant. This reveals how animals and humans live in close proximity to one another and how at times the boundaries between humans and animals become socially and politically charged. These animal–human relations are situated within broader political economies of animal bodies. Finally, all these relationships are subject to examination from an ethical perspective.

They provide an interesting and informative analysis of why the 'animal moment' has occurred in social theory. This is tied in with economic questions and developments:

> Over the past two decades, the animal economy has become simultaneously both more intensive and extensive. More profits are squeezed out of each animal life, while the reach of animal-based industries has grown to include most of the developing world.
>
> (Wolch and Emel, 1998: 2)

Specific elements of this include the processes of economic globalisation and the changes entailed in the world diet, processes of economic development and habitat loss, the trade in wild animals, and the emergence of the biotechnology industry and the genetic modification of animal bodies. These economic developments have raised questions about the human use of animals:

> The threats of massive environmental degradation and species extinction, and the commodification of billions of animals as the economy goes global, have led to a turbulent politics surrounding animals.
>
> (Wolch and Emel, 1998: 8)

This politics is varied and complex. There are conservation struggles, the protection of wilderness and wilderness species, and moves towards animal welfare – based on the idea that individual animals should not suffer. This type of politics has increasingly been linked to debates about the types of food people eat and the conditions of its production. Animal politics can be linked to some developments in social theory, which have centred on critiques of modernity. Western modernity as a historical epoch was characterised by rapid developments in science, machine technology and modes of industrial production that together led to unprecedented living standards, dependence on inanimate energy sources, the political system of nation-states, and the rise of massive bureaucracies. By the 1970s, the legacies of modernity and modernist ways of knowing were under severe attack. Critics argued that the achievements of modernity rested on race, class and gender domination, colonialism and imperialism, anthropocentrism and the destruction of nature. This is reflected in the 'cultural turn', the de-centreing of the subject and the critique of dualism, and the exposure of modernist myths of Western progress. It is important to note the political nature of these concerns. Clearly, an analysis that points out the ways in which animals have been excluded from ethical and moral concerns seeks to redress this. Wolch and Emel state that 'Our political project is the creation of many forms of shared space':

> With barriers to emotional engagement eroding, battles over material and cultural goods increasing, and global capitalism expanding, democratic communication and decision-making will be absolutely necessary to maintain any sort of social, economic

and ecological balance. For us, building a progressive politics for the twenty-first century means combining critical analysis with a commitment to inclusive, caring and democratic campaigns for a justice capable of embracing both people and animals.

(Wolch and Emel, 1998)

For further study

1.   Undertake an analysis of the schemes of work taught in geography in your department. How far do they reflect the invisibility of animals? What might it mean to teach a geography that reflected the importance of animals?

Post-natures

Finally, in this section we should mention the development of what Castree (2005) calls 'post-nature' geographies, which take issue with the society–nature dualism that has characterised geographical thinking. A good example of this type of approach is found in the edited collection *Technonatures* (White and Wilbert, 2009). The book starts from the implicit recognition that critical discourses formulated around strong, power-laden oppositions and distinctions (organic versus synthetic; human versus animal or machine; natural versus technological, etc.) have become not just much harder to maintain in recent years, but also much less politically desirable to maintain. Our lives are increasingly a complex mix of nature and technology (think of a car). The term 'technonatures' is designed to draw attention to this complexity. It is linked to Raymond Williams who, in his book *Keywords* (1976), argued that words such as 'nature', 'culture' and 'technology' shift their meanings as society changes. Thus the term 'technonatures' serves to signify that we can no longer see nature as a space free of societal and technological practices. It also signifies the extent of the humanisation of nature, and represents a development of the idea of social natures associated with Braun and Castree. Thus technonatures is an 'organising myth and metaphor for thinking about the politics of nature in contemporary times' and highlights a growing range of voices

> ruminating over the claim not only that we are inhabiting diverse social natures but also that knowledges of our worlds are, within such social natures, ever more technologically mediated, produced, enacted, and contested, and, furthermore, that diverse peoples find themselves, or perceive themselves, as ever more entangled with things.
>
> (White and Wilbert, 2009: 6)

A simple example of this may help to clarify. I recently visited a tourist attraction in south-west England called the Combe Martin Wildlife and Dinosaur Park (www. dinosaur-park.com). It was a disconcerting experience. The park is located on the side of a secluded valley and represents a form of diversification away from its former economically precarious agricultural use. The animals that may have previously been found on this hillside have been replaced by more exotic species. There are lions, kangaroos, monkeys, sea-lions and wolves. The park is involved in a variety of conservation projects. At the entrance to the park there are a series of 'life-size' mechanical dinosaurs which, every hour on the hour, become animated and roar. In a reference to the film *Jurassic Park*, these dinosaurs are chained. Ironically, this suggests an implied critique of the whole wildlife park, because the animals we pay to see have been subject to the same processes of capture, transport and display as the dinosaurs experience in the film, and thus raise the question of whether humans may get their 'just desserts' in exploiting nature as a means to extract economic value from the land. In many ways, the Wildlife and Dinosaur Park is an example of Neil Smith's (2007) discussion of how nature is used as an 'accumulation strategy'. Smith notes that, beginning in the 1980s and 1990s, an extraordinary range of new 'ecological commodities' came onto the market. Ironically, these owed their existence to the success of the environmental movement in the 1960s. They relied for their exchange value on the idea of nature as a sign:

> Green capitalism may be touted as a means of softening the environmental impacts of the capitalist exploitation of nature, or criticized as simply environmental veneer for sustained exploitation, yet whatever the truth of these propositions the significance of 'green capitalism' is far more profound. It has become nothing less than a major strategy for ecological commodification, marketization and financialization which radically intensifies and deepens the penetration of nature by capital.
>
> (Smith, 2007: 17)

For further study

1. What do you understand by the term 'technonatures'? Are there examples of technonatures that you could use in your teaching?

Conclusion

This discussion of how geographers have developed their knowledge and understanding of the relationship between society and nature has important implications for curriculum planning in schools. In particular, it suggests that 'geographical thinking' offers a set of frameworks and perspectives that teachers can use to deepen students' knowledge and broaden their understanding of these issues.

Finally, it may be useful to summarise the current ways in which issues of people–environment or society–nature are dealt with in school geography. First, there is physical geography, where it is assumed that there exists a physical world or nature that can be studied objectively using the methods and approaches of science. This is evidenced in school geography, where students learn about the processes that shape particular landforms and environments. Few geography lessons today assume that physical geography should be studied without reference to the broader human contexts in which natural processes take place. In this way, people are seen to have an impact on the physical environment, often in ways that are disruptive to physical systems. The reasons for the heightened conflict between society and nature are generally explained as the result of increased population, and the desire for increased use of resources as the result of improved standards of living (for example, the desire to live on the coast leads to modification of coastal systems). In this type of environmental geography, there tends to be much more focus on the processes at work in the physical environment than on the processes that shape society. This leads to oversimplified statements about the operation of society (for example, pupils may have a fairly complex understanding of the workings of rainforest ecosystems, but a limited understanding of the ways in which Brazilian society is structured so as to place pressure on the forests).

The discussion of academic geography's engagement with the question of the relationship between society and nature in this chapter suggests that many human geographers reject the consensus politics associated with sustainable development because this tends towards an all-too-easy story of progress and closure. The chapters in the next section explore the implications of this for commonly taught geographical themes including hazards, population, resources, food, cities, the economy, climate change and transport.

Activities

How do you respond to the argument that it is more important for students to learn how geographers understand the relationships between society and nature than how to act as environmentally concerned citizens?

Section two: Themes

4

Inescapable ecologies?

Most geographers seem to go about their work with an easy conscience. The self-image of the geographer at work appears to be one of doing good. Tune into any discussion among geographers and as likely as not the discussion unfolds from the standpoint of the benevolent bureaucrat, a person who knows better than other people and who will therefore make better decisions for others than they will be able to make for themselves.

(Harvey, 1974: 22)

In 1974, David Harvey wrote an article entitled, 'What kind of geography for what kind of public policy?' Harvey discussed the ways in which geography as an academic discipline had become incorporated into the concerns of the state. According to Harvey, in the period 1930–70, education became increasingly geared to producing individuals who contribute to the 'national interest'. For instance, universities produced geography graduates trained in the fields of urban, regional and environmental management. Education was increasingly seen as training in technical competence. These tendencies seem to contradict the image of the benevolent bureaucrat that Harvey suggests is the preferred image of geographers, but humanism in geography developed as a necessary counterpoint to the creation of wealth. Humanism thrived and prospered in universities, and though Harvey thought that it was threatened, he argued that the concern with the technics of urban and environmental management brought geographers into contact with other humanistic strands of thought associated with social reform and welfare. Harvey argued that these two strands – the economic and the humanistic – were in tension, but at the individual level were resolved through the strategy of separating 'fact' and 'value'. If geography is a science, and therefore concerned with facts and models, we can relegate our humanism to personal opinion, to be expressed outside geography but not within. Harvey argued that the problem with this approach was that, from the late 1960s, the idea that science is neutral or value-free was challenged by the idea of science as ideology. This meant that the struggle over relevant geography was not really about relevance, but about what was relevant geography, and to whom? Were geographers to serve the interests of capital and the corporate state, or other interests? In other words, what type of geography for what type of public policy?

The question of relevance figures strongly in present-day discussions of school geography. Teachers and curriculum planners routinely talk about making the subject relevant to the lives of students. Harvey argued that the geography of the time served to produce a technically efficient bureaucracy that could manage the market economy in the interests of powerful groups (the ruling elite). It was therefore relevant to the needs of that elite, but it was not relevant to what Harvey regarded as the wider public interest. It did not, for example, teach students what to do about social injustice or ecological disharmony. This raises the question of to whom current forms of school geography are relevant.

In the 1980s, a small number of geography educators took up Harvey's ideas and explored them in relation to the school geography curriculum. It is important to understand something of what was happening at that time. The social consensus in which it was assumed that all groups in society were broadly progressing in wealth and welfare was being fractured. In 1976, the Labour Prime Minister James Callaghan had inaugurated the so-called 'Great Debate', in which he argued that education was not meeting the needs of employers. Education, he argued, should be more vocational and geared to the world of work. On top of this, society seemed to be becoming a more violent and unruly place. Adult authority seemed to be eroding in the face of an irreverent media culture, and there was talk of a 'crisis of youth'. As the 1970s ended and the 1980s started, economic recession led to high young unemployment, rapidly rising social inequality, tensions in inner cities and environmental deterioration; teachers and schools were increasingly urged to teach a curriculum that was relevant to the needs of capital. Education was to be more vocational and focus on basic skills. Some geography teachers, especially those teaching in large urban centres, questioned the relevance of school geography, which seemed remote from the lives of young people growing up in a divided society. One part of this was the emergence of ecological issues. Nuclear power, agricultural intensification, factory closures all seemed to be marginal to an outdated geography curriculum.

These 'radical' geography teachers challenged the idea that geography lessons offered a neutral representation of reality. For example, in the conclusion to his book *The roots of modern environmentalism*, David Pepper (1984) argued against the idea (proposed in 1973 by the green economist E.F. Schumacher) that, in the drive to realise a socially and ecologically balanced world, education is the greatest resource. Instead, in line with Harvey's argument, Pepper stressed that education is geared to the needs of capitalist society and promotes ideological views of society and nature.

According to Pepper, one of the most important ways it does this is through *omission*, by which education frequently fails to encourage critical awareness and an ability to think in new and creative ways. It does this by emphasising the techniques of how to do things, but neglecting consideration of values and morality. Hence it does not encourage pupils and students to question received and conventional wisdom. In the school curriculum, the ideology and methods of empiricist science hold a good deal of influence, and this encourages the separation of fact and value. It makes values a matter of opinion for our spare time, while 'facts' constitute the legitimate object of the academic's professional pursuit.

However, ideological teaching is not simply a matter of omission. In addition, Pepper argues, the dominant ideas taught in education are the ideas of the dominant capitalist group in society. This group is represented by the corporate state. Education is used to transmit information down to individuals about what is right for the 'national interest'. Like the corporate state, education is dominated by the ethics of rationality and efficiency – it seeks to enhance the interests of the corporate state through (1) enhancing competition and economic growth; (2) managing cyclical crises in the economy; and (3) defusing or containing discontent. One way in which this happens is to neglect or discourage any serious thinking about the social and political organisation of society. More positively, this may be through teaching certain values that support capitalist ideology (for example, in geography exercises that encourage students to act as entrepreneurs to decide the best location for a factory; or that assume that firms should decide for themselves how to reduce pollution).

As well as the content of the curriculum, school work is organised to prepare students for the demands of the world of work. The curriculum is written and handed down from on high by 'experts'. School subjects are presented as a package or product – received consensual knowledge – and not as a process that mediates an active reading and writing of the world. School work is fragmented, standardised and routinised (and, some would argue, this is increasingly true of university education). Externally imposed curriculum goals are carried out in a standardised and fragmented way, and that 'knowledge', reduced to the status of a commodity, is consumed by more or less passive students, or 'customers'.

The result of all this is that, despite many hours spent in school classrooms and geography lessons, the vast majority of students leave without a realistic grasp of the social and political forces that shape their lives. In a subsequent article entitled 'Why teach physical geography?', Pepper (1986) analysed the London Board's A level examination syllabus and papers, and argued that, because they failed to encourage critical questioning, the physical geography taught was 'conducive to the stability of the existing economic and political order' (Pepper, 1986). In addition, it was based on a model of learning that encouraged students to learn and adapt to a particular role in society. As Pepper argues, 'To do well you "mug-up" information and uncritically regurgitate it without reference to the broader system of which that information is part' (Pepper, 1986).

Pepper's analysis suggested that the physical geography papers did not allow pupils to set knowledge within the context of human society and problems. The physical environment was not seen as part of a system that also contains human society. Students were encouraged to be analytical rather than synthetic; reductionist rather than holistic. The questions split knowledge into little information 'bits', such as how stream load and discharge are related, or the 'five stages of coastline development'. There was little room for seeing how these bits fit together. Pepper concluded:

You need neither technical skill nor critical faculty to do the paper; no comprehensive overview, no sense of 'relevance', application or synthesis, and above all no opinions about anything. All you need is the ability to memorise and recall textbook information and recognise what pages of the book you are being asked to regurgitate.

(Pepper, 1986: 64)

In order to overcome these problems and develop a relevant physical geography, Pepper provided some examples of how topics within physical geography can be linked to broader social contexts. For example, knowledge of soil structure, texture, porosity and cation-exchange capacity is important because they are components of long-term soil fertility, which are being damaged by modern business farming, perhaps forming the deserts of the future. In arguing that the physical basis of geography is important to study, Pepper goes on to suggest that without a social purpose, there is little justification to teach physical geography. The London examination discussed by Pepper fostered 'an uncritical, atomistic and functional approach to the physical environment which is quite divorced from its socio-economic context' (Pepper, 1986). The physical geography described by Pepper is derived from dominant models of science education, which fail to address the societal context in which decisions are made. This type of education focuses on 'fact' gathering and rote learning, making students puzzle-solvers within a paradigm, rather than investigators of the paradigm itself.

These points were further developed in a series of articles by John Huckle (1983, 1985, 1986). Huckle argued that school geography served to legitimise existing economic and environmental relations. He warned that:

The ecological crisis is worsening. In recent years a series of national and international reports, including the world and UK conservation strategies, have warned of this. They have documented the growing threat to the planet's life support processes and genetic diversity, and have called for new policy initiatives on both conservation and ecologically sustainable development.

(Huckle, 1986: 2)

Huckle adopted a materialist analysis of these developments, noting that human history is one of increasing control of nature using technology. In the process of this development, people's relations to one another (social relations) changed, as well as their relations to the natural world. This means that it is important to understand environmental change as closely linked to changing economic structures of society. Capitalist social relations entail particular attitudes and practices towards nature. As Huckle states:

Capitalist culture is competitive, forceful and manipulative; it leads to an instrumental approach to nature which is functional, pragmatic, piecemeal and short-term.

(Huckle, 1986: 5)

This argument has important implications for education, since it suggests that to understand environmental issues, it is necessary to have an understanding of how these are linked to the political economic system that produces them. The problem is that school geography has developed in ways that prevent this type of understanding:

> By diverting attention away from human agency and social explanation, school geography [...] clearly acts as ideology supportive to capital. This role is reinforced by an associated economic determinism and a progressive view of social change. The image so often presented is of people and society subject to the laws of nature and market economics. Progress comes about through their progressive adaptation to these laws using ever more advanced technology. The resulting costs and inequalities are largely ignored in the benign images often presented, and the planning of such change is generally presented as a rational, consensus activity, free of conflict, racism, sexism or class struggle. Where controversy is acknowledged it is often treated superficially. Pupils are asked to discuss issues or form opinions without analysis of the relevant political history.
>
> (Huckle, 1986: 9)

This was a far-reaching and hard-hitting critique of school geography. It is important to realise that Huckle was not seeking to criticise individual geography teachers, but was suggesting that the historical development of geography had isolated the subject from the mainstream of political and social theory that is central to understanding the causes of environmental problems. The result was that explanations in geography lessons of environmental problems related to famine, natural disasters or resource crises tended to rely on the types of 'apolitical ecologies' described by geographers such as Paul Robbins (see chapter three). Huckle argued that:

> The ideas taught in schools too are generally based on an unquestioning view of social change and economic forces. Lessons on environmental problems tend to blame purely natural causes, or regard them as global or universal problems attributable to such causes as overpopulation, resource scarcity, inappropriate technology, overconsumption or overproduction. All such teaching fulfils an ideological role. It fails to relate issues to the different social settings in which they arise, and fails to explain how technology, consumption and production are structured by economic and political forces. Blame is effectively transferred; the crisis is attributed to nature, the poor, or inappropriate values.
>
> (Huckle, 1988: 64)

This discussion of the concerns of writers such as David Harvey, David Pepper and John Huckle about the relationship between geography and the capitalist state, the nature of education, and how environmental crises are taught in school geography is not a historical indulgence. As I write this in 2010, these questions are central to discussions about the future of schooling. It is becoming increasingly clear that we are living at the meeting point of two interrelated crises. First, the slow emergence of recognition of the environmental limits to capital that has dawned since around 1970s; second, the more rapid onset of the financial crisis that has raised significant questions about the long-term sustainability of economic growth. The most capable of analysts, such as David Harvey in his 2010 book *The enigma of capital (and the crises of capitalism)*, are clear that the two are related. In addition, doubts are openly raised about whether the significant improvements in school examination performance are leading to a more educated population. To offer two examples: Ainley and Allen go so far as to suggest that 'A generation of students and teachers at school, college and university are working harder, but not necessarily learning more' (Ainley and Allen, 2010); while geographer Daniel Dorling, reviewing the evidence that points to the return of elitism in education, comments that 'People who have taught the children of the higher classes at the universities they go to see the result of the growth in elitism. These children have been educationally force-fed enough facts to obtain strings of A grades, but they are no more genii than anyone else' (Dorling, 2010). Given that effort to improve the quality of schooling in contemporary capitalist Britain does not appear to translate readily to a more 'intelligent' society, it seems worthwhile to examine more closely what is taught in geography lessons. Specifically, I want to examine the question of whether and how the content of school geography curriculum continues to present ideological views of the relationships between society and nature.

For further study

1. How would you define 'relevance' in school geography? Relevant to whom? For what purposes? Do you think that David Harvey's argument that geography serves the interests of the ruling elites still stands?

2. In the light of David Pepper's criticisms of physical geography as taught in schools, undertake a review of the content and approach to physical geography in your department. To what extent do you think Pepper's argument is still relevant?

3. Pepper argued that without a social purpose, there is no justification for teaching physical geography. Complete the following table to explain how the topics listed could be justified. Think carefully about whose purposes the knowledge of physical processes serve. For example, river or coastal flood defence schemes paid for by taxation may serve to protect the interests of wealthy property owners.

Topic	Justification for teaching it
Weather	
Climate	
Slope shapes and processes	
Soil properties	
Movement of water through the landscape	
Ecosystems	
Biomes	
Coastal landforms and processes	
Glaciation and periglaciation	

Reading specifications

In a review of the influential 16–19 Geography Project A level syllabus in the 1980s, Andrew Sayer (1986) commented that syllabuses generally make frustrating reading. This is because they have to offer guidelines for teaching, yet cannot be too restrictive. In practice this tends to lead to rather bland and anodyne statements. However, Sayer suggested, beneath these statements it is possible to discern 'a distinctive approach to geography'. In what follows I offer a reading of three specifications (two GCSE and one AS/A2 level) provided by Edexcel, paying attention to their treatment of two themes concerned with environmental issues (natural hazards and resources), in order to discern something of their distinctive approach to geography, and to ask how far they encourage geography teachers to teach as if the planet matters. Before that, however, I offer some brief reflections on the view of the relationship of society and nature that underpins the specifications.

There is a clear approach to society and nature in the specifications. It is one that assumes that there is a pre-existing natural world that is being used and affected by human beings. There is a clear separation between the two. In general, this human impact is undifferentiated – 'we' (humans) are overexploiting resources. The only distinction between people that seems to occur with any degree of regularity is that between 'high-income' and 'low-income' countries, or countries in different states of development. Though it is recognised that there are different viewpoints, these are never expressed in terms of the actual social groups involved. This is despite the fact that human geography increasingly recognises the differences that exist between social groups on the basis of, for example, gender, ethnicity or class.

Interpretations of disaster

Global Challenges is a compulsory unit of the Edexcel AS specification. *Global Challenges* is made up of two units – World at Risk (which has two elements, Global Hazards and Climate Change); and Going Global (which also has two elements, Globalisation and Population Migration). According to the overview:

> The unit poses questions which seek to explore the meaning, causes and impacts of a number of headline global issues. It gives students the opportunity to evaluate existing attempts to manage the problems they bring and challenges us to find solutions for the 21st century. Whilst its scale is global it is important that students can relate these issues to their own situations, becoming aware that they too can have a say in and play their part in meeting these global challenges.
>
> (www.edexcel.com)

In reading this, the first question that emerges concerns the priority given to the scale of the 'global' in this unit, and in particular the notion of 'headline global issues'. Although it may appear common sense to think in terms of global issues, in fact this represents an important shift in the scale of geographical enquiry, since, in the past, geographers have tended to focus on the scale of the nation or region. A critical perspective on geographical education suggests the need to focus on the origins of this scalar shift in school geography. A useful clue is provided by Ron Johnston and Peter Taylor (1986) in their introduction to *A world in crisis?* They correlate the 'distinct shift in the geographical scale of emphasis, from national to global' with the replacement of post-war optimism with a 'new realism' towards the end of the 1960s:

> Suddenly crisis seemed to be the word on everybody's lips, and the adjectives applied to it (ecological, environmental, demographic, urban, rural, debt, food, energy, etc.) were so wide-ranging that they contributed to a general sense of despondency.
>
> (Johnston and Taylor, 1986: 1–2)

Global Challenges may thus be read as the logical out-working of this scalar shift in school geography. However, this requires a little more discussion, not least because the unit overview gives us a hint of how the particular issues, or challenges, were selected. These are 'headline global issues', and this suggests that there is a question of representation at work. These global issues are the kinds that teachers hope students might encounter in reading newspapers or watching quality news programmes. But the idea of geographical scale is not as obvious as it appears. Indeed, in the past two decades, geographers have debated how we should understand scale. In *Geographies of globalization*, Andrew Herod (2009) summarises the different ways in which geographers have conceptualised the idea of scale.

- Scales do not exist outside of our minds – when we say something is local or regional, we are imposing our own mental schemata.

- Scales are natural or logic units or containers through which we understand the world. Thus geographers' tendency to talk about local, national and global scales reflects the way the world is.

- Scales are social products – they are actively created, rather than simply mentally imposed or logical/natural ways to divide up the world.

Finally, Marston *et al.* (2005) have proposed that scale should be abandoned because it privileges views which see the world in hierarchical terms – and this tends to promote one scale (usually the global) over others.

These different ways of thinking about scale become important in thinking about the political implications of the worldview offered by the exam specification. Do these issues represent an actual process whereby the world is becoming more globalised, or is this simply a shift in the way we look at the world? If it is the former, is this the result of an active social production, or is globalisation seen as a natural and inevitable product of economic development? (It is notable that in their book *Spaces of work*, Castree *et al.*, 2003 insist on using the term 'global capitalism' as opposed to 'globalisation' so as to highlight the political project that lies behind it.) In addition, following Marston *et al.*, it could be asked whether the specification's requirement for students to view the world from a global perspective serves to place them in a position of power, from which they look down from above and survey the lives and misfortunes of other people. These are, after all, Western conceptions of global challenges, and prompt us to reflect on how the list might look different when viewed form the 'global South'. One of the problems of adopting a 'God's eye' view of the world is that it seems to remove problems to a world beyond our own agency and control. The other question, unanswered here, is that of the relationships between the different scales. It might be argued that this is all set within a global managerial framework which assumes that the world is full of challenges, and the geographer can help solve them (reminding us of Harvey's comment about the benevolent bureaucrat at the start of this chapter).

With these comments in mind, let us turn now to the Global Hazards section of World at Risk. Students are required to examine three enquiry questions:

1. What are the main types of physical risks facing the world and how big a threat are they?

2. How and why are natural hazards now becoming seen as an increasing global threat?

3. Why are some places more hazardous and disaster-prone than others?

(www.edexcel.com)

Natural hazards are a relatively recent addition to the school geography curriculum. As a field, natural hazards research dates from the 1970s, and was a response to the apparent increase in frequency and magnitude of natural disasters. Insights from academic research were incorporated into examination syllabuses, which adopted an issues-based approach and stressed the theme of people–environment relations. The broader context for this was the development of a global media culture, which increasingly constructed news stories on the basis of global crises. Within a media-dominated popular culture, natural hazards serve to remind us of the unpredictability of nature and provide evidence of the power of forces.

The specification distinguishes between 'disasters' and 'hazards', a disaster being when natural hazards 'threaten the life and property of increasing numbers of the world's population'. Students are to make use of the 'disaster risk equation', which holds that 'the risk of disaster increases as hazard frequency and people's vulnerability increases, while their capacity to cope decreases'. Students are to learn that some types of hazards are increasing in magnitude and frequency, and having greater impacts upon people and their lives, and that natural disasters are increasing because of a combination of physical and human factors. The physical factors include unpredictable events such as global warming and El Niño events, while the human factors include the exploitation of resources (e.g. deforestation), poverty, rapid population growth and urbanisation.

Since the 1980s, it has become increasingly rare to come across accounts of natural disasters that attribute the effects purely to natural forces. In 2010, earthquakes in Haiti and Chile had very different death tolls, and this was widely understood as the result of different levels of preparedness and resources to cope. Svensen (2009) notes that a milestone in international disaster research has been the realisation that it is not 'perilous nature' that causes natural disasters. Instead, these are just as much a result of how societies are organised as they are of geophysical factors or extreme weather conditions. This realisation came in the 1970s, in response to events such as drought and famine in the Sahel, earthquakes in Nicaragua and Guatemala, and cyclones in Bangladesh. Researchers posed the questions as to whether the magnitude and frequency of these events had increased, and why it was the poorest countries that were most severely affected.

These questions were addressed by radical geographers such as Phil O'Keefe *et al.* (1976) in an article in *Nature* entitled 'Taking the naturalness out of natural disasters'. They argued that natural disasters are not created primarily by nature, but arise as the result of an unequal distribution of Earth's resources. This argument posed a challenge to earlier forms of research on natural hazards, which assumed that people and societies can adapt to natural forces so as to reduce the extent and impact of the disaster. For instance, the influential 'Chicago school' of hazard research had stressed how this reduction could be achieved through mapping the risks associated with particular hazards, monitoring natural processes, drawing up evacuation plans and developing new technology. In this managerial or technocratic approach, the key was knowledge of nature and the development of the Earth, since natural hazards are seen as the inevitable consequences of the extreme processes of nature. The introduction of technological solutions was central to the United Nation's International Decade for Natural Disaster Reduction of the 1980s, which involved the transfer of Western knowledge and technology to underdeveloped countries.

Building on O'Keefe's insight, this dominant view of natural disasters was challenged in the 1980s. A landmark was Kenneth Hewitt's (1983) edited collection *Interpretations of calamity*. In his introduction, Hewitt identified a number of features that characterised the dominant view. These were:

1. There is generally a straightforward acceptance of natural disaster as a result of 'extremes' in geophysical processes. This means that causality is seen to run from the physical environment to its social impacts.

2. The geography of risk is usually treated as synonymous with the distribution of natural extremes.

3. There is an equally strong conviction that something can be done, but this something is viewed as strictly a matter of public policy backed up by the most advanced geophysical, geotechnical and managerial capability. The goals are prediction planning and management, and the main expertise comes from the physical sciences and engineering.

(Hewitt, 1983: 5–6)

For Hewitt, the dominant view creates a 'disaster archipelago', in which natural hazards have been carefully roped off from the rest of people–environment, and this suggests that hazards are extreme events or accidents rather than part of ordinary experience for large numbers of people.

Susman *et al.*'s (1983) chapter in *Interpretations of calamity* was entitled 'Global disasters, a radical interpretation'. They noted an increase in the incidence of disasters over the previous fifty years, especially large-scale disasters, and an increased loss of life per disaster. However, in the absence of any major geological or climatological changes over this period, they conclude that the explanation must be sought in the conditions that increase the growing vulnerability of the population to extreme physical events. This vulnerability is due to human changes, and these changes are linked to the idea of development and its failures.

Susman *et al.* pointed out that it was commonplace to divide the world into 'developed' and 'underdeveloped' countries. Underdevelopment was usually seen as resulting from the intrinsic limits of a particular country, and explained in terms of insufficient integration of the different sectors into the modern economy. Thus lack of development was explained in terms of demographic features such as an imbalanced population structure, lack of natural resources and lack of capital. Susman *et al.* rejected this account of underdevelopment, instead stressing the process of the development of underdevelopment in relation to other places and the world economy:

[...] the present revolution in thinking about disaster is related to a far wider revolution of thought about underdevelopment. What had previously been seen as a state out of which the poor country had to emerge is now widely seen as a continual process of impoverishment based on a world economy which perpetuates technological dependency and unequal exchange.

(Susman *et al.*, 1983)

The major contribution of their paper was the theory of marginalisation. Marginalised people or groups are positioned on the edges of the economic system, and this economic marginality often leads to geographical marginality, as these groups are forced off the land or onto poor or insufficient land. The result is that the poor, with little economic and/or political power, are compelled to live in the most dangerous or unhealthy places. For example, in Rio de Janeiro poor people live in *favelas* on slopes of 'alpine difficulty'; the poorest urban squatters in Asia live on hazardous floodplains; in Recife (north-east Brazil) large numbers of people live in, and on, the mud of the tidal estuary, living off crabs; and a quarter of Kenya's population live in that country's drought-prone marginal lands. In concluding their chapter, Susman *et al.* offered a series of predictions and recommendations (all of which could be turned into a worthwhile set of enquiry questions for geography students):

■ Disasters will increase as socioeconomic conditions and the physical environment deteriorate.

■ The poorest classes will continue to suffer most losses.

■ Relief aid reflects dominant interests and prevents political upheaval – generally working against the interests of those who suffer most.

■ Disaster mitigation relying on high technology merely reinforces the conditions of underdevelopment and increases marginalisation.

■ The only way to reduce vulnerability is to concentrate disaster planning within development planning (which must be broadly socialist).

■ The only models for successful disaster mitigation are those conceived in the struggle against exploitation.

(Susman *et al.*, 1983: 279–80)

These arguments about the need to move away from a focus on the idea of disasters as extreme events, and instead to see them as triggers underpinned by a whole set of human and social processes, became influential in the 1980s. An example of this argument is Lloyd Timberlake's (1985) *Africa in crisis*, a study of what he termed 'environmental bankruptcy'. In the context of drought and famine in the Sahel in the early to mid-1980s, Timberlake set out to challenge the popular view that the cause was lack of rainfall. Instead, the drought was the trigger that tipped the most marginal groups in societies based on rain-fed subsistence agriculture into crisis. The drive to develop through the use of export-led crop production meant that governments had taken on debt from the World Bank. Commercial crop production meant that the best and most fertile land was used up, and subsistence farmers were forced to graze their animals and grow their crops on marginal land.

These approaches indicate a concern to locate natural disasters in their circuits of political economy. From this perspective, the human factors that are offered as causal explanations for the increased impact of natural disasters should be seen as consequences of deeper structures that shape the relations between societies and lead to the increased vulnerability of marginalised people. With this in mind, we might suggest that the focus of 'Global Challenges' on these spectacular and highly mediated events serves to distract students and teachers from developing understanding of the social processes that shape people's lives. In practice, this means that a good deal of students' time is spent quantifying and mapping the frequency and distribution of events that affect 'vulnerable' people, at the expense of studying the historical, economic and political processes that construct some people as vulnerable. As Piers Blaikie *et al.* (2004) state at the start of their book *At risk*, it is crucial to grasp that disasters, especially natural hazards, are 'not the greatest threat to humanity', and that, although they can be lethal, many more of the world's population have their lives shortened by 'unnoticed events, illnesses, and hunger that pass for normal existence in many parts of the world' (Blaikie *et al.*, 2004).

In this sense, the final question that requires students to understand why some places are more hazardous and disaster-prone than others would become less the mapping and correlation of hazardous events suggested in the specification, and more an enquiry into the social production of risk:

> There is a danger in treating disasters as something peculiar, as events which deserve their own special focus. By being separated from the social frameworks that influence how hazards affect people, too much emphasis in doing something about disasters is put on the natural hazards themselves, and not nearly enough on the social environment and its processes
>
> (Blaikie *et al.*, 2004: 3–4)

For further study

1. Make a study of how natural disasters are represented in the media (television, newspapers, internet, etc.). How are they framed? (A good source here is Cottle, 2009.) How could you use your findings to inform your teaching of disasters in geography lessons?

2. How do you respond to the argument that 'there is a danger in treating disasters as something peculiar, as events which deserve their own special focus' (Blaikie *et al.*, 2004)? How might you reconfigure your own teaching of this part of the exam specification?

Consuming resources

All three of the specifications discussed in this chapter have a focus on the question of resources. Within the AS specification, it is recognised that many researchers recognise that globalisation is creating an 'unfair world in which rich consumers exploit the world's poorest people' and that 'there needs to be a realisation that global agreements, green strategies and ethical purchases can modify the negative results of globalisation'. Edexcel GCSE B has a unit entitled Consuming Resources that asks students to consider 'How and why does resource consumption vary in different parts of the world?' and 'How sustainable is the current pattern of resource supply and consumption?' (www.edexcel. com).

Students are to learn that 'resources are classified as renewable, sustainable and non-renewable, and this has implications for their consumption', and that 'patterns of resource supply and their consumption have produced a changing world of haves and have nots'. In addition they are expected to know that 'different theories exist about how far the world can cope with the current consumption of resources', and that 'the challenges for future resource consumption centre on achieving sustainability'.

In these specifications, it is possible to see why some commentators (see the discussion in chapter one) consider that school geography has become a vehicle for promoting green lifestyles and suggesting to students that current Western models of development are unsustainable (e.g. Standish, 2009). It might be noted that the notion of sustainability is so ingrained in the collective common sense that specification writers do not feel the need to offer a definition. Indeed, the word 'sustainable' is used so liberally and without focus that we are reminded of Swyngedouw's comment that:

> I have not been able to find a single source that is against 'sustainability'. Greenpeace is in favour, George Bush Jr. and Sr. are, the World Bank and its chairman (a prime warmonger on Iraq) are, the Pope is, my son Arno is, the rubber tappers in the Brazilian Amazon forest are, Bill Gates is, the labour unions are.
>
> (Swyngedouw, 2007: 20)

In some ways, the specifications signal an important shift in how school geography represents environmental problems. Whereas in earlier times geography texts might have blamed the failings of the 'poor' or 'less developed' for their plight, instead blame is attached to the profligacy of Western societies and their demands for consumer goods and resources such as oil. For instance, in GCSE A's Environmental Issues – A Wasteful World, students are to learn that greater wealth is a major contributor to increasing waste (especially in higher-income countries), and this is linked to the development of the consumer society, which leads to a throw-away society. Students are to make a case study of recycling on a local scale and to investigate their carbon footprints before exploring the possible solutions to energy wastage in the home or in schools.

Despite these developments, the specifications remain set in a problem-solving rather than a problem-posing mindset, and fail to offer students the types of knowledge and perspectives required to make sense of ideas such the consumer society and to evaluate the potential for action to reduce society's impacts on nature.

This can be seen through a discussion of the choice of theories that are on offer to examine how far the world can cope with the current consumption of resources. Three are stated in the GCSE B specification. These are: Malthusian, Boserupian, and Limits to Growth. All three can be seen as part of a set of explanations that focus on the relationship between population and resources. Robbins (2004) notes that

> In Western Europe since the late 1700s, when human influence and response to the environment was first submitted to scientific scrutiny, the central driving explanation for social/ecological crisis has been increasing human population, measured in absolute numbers.
>
> (Robbins, 2004: 7)

Neo-Malthusian approaches developed with the report *The Limits to growth* of the early 1970s, but what the perspectives have in common is that 'all hold to the ultimate scarcity of non-human nature and the rapacity of humankind's growing numbers'. The agricultural economist Esther Boserup's (1965) *Conditions of agricultural growth* offered the classical rebuttal of the Malthusian argument about limits; through analysis of historical data on agricultural production, she suggested that the amount of food produced on the same amount of land has increased exponentially. More people means more food, and the argument is that the innovative nature of humanity will ensure that what is seen as useless today may become an important resource tomorrow. In the case of agriculture, it is the induced intensification and technological fixes such as the Green Revolution that give rise to optimism about increased food supplies. However, even Boserup's argument does not necessarily lead to a rejection of the idea of limits. The Green Revolution led to the breaking up of the prairies, leading to soil erosion and the loss of biodiversity. What is more, this form of agricultural intensification required large inputs of fertilisers supplied by the petrochemical industries, and tractors are dependent on fossil fuels, so the idea that there can be increased output with little cost does seem 'cornucopian'. Boserup's thesis does throw doubt upon validity of Malthusian or *Limits to growth* perspectives that there are natural limits.

In their book *Environment and society*, Robbins et al. (2010) identify seven sets of theoretical perspectives that focus in the links between society and nature. These include:

1. Population and scarcity perspectives (such as those discussed so far), which focus on how human population growth presses against the limits of nature.

2. Economic ways of thinking that stress the power of markets to respond to scarcity and drive inventive human responses.

3. Institutional approaches, which address environmental problems largely as common property problems that are amenable to creative rule-making, incentives and self-regulation.

4. Ethics-based approaches to the environment, which offer radical ways of rethinking the place of humans in a world filled with other living and non-living things.

5. The environment as a problem of risk and hazard.

6. Political economy approaches, which insist that the environment is linked to access to power over resources and inequalities – stressing the environmentally corrosive impacts of market economies.

7.   Social constructionist approaches, which stress the importance of language, images and stories in constructing and disseminating ideas of environmental issues.

All these theoretical perspectives could be used to shed light on the meaning of 'sustainable' as used in the GCSE specification. They would help to examine the claims that are made about resource use in texts used to support the specifications. These specifications seem to imply that rising to the 'challenge' of sustainability is essentially a technological fix, along with some governmental agreements and some sensible consumer choices on the part of individuals. These examination specifications are the educational equivalent of the discourse of ecological modernisation, which posits a win–win between economic growth and environmental management. It is possible, of course, that this is a rather harsh critique, and that there are signs of a developing critique in the use of the phrase 'the consumer society'. It would be very useful for students and teachers to engage in analysis of the origins of this consumer society and its implications. However, it is hard to avoid the conclusion that, in the exam specification, the term is used as a vague euphemism that serves to shroud the deeper forces that drive the expansion of consumption.

In view of the fact that there are some serious doubts as to whether the capitalist drive for growth is reaching its physical limits, it might be suggested that geography teachers would be advised to engage students in a more disciplined discussion of the geography of resources and the development of a consumer society. As Jared Diamond (2005) argues in *Collapse: how societies choose to fail or succeed*, previous societies have also faced their own environmental limits, and the evidence is that these moments often end up in societal collapse (see also Tainter, 1988). Environmental historian J.R. Neill (2000) notes that after around 1820 the world's economy became increasingly based on work done by non-muscular energy. By 1950, any society that did not deploy large amounts of energy was doomed to poverty. The fuelwood crisis of the later Middle Ages was solved by the discovery and development of a new source of energy: coal. This was the basis for the expansion of industrial development. By the early twentieth century, coal met 90 per cent of the world's energy resources. Prior to the Second World War in the United States and after the war in Europe, coal came to be superseded by oil and gas as the energy source of choice. This led to significant shifts in geopolitical power as previously marginal areas came to play a major part in the global economy. The world now literally runs on oil and gas, and in historical terms it may be argued that the primary reason for the high rates of global economic growth through the 1990s was the availability of cheap oil. The implications are stark: no cheap oil means no growth; or, starker still, no oil means no global economy (for a stark account see Kunstler, 2005).

For further study

1.   Robbins *et al.* (2010) identify seven different theoretical approaches to understanding the relationship between environment and society. Clarify for yourself the main features of these approaches. Which theories are found in media coverage of environmental issues? Which are found in the resources used to teach geography in your school?

2.   In what ways might a historical perspective on the development of the 'consumer society' help students to gain a clearer understanding of society's use of resources?

Conclusion

This chapter has taken the form of a critique of aspects of existing examination specifications in geography, paying particular attention to how students are introduced to the themes of natural hazards and resources. It draws upon earlier analyses of the ideological nature of geography teaching, and attempts to see whether the criticisms made by these commentators are still relevant. There is little doubt that economy and society have changed in the past three decades, and ideas of teaching and learning and curriculum planning have also shifted. However, the argument of this chapter is that school geography still fails to provide students with a realistic understanding of the forces that shape their lives and the lives of others. Of course, teaching and learning in school geography does provide students with other things. The home page of the Edexcel website invites teachers to adopt its specifications on the grounds that they promise 'better results for all your students'. To teach geography as if the planet matters insists that there is something more important to be gained in undertaking a relevant and meaningful geographical education.

Activities

1.   To what extent to you think the promise by exam boards to offer 'better results for all your students' is a corruption of the aims and purposes of geographical education?

2.   Undertake an analysis of the examination specifications for geography taught in your school. How far do they support John Huckle's argument that:

The ideas taught in schools too are generally based on an unquestioning view of social change and economic forces. Lessons on environmental problems tend to blame purely natural causes, or regard them as global or universal problems attributable to such causes as overpopulation, resource scarcity, inappropriate technology, overconsumption or overproduction. All such teaching fulfils an ideological role. It fails to relate issues to the different social settings in which they arise, and fails to explain how technology, consumption and production are structured by economic and political forces. Blame is effectively transferred; the crisis is attributed to nature, the poor, or inappropriate values.

(Huckle, 1988: 64)

5

A question of food

> It is hard, if not impossible, to be neutral about food. Food is essential for life yet contributes to premature death everywhere – even in rich societies. It brings pleasure and lubricates social interaction but carries risks and cements social divisions. Its production reflects a wondrous mix of natural and human actions. Yet it results in increasingly well-documented social, health and environmental costs.
>
> (Lang *et al.*, 2009: 1)

This statement draws attention to the cultural and social importance of food – what, how much (or how little), and where we eat. Food has become increasingly central to policy-makers in the contemporary world. Although this is not to suggest that this is a wholly new development, heightened concern that all is not well in the food system is reflected in the sheer number of popular books published in recent years that explore aspects of food (a selection of which include: Eric Schlosser's (2002) *Fast food nation* and Schlosser and Wilson's (2006) *Chew on this*; Colin Tudge's (2004) *So shall we reap*; Michael Pollan's *The omnivore's dilemma* (2004) and *In defence of food* (2008); Raj Patel's (2008) *Stuffed and starved*; Carolyn Steel's (2008) *Hungry city*; and Paul Roberts' (2009) *The end of food*. A large number of popular television programmes, such as *Jamie's school dinners* (Channel 4, 2005); *Honey, we're killing the kids* (BBC, 2005–07); and *You are what you eat* (Channel 4, 2004–07) focus on the dysfunctional food choices made by individuals. Academic work discusses the commercialisation of childhood and the way in which children's food consumption is shaped by large corporations; and academic studies contribute to the fast-growing interdisciplinary field of food studies. These concerns are reflected in the field of social policy, where there are myriad schemes designed to change consumer behaviour, reflected in the UK government's Food 2030 strategy (www.defra.gov.uk/foodfarm/food/strategy).

These developments are part of a wider set of changes in how people in advanced Western economies live their lives. Sociologists and social geographers have noted that in the past three decades, society has become more home-centred, and that the home is the place where people express their identities. These identities, it is suggested, are more and more shaped by consumerism, so buying the right food, knowing the right cut of meat for *that* dinner-party, becomes an important source of self-branding. It is a way of showing that we are 'fit for consumption'. Through consumption, we express something about ourselves as individuals. An important aspect of this is attention to the quality of the food that we eat, and over the past few years there have been programmes that stress the importance of understanding where our food comes from. Knowing what you are eating and where it has come from is part of a broader politics of food, which raises questions about the nature of food production. In addition, this is linked to the politics of food consumption and widespread concerns about the health and social costs of rising childhood obesity and the rise of disordered eating, especially among young women. More generally, there is growing interest in the idea of linking consumers with the producers of food through the idea of Fairtrade; and at the other extreme, there are concerns about the so-called McDonaldisation of society, or 'coca-colonisation', as Western food systems replace local or indigenous food cultures. Schools themselves are not free from this set of concerns or 'moral panics' about food, and indeed are becoming carefully targeted as being important sites where a new food culture might be developed. This is reflected in campaigns such as *Jamie's school dinners* and the Soil Association's 'Food for Life' campaign to 'change food cultures, one school at a time'.

This is the complex cultural landscape in which geography teachers' efforts to teach about the geographies of food is located. This chapter seeks to sketch out an agenda for geography's contribution to pupils' understanding of 'the food question', and to wider efforts to change school food cultures. It starts by examining the way that common post-Second World War approaches to teaching about agricultural geography in schools were challenged, during the 1980s, by changes in the nature of UK agriculture based on assumptions of increasing production. The advent of a post-productivist agricultural transition provided space for a broader discussion of the geographies of food, most notably through the development of insights from cultural geography and food studies. In recent years, the wider cultural concern with what we consume has led to many schools seeking to bring about changes in their school food culture, and this chapter suggests ways in which geography teachers might contribute to a more critical approach.

For further study

1. Undertake a week-long survey of popular media culture coverage of food (news, newspapers, entertainment shows, soap operas, etc.). How are food issues and food culture represented? How might you use these resources to teach about the geography of food?

The geography of agriculture

In Dudley Stamp and Stanley Beaver's *The British Isles: a geographic and economic survey*, the chapters on agriculture set out the basis for study of the geography of agriculture that informed teaching of the subject in schools in the post-war era:

It is important to realise the position which farming today occupies in the life of Britain. In the course of the great industrial expansion of the industrial revolution and after, when Britain became more and more engaged in the task of supplying manufactured goods to an ever-expanding world market, home production of food came gradually to be neglected, almost forgotten by the growing number of town dwellers.

(Stamp and Beaver, 1954: 163)

This perilous situation came to a head during the Second World War, when Britain's reliance on the import of foodstuffs and raw materials threatened national security. In light of the food shortages during the Second World War, there was a political premium on increasing agricultural production. Farmers, who had served the nation in a time of crisis, were entrusted with stewardship of the land. The result was that, for the first time since the onset of the great agricultural depression of the 1870s, all sectors of agriculture were prospering. The story of Britain's agricultural geography in the post-war period has been the modernisation of farming. From the 1950s to the 1980s, the organisation and practices of farming were transformed, with dramatic results. This resulted in vastly increased yields of arable crops such as wheat and barley, and a growth in the overall area under the plough. In addition, improved grassland pasture has allowed for an increase in livestock, with improved yields of milk per cow. Although the overall map of agricultural activity may appear to have changed little – with the development of large-scale, efficient farms in the east of the country with its flat land and rich soils, and the continued survival of family farms in the north and west based on pastoral farming – changes in processes and productivity have been profound. The basis of these changes were the mechanisation of agriculture, the use of artificial fertilisers and pesticides, selective plant and animal breeding, and more efficient and capital-intensive farming. There is also a focus on the idea of intensive arable farming, with higher levels of inputs and outputs per hectare.

For much of the post-war period, geography teaching in schools, focusing on the distribution of farming types, the processes of agricultural production, and the shift to modern, efficient farming, contributed to a wider ideology about proper use of rural space and agricultural improvement. However, by the 1980s an alternative narrative had developed about the process of modern agriculture. It was no longer assumed that the expansion of agricultural production for its own sake was a desirable thing. Instead, the economic, social and environmental costs of modern farming were stressed. Whereas previously the geography of agriculture could be taught in ways that stressed the neutral development of technology, critics pointed to the political nature of the changes involved, and the uneven share of costs and benefits of modern agriculture. This 'crisis of agriculture' is discussed in the following section.

The crisis of agricultural productivism

In *Countryside conflict: the politics of farming, forestry and conservation*, Phillip Lowe *et al.* (1986) argue that 1984 marked the end of the post-war era of agricultural expansion. This was symbolised by the decision of the EEC to cut back milk production, prompting some dairy farmers to pour 'surplus' milk down the drains. However, in retrospect, this signalled the end of a gradual process in which there were intensifying conflicts between farmers and conservationists, newcomers to rural areas and the largely urban public. Bowers and Cheshire's (1983) *Agriculture, the countryside and land use* offered an economic critique of policies that favoured continued increases in agricultural production and that denied any conflict between the goals of production and conservation. The key to this was the system of grants and guaranteed prices, which ensured that farmers had a market for their produce. This encouraged them to increase production by extending onto marginal lands (for example, by draining wetlands and removing woodland and hedgerows), and to intensify production through the use of machines, artificial fertilisers and pesticides. This linked them to an industrial market for chemical products and reduced the need for human labour. There were important consequences for the viability of rural communities:

> These changes have [...] destroyed important wildlife habitats. They have damaged the beauty of the British landscape, itself the creation of generations of farmers practising agricultural techniques in harmony with their environment. They have caused serious environmental pollution, threatening wildlife and, at the extreme, causing one water authority to import bottled, nitrate-free, drinking water supplies for young babies.
>
> (Bowers and Cheshire, 1983: 4)

Public concerns about these developments were expressed in a number of influential studies. The sociologist Howard Newby's (1979) *A green and pleasant land?* provided an account of the transformations that had taken place in rural England in the light of agricultural modernisation, which eschewed the romantic and nostalgic views that were held by a largely urban population. He portrayed a social order that had once been defined by deference to the land-owning classes by the agricultural labour force, but which had come under strain as the result of the reduction in the agricultural workforce and the subsequent arrival of newcomers, who lived in the country but were not of it, and did not share the same values. Similar, Marion Shoard's (1980) *The theft of the countryside* was a well aimed broadside at the effects of agricultural intensification:

> Although few people realise it, the English landscape is under sentence of death. Indeed the sentence is already being carried out. The executor is not the industrialist or the property speculator, whose activities have only touched the fringes of our countryside. Instead it is the figure traditionally viewed as the custodian of the rural scene – the farmer.
>
> (Shoard, 1980: 9)

As Lowe *et al.* (1986) document, the 1970s and 1980s saw the emergence of a series of significant countryside conflicts, in which environmental concerns were raised about the impact of agricultural production. These included well-publicised disputes, in the early to mid-1980s, over the draining of the Somerset Levels and the Halvergate Marshes, both of which became environmental *causes célèbres*. In addition, the workings of the European Common Agricultural Policy, which generated food mountains and wine lakes, captured the public imagination. In light of these developments, it was no longer possible to adopt such a positive tone in teaching geographies of farming, and this was added to by a growing awareness of the uneven internationalisation of food production and consumption. In the famine in the Sahel region of Africa in 1983–84 (which gained worldwide media attention and led to the global Live Aid events of 1985), the operations of international trade became apparent as countries continued to export 'luxury' crops to the developed world at the same time as their populations were struggling to meet subsistence food levels. By the mid-1980s it was possible to speak of the 'countryside in crisis', in which deeply held assumptions about the role of farmers and agriculture were questioned:

> The farmer is no longer the fence-gazing rustic, if indeed he ever was; he is a capitalist whose practices are determined by the markets of the big cities. Since the last war successive governments have poured money into boosting agricultural productivity, with the ostensible aim of making Britain self-sufficient in temperate food products. The resulting intensification, particularly in the lowlands, has had a major impact on both rural communities and our wildlife.
>
> (Pye-Smith and Rose, 1984: 17)

The texts cited in this section, all dating from the early to mid-1980s, are indicative of the fact that the ideology of agricultural productivism was in the process of breaking down. This ideology equated agriculture with the countryside; food with farming; and the farmer with stewardship of the land. But these assumptions were widely challenged as farming came to contribute a small and declining part of the rural economy. The most theoretically developed attempt to teach about these issues in school geography was found in John Huckle's (1988–93) *What we consume*, particularly the unit on UK Agriculture. As Huckle noted, the 'treadmill of agricultural production, which developed after the Second World War and continued to gain momentum until the early 1980s, was justified by an ideology which equated rural space with agricultural production'. In light of the collapse of this relationship, Huckle argued that there are:

> opportunities to promote alternative ideas about the nature and sustainable use of the countryside. Indeed, the collapse of farm incomes has been a major impetus for farm diversification, and the alienation from nature associated with an urban world increasingly associated with consumerism means that the rural takes on many meanings in the cultural landscape and is contested and debated.
>
> (Huckle, 1988: 93)

Huckle's unit on UK Agriculture and Wetland Drainage was an attempt to teach about the economic and political processes that were shaping agricultural production during the mid-1980s and to show how these were subject to contest and challenge. The key idea that underpinned the unit was that of the agricultural treadmill. This shows farmers as benefiting from a regime of expansion supported by government subsidies, and encouraging the mechanisation and intensification of farming processes. Once the treadmill gathers momentum, it is hard to get off. The activities in the unit sought to show how there are significant social and environmental costs associated with the treadmill of agricultural production. This is illustrated in the activity on rural communities, which draws upon the analysis of Bowers and Cheshire (1983); an activity on nitrate pollution, which allows pupils to explore the ways in which large corporations offer selective representations of agricultural practices; and a decision-making exercise that explores the dilemmas involved in the draining of the Halvergate Marshes, an area of wetland – the last remaining extensive stretch of open grazing marsh in eastern England – that was threatened with drainage and cultivation in the mid-1980s. The final activity involves pupils in thinking about the countryside they would like to see in the future. They compare the countryside in 1947 and in 1986, and are asked to consider how they would like the countryside to be in 2000, using the following questions:

■ What might the countryside be used for?

■ What sorts of work might be done in the countryside?

■ How many people will live there and how will they live?

■ Will there be more or less wildlife and landscape to enjoy?

■ Will access to the countryside be easier or more difficult?

■ Who will pay for countryside conservation and how will it be carried out?

(Huckle, 1988: 117)

With hindsight, these developments in the teaching of agricultural geography fit the regimes of productivist and post-productivist agriculture now commonly found in the literature on rural geography. Ilbery and Bowler summarise this shift:

Agriculture in developed market economies has undergone a substantial restructuring in the postwar period and two major phases of change can be identified. The productivist phase, where the emphasis was placed on raising farm output, lasted from the early 1950s to the mid-1980s and was characterised by a continuous modernization and industrialization of agriculture. The post-productivist phase [...] where the aim is to reduce farm output, is now a decade old and characterised by the integration of agriculture within broader economic and environmental objectives.

(Ilbery and Bowler, 1998: 57)

They suggest that three shifts characterise the transition to post-productivism: from intensive to more extensive land use; from concentration of ownership to dispersed ownership; and from specialisation of production to diversification. It is important to note that the evidence for this transition is not always clear, and that in reality they are part of the development of a new emerging political economy of agriculture or food regime. These developments required a rethinking of the relationships between agricultural production, increasingly organised on a global scale, and patterns of social and cultural change. An important text in developing an understanding of the geography of food production and consumption was David Goodman and Michael Redclift's (1991) *Refashioning nature*, which can be read as an early statement about the social construction of nature. Indeed, it argues that the conditions of modern food production have led to a realisation that nature is not natural and that it has a variety of meanings. They argue that we cannot think of food, ecology and culture in separate categories, rather that they are interdependent on each other. Thus the development of an industrialised agri-food industry is closely linked with the shift of women's employment and the decline of the family farm. They stress the need to integrate political economic approaches and those associated with cultural perspectives. These insights were important in the subsequent development of the cultural geographies of food, discussed in the next section.

For further study

1. Examine a selection of school geography textbooks from the 1970s to the present day. How is the geography of agriculture represented in these books? Is more or less space devoted to this topic over time? Have there been changes in how farming is represented? What are the key ideas presented to students? How and why have they changed over time?

The cultures of food

It is possible to argue that these shifts in the nature of food production have led to important changes in our understanding of food consumption. For example, the development of a global food regime and processes of globalisation have led to significant changes in how people eat and the sense they make of food consumption. This is reflected in the emergence, in the 1990s, of the field of food studies. Warren Belasco suggests that the emergence of a scholarly interest in food is following wider urban middle-class culture which, since the 1970s, has become 'much more interested in food-related matters of taste, craft, authenticity, status, and health' (Belasco, 2008). Belasco's comments alert us to the need to consider how the objects of study in geography classrooms may (consciously or unconsciously) reflect the interests and concerns of geography teachers. In other words, geographers interested in food belong to the same affluent social class that has fuelled the expansion of restaurant and supermarket options, and are effectively engaged in studying themselves. More generously, the political instabilities and crises that seem to shape our lives seem out of control, while paying attention to what we eat may be an attempt to assert some control over our lives.

Geographers interested in food have insisted on the need to make the connection between everyday consumption choices and their 'invisible' links to global food commodity chains, and in doing so have raised questions about hunger, inequality, neocolonialism, corporate accountability, biotechnology and ecological sustainability.

A significant aspect of work concerned with the cultures of food is a focus on 'ordinary lives', or the spaces of everyday life. This is reflected in the so-called cultural turn in geography. The cultural turn was linked to broader shifts in social science. Peter Jackson's (1989) *Maps of meaning* was the classic statement, drawing upon work in British cultural studies that focused on ideas of hegemony, ideology and resistance. Central to this approach is the idea of 'cultural politics' – that everyday acts of consuming goods, services, sounds and images can have political meanings. Although food did not feature to any great extent in Jackson's book, the subsequent development of cultural geography was marked by a large volume of work on food. The cultural turn that took place in human geography had a number of features. These included:

- respect for ordinary life

- willingness to explore alternative spaces

- openness to the textuality of everyday life

- interest in media and pop culture

- propensity to focus on consumption

- interest in how people negotiate the management of their everyday lives and bodies

- strong devotion to notions of difference.

All these features are present in the book that best represents this focus on food: David Bell and Gill Valentine's (1997) *Consuming geographies: we are where we eat.* Bell and Valentine offered a unique approach to thinking about the geographies of food, organising their study using Neil Smith's (1993) notion of the social construction of scale. Thus they present chapters that explore how food is related to the scales of the body, the home, the community, the city, the region, the nation and the global. This allows for a discussion of issues as varied as body image and disordered eating, the gendered nature of food preparation, the role of food in the development of ethnic identity, the construction of the national diet, regional food cultures, and food tourism. The approach is deliberately concerned to highlight the social construction of food cultures, or the idea that food consumption has meanings that are wrapped up with social, economic, political and moral systems, and stresses the importance of understanding the cultural politics of food. Having offered a brief introduction, the remainder of this section provides some examples of how the cultures of food might be approached.

A useful introduction to the cultures of food is found in Ashley *et al.*'s (2004) *Food and cultural studies*. Elements of their approach can be seen in their chapter on the national diet. Following relatively recent historical commentators, they reject the idea that nations exist as primordial, natural units, holding that they should rather be understood as social constructions or 'imagined communities'. While grand politics may be an important part of this, it is in more mundane everyday activities that a sense of nation is shaped, and food is one example of this. For example, in defining the British national diet:

> A day's 'menu' might be: the full English breakfast (fried egg, bacon, sausage, tomato etc.); roast meat (especially beef) with all the trimmings; afternoon tea with scones and/or homemade cakes; and fish and chips for supper. Remote though this may be from the daily food consumption of most British people, there is nonetheless a case for arguing that this constitutes a national diet as defined by the collective imaginings of the people.
>
> (Ashley *et al.*, 2004: 76)

A common assumption in cultural geographies is to argue that the mundane and everyday practices of food preparation and consumption in fact denote more deep-seated aspects of identity formation. For example, Gilbert Adair (1986) argues that 'fish and chips [...] constitute what one might call [...] a force for national unity'. Identities are often forged as distinct from various 'others', and it is this that explains popular worries about the 'Europeanisation' of British food, including the replacement of the pint of milk with a litre. From this position, it then becomes possible to deconstruct the assumed unity and authenticity of the nation. This approach is found in Panikos Panayi's (2008) *Spicing up Britain*. Panayi offers a counter-historical account of British food, following contemporary historians in demonstrating how the idea of a distinctly British diet was, from the start, closely interlinked with the project of Empire and the two-way traffic in people, commodities and ideas between the 'mother' country and her colonies. He provides a wealth of evidence to show how so-called foreign food found its place in the urban centres and increasingly the homes of the 'host' nation. He divides his account into two periods: 1850 to 1945, and 1945 to the present. In the latter period, processes of globalisation, along with the attendant changes to social and cultural life, have led to a fragmented national food culture, and the new threat is seen to come from fast-food developments such as McDonald's, thus raising the ever-near spectre of 'Americanisation'.

An example of how social and cultural changes are closely linked is provided by an examination of cookery texts. Sherrie Inness' (2006) *Secret ingredients: race, gender and class at the dinner table* is an exploration of how American cookery books have reflected and shaped perceptions of different social groups, especially women. She argues that these texts contain important messages about what it means to be a woman in American society. She examines the development in the 1950s of convenience food literature. She suggests that many women welcomed the freedom from having to cook 'just like their grandmothers' because it seemed to suggest that they could have a life free from family obligations and household chores. These books could be read alongside classic texts such as Betty Friedan's (1963) *The feminine mystique*, which reported women's sense of restlessness and dissatisfaction with a home-centred life of child-rearing. Inness discusses texts such as Frances Moore Lappé's (1971) *Diet for a small planet*, which helped spread the ideology of natural foods for a simpler and healthier lifestyle. Not only did these books pass down recipes for lentil loaf and tofu casserole, they shared a 'political agenda about the necessity of changing mainstream American's consumer-driven mindset and making them think about how their actions impacted people around the world environmentally and otherwise'. Inness' is an excellent example of a textual approach to cultural studies. It combines detailed and close readings of a variety of cookery texts along with a discussion of the wider social contexts in which they were produced. These readings illustrate what is at stake in the development of food cultures, but also demonstrate how this culture is never singular – there are dominant, emergent and residual cultures. In the British context, Nicola Humble's (2005) *Culinary pleasures* charts the transformation of British food as reflected in cookbooks (see box).

The transformation of British food

'THE WONDERFUL WORLD OF BREAD. I'm still really mad about bread – I love it. It's so exciting. While me and my mate, Bernie, who's a great baker, were trying to perfect our sourdough recipe it was hilarious 'cos we were like a couple of pregnant women on the phone each day seeing how our buns were proving. But that's what bread does to you. It's such a rewarding, therapeutic, tactile thing and you'll be so proud of yourself once you've cracked it.'

This is the introduction to an entry on bread baking from Jamie Oliver's book *Happy days with the naked chef*. Oliver has become an important celebrity in Britain's food culture. His down-to-earth, matey style endears him to men and women, young and old. As Humble (2005) notes, this recipe was very much of its time, highlighting the 'turn to baking at the millennium and the continuing love affair with all things Italian'. There is a common-sense enthusiasm for the bread, and a sense of trespass on a feminine terrain (the joke about pregnant women). The laddish tone is part of Jamie Oliver's appeal, and one he has used to further his projects of providing culinary skills and a taste for good food in the population as a whole. These projects culminated in two programmes – *Jamie's school dinners* and *Jamie's Ministry of Food* (Channel 4, 2008), in which he sought to make Rotherham, an industrial town in South Yorkshire, 'the culinary capital of the UK'. Appalled by the poor quality of the diets of local people, Oliver set out to provide a number of residents with basic skills in food preparation and a number of simple but nourishing recipes. The idea was that these people would use their new-found skills and pass them on.

Hugh Fearnley-Whittingstall's River Cottage brand is a response to concerns about the quality of food available in supermarkets. His *River Cottage* cookbooks and TV programmes are based on the idea of self-production of fruit and vegetables and the rearing (and slaughtering and butchering) of livestock. Over the decade, Fearnley-Whittingstall's projects have moved away from his River Cottage farm to explore alternative forms of food provision. One was a high-profile campaign to encourage

Tesco to offer reasonably priced free-range chicken; and another is the use of an area of waste ground in suburban Bristol as an urban smallholding maintained by local residents.

As these examples suggest, television cookery programmes offer an accessible way of engaging with questions about the politics of food. Jamie Oliver's programmes raise a number of questions for geography teachers and students to explore. For example, as the next section discusses, his work on school dinners is part of a wider concern about the quality of food in schools, while the *Ministry of Food* programmes raised important issues about the reasons behind individuals' food choices and the availability of fresh, high-quality food in deprived urban centres.

For further study

1. Undertake a study of current food shows on television. Attempt to map the food cultures on display. What are the cultural politics of food? Are there issues and questions that you think should be discussed in geography lessons?

A comprehensive discussion of the emergence of lifestyles organised around food in Western societies is found in Josee Johnston and Shyon Baumann's (2010) *Foodies: democracy and distinction in the gourmet foodscape*. They suggest a number of reasons for the emergence of this obsession with food:

- great pleasures offered by the contemporary gourmet foodscape

- concern about the industrial food system and its implications for health problems, ecological devastation and social injustices

- processes of globalisation have served to heighten transnational migration and increased cross-border travel, with the result that food culture has become more cosmopolitan

- the rise of food media – especially food television and internet sources – mean that it is possible to access a wealth of information about the food we eat (or may plan to eat in the future).

Johnston and Baumann indicate that, since the 1950s, an important shift has occurred in elite 'foodie culture', away from a concern with high-status French cuisine towards a more democratic, omnivorous approach that has a hunger for regional and local cuisines. They provide an interesting account of the development of this foodie culture, which is related to the role of restaurant critics, who served to popularise knowledge of food and cooking techniques. Significant shifts occurred in the 1950s, with the publication of Elizabeth David's books on working-class and peasant cooking in the Mediterranean, Italy and France; and within the counter-culture of the 1960s, with its concern with ecological health and the publication of alternative cookery books such as *Diet for a small planet* (Lappé, 1971). While the food cultures of the 1980s were marked by the features of 'yuppie' culture, with a concern for status and conspicuous consumption, there was a concomitant interest in 'ethnic' cuisine, and the 1990s and 2000s were marked by a growing concern for ecological sustainability and locally sourced food. The general move is towards one of breaking down status hierarchies and the quest for authenticity in food consumption.

At the same time, there is a counter-trend towards distinction, as foodies use their consumption choices to signal their good taste. This means that the politics of foodie culture are contradictory. Johnston and Baumann are upfront about this, recognising how 'foodie culture operates as a form of cultural capital that enables and legitimises social inequality'. They note that, at that same time as they participate and revel in foodie culture, they are reminded that 80 per cent of the food in the world is consumed by just 17 per cent of the world's population. This global food inequality is often imperceptible in the gourmet foodscape. At the same time, there are challenges to this, most notably in prominent concerns with organic food and a focus on local eating, and expanding public consciousness of the concept of food miles. These 'green' challenges – those concerned with ecological sustainabililty – are not matched, however, by 'red' challenges of social justice – those concerned with social inequality based on class and income.

The examples in this section are merely a taste of the potential for school geography to develop insights and approaches linked to popular cultures of food. They should be located in the context of what Barry Smart (2010) unequivocally calls 'the consumer society', which means they are concerned with reflecting on the values and identities, and occasionally ethical choices, involved in food consumption. As in all cases where pleasure and politics are mixed, there are no easy pedagogical approaches. In the final part of this chapter, we link the geographical perspectives developed so far to attempts to change the nature of what are labelled school food cultures.

For further study

1. How would you characterise the food culture of where you live? What are its main features? How do ideas of geographical scale affect your understanding of this food culture? How has the food culture changed over time? With what effects?

Changing school food cultures

The first part of this chapter discussed the apparent breakdown of a productivist food system, and suggested that this meant it was no longer possible simply to assume that food production could be left to the 'experts' in farming. These developments are the result of important shifts in the nature of food production and consumption. Geographical and sociological studies have stressed the fact that the food system is linked to processes of economic, political and cultural globalisation. The productivist agricultural systems that emerged in the post-war period guaranteed food production through intensification and industrialisation of the agro-industrial complex, which meant that in an era of post-war abundance, food moved to the back-burner of consciousness for many people. For large sections of society, food became plentiful, inexpensive, convenient and relatively nutritious. Trust was placed in the agri-food industry: in farmers, nutritionists, food corporations, agribusinesses and the state. The 'food experts' were in charge. The result was that the issue of how, where and by whom our food was produced was not the subject of conversation.

As a higher proportion of people came to live in urban and suburban locations, their direct experience and hence consciousness of the processes of food production declined, mediated though television and advertisements; women entered the workforce in increasing numbers, meaning that food provision was assured through supermarkets and processed food. There was confidence in the white-coated 'experts' in science and technology; and changes in the retail system meant that this was widely regarded as an era of choice.

However, as early as the mid-1970s, sociologists of the rural were writing about the way modern urban dwellers felt alienated from contact with the countryside; the publication of Rachel Carson's (1962) *Silent spring* drew attention to the impact of pesticides and chemical use on wildlife and human health; books such as *Diet for a small planet* (Lappé, 1971) drew on fears of overpopulation and Malthusian resource crises; and later, Ulrich Beck (1992) described how we lived in a risk society, where people were increasingly forced to reflect upon decisions without faith in 'expert systems'. These changes ushered in an era of heightened reflexivity about many aspects of our lives. Where previously there was assured guidance on hand to advise people on how to live their lives, individuals were increasingly thrown back on their own resources.

According to some commentators, the contemporary global food system is marked by two contradictory trends. On one hand, we see the continuation of trends of agricultural intensification, retail concentration and the commoditisation of food; on the other, we see the development of a 'new moral economy', based on an alternative food system that attempts to exist outside the mainstream of the commodity-driven network (this would include organic foods, eco-labelled foods, direct marketing, fair trade, local food, community kitchens and gardens, community-supported agriculture, food box schemes and farmers' markets). All these signify a mounting reflexivity and new modes of action among producers, consumers and activists in the production and consumption of food:

> Food, along with its attendant production processes, is moving to the forefront of our consciousness [...] Many of our long held assumptions about food – from the way it is produced to the way we eat – are now in flux.
>
> (Wright and Middendorf, 2007:)

Schools are not immune from these developments, and recent years have seen a growing number of initiatives focusing on changing aspects of the food culture of children in schools. The 2008 National Curriculum included a cross-cutting dimension concerned with 'healthy lifestyles'. The Department of Health/Department for Children, Schools and Families Food in Schools Programme (www.foodinschools.org) included advice on curriculum initiatives, whole-school guidance, continuing professional development for teachers, guidance on sustainable school meal procurement, minimum nutritional standards for school meals, qualifications for school cooks, and the school fruit and vegetable scheme, which provided four- to six-year-olds in state primary schools with a free portion of fruit or vegetables per day. In addition, the national Healthy Schools programme (http://home.healthyschools.gov.uk) sought to promote a 'whole school/ whole child approach to health', and was seen as a key means of achieving the goals of the Children's Plan and of the 2008 White Paper *Healthy weight, healthy lives*. Finally, the School Food Trust (www.schoolfoodtrust.org.uk), established by the (then) Department for Education and Skills in 2005 with a remit to 'transform school food and food skills', promoted the education and health of children and young people and aimed to improve the quality of food in schools.

There are also various campaigns, some of which are highly publicised. One is *Jamie's school dinners*, which was 'all about making radical changes to the school meals system and challenging the junk food culture by showing schools how they can serve fresh nutritious meals that kids enjoy eating'. Another campaign, developed by the Soil Association (along with a series of partners), was the Food for Life Partnership (www.foodforlife. org.uk), which seeks:

> To reach out through schools to give communities access to quality local and organic foods and the skills they need to cook and grow fresh food for themselves. We want all young people and their families to rediscover the pleasure of taking time out to enjoy good food that makes them feel healthy and connected to the changing seasons.

The programme is based on six steps to transform school food culture.

- Every pupil to eat healthy and climate-friendly school meals by 2015.

- School meals to be run as an education service, not a commercial business.

- Government to invest 50 pence per pupil per school meal to achieve a £1 ingredient spend while allowing take-up to rise.

- More paid hours for school cooks to prepare fresh food.

- At least twelve hours of cookery lessons a year for every pupil up to Key Stage 3 by 2011.

- Every pupil to have direct experience of food growing and production, in school gardens and on farms, by 2011.

These six steps represent a significant transformation in the cultures of schooling. To ask schools to help 'young people and their families to rediscover the pleasure of taking time out to enjoy good food that makes them feel healthy and connected to the changing seasons' suggests a reversal of the cultures of speed that shape modern life and schooling (http://www.jamieoliver.com/tv/school-dinners). In surveying this complex landscape of initiatives, it is clear that the Food for Life Partnership suggests a rather different and more nuanced definition of food culture, one that makes reference to health; the impact of modern agro-industrial food production on climate; and the changes in eating habits that promote reliance on convenience foods, processed food and eating alone. Its mission statement recognises the need to go beyond targeting young people with messages about health and sustainability.

The Food for Life Partnership characterises its work as 'transforming school food culture, one school at a time'. As Raymond Williams (1976) famously noted, 'culture' is one of the most complex words in the English language. Williams demonstrated how culture – how people think, feel, act – is inextricably linked with the material forces shaping society. This means that 'food culture' is a complex term. It is shaped by powerful economic forces. For example, there is concern about the globalisation of food as the world diet becomes Westernised and traditional ways of producing and preparing food are colonised by agro-industrial corporations; but there are also notions of a national diet and the way food represents the way of life of people in particular places. Processes of industrialisation and urbanisation led to changes in food consumption as more and more people were separated from the land, and social changes such as the gender division of labour have meant that women are increasingly employed away from the home; migration and movement lead to changes in what is eaten.

The Food for Life Partnership model offers the vision of a slower, more ecological approach to schooling. The issue at stake in this evaluation is how far the initiatives and actions associated with the Food for Life Partnership have the potential to transform school culture (which is defined widely to include children, families and communities). It would be possible for schools to adopt the language of the project as an 'add-on'. At the other end of the spectrum, it might be that the whole school culture is transformed to reflect the values of the project. Where, we might ask, is food discussed within the school environment? What messages about food are promoted, and how do children, teachers and parents make sense of the plethora of current (often inconsistent) messages about food that they receive from media, school and wider community?

Any attempt to map a school's food culture must see it as emerging, in transition and contested. The implication is that, rather than seeking to develop an a priori model of school culture, we should adopt a more flexible heuristic that can allow us to characterise the school food culture. Bell and Valentine (1997) provide a useful conceptual framework for thinking about food, based on the idea of geographical scale. Table 5.1 presents a scalar model of school food cultures and offers a framework for evaluation and analysis of a school's food culture.

Table 5.1 A scalar model of school food cultures – a framework for analysis

Body	To what extent is there is a focus on developing healthy lifestyles – encouraging students to exercise, eat healthily, and develop comfortable and relaxed ways of living? Are classroom environments conducive to health? Is the curriculum designed accordingly, with food being a prominent theme within the academic and social curriculum? Do students have good knowledge and skills concerning food?
Home	What do children eat at home? Where do they eat? Under what conditions? Who is responsible for food purchasing and preparation? What is eaten on special occasions? What is the 'perfect meal'? What is the relationship between school and home? Is learning situated within discussions of health and well-being? What is the meaning of food within family life? To what extent do schools find ways to discuss food issues with parents and family?
Community	Does the school have strong and developed community links? Is the school open to the community, and do pupils regularly spend time in the community? Does the school sees itself as actively shaping the development of its community, rather than responding to it? Are there distinctive 'food communities' within the school? How are these related to social categories of gender, social class and ethnicity? To what extent are these groups addressed by the food culture of the school? To what extent do pupils get the chance to participate in local food production in the school or community?
City	How accessible and affordable is healthy eating to residents in different city neighbourhoods? How much do urban residents know about how their food is produced and where it comes from? To what extent are students involved in the production of food in urban areas? What is the quality of food outlets within the city?
Region	Are there regional (and ethnic) differences in food cultures? Are these differences diminishing due to the globalising tendencies of modern society (the 'McDonaldisation' thesis), or are local and regional cultures of consumption resilient to such forces? Does the school encourage the development of a regional identity, or are pupils subject to globalisation?

Nation	Should there be a national food policy, cognisant of urban and regional differences?
	If so, how should this be accomplished within the different levels of UK government?
	Should Britain aim to be more self-sufficient in food provisioning, or can food security be ensured through eliminating the barriers to trade and promoting fairer and more sustainable means of production?
	How does the school interpret debates surrounding the commercialisation of childhood and how children's food consumption is shaped by commercial forces?
Global	What are the global forces shaping current food cultures, from the neoliberalisation of economies to the impact of climate change?
	What institutions will shape these changes, and how can they be resisted or challenged?
	To what extent does the school encourage students and teachers to make connections between patterns of food consumption and food production in other places?

This scalar analysis enables geography teachers and students to examine how school food cultures are being produced in actual schools, and to illuminate the choices that are made in seeking to transform school food cultures. The following case study (see box) hints at the complex nature of the geographies of school food culture.

Case study – a school's food culture

Bedford Park School is a comprehensive school located in Bristol, a large city in the south-west of England. It draws the majority of its students from two inner suburbs, one an industrial suburb with a history of tobacco manufacturing, paper and packaging, and food processing; the other a neighbourhood that has experienced recent gentrification. The school is striving to improve its performance in national league tables of examination results, which are still below the national average. However, the headteacher and school leaders are increasingly aware of the existence of a 'culture of underattainment' among the predominantly white, working-class pupils in the school (especially, though not exclusively, boys). There are moves to ensure that the welfare of all pupils is maximised and attempts are made to develop home–school links. This involves taking a wide definition of pupils' well-being.

Food is playing an increasingly prominent role in attempts to shift the school culture. There is a school canteen, and lunchtime is a time of release for many pupils. Currently 19 per cent of pupils eat school dinners. Among those who use the school canteen, the most popular purchases are warm baguettes and sandwiches. The most popular days are Wednesday, when there is a roast meal, and Friday, when fish and chips is on the menu. The school meals are provided by a company contracted by the local authority, and the school leaders argue that there are

---

tensions between the needs to minimise costs and the quantity and quality of food available to pupils (currently meals are provided at 40 pence per unit and sold at £1.75). Discussion with a senior teacher revealed that many pupils were put off by the healthy content of the meals (a no-salt edict has even led to one or two pupils 'supplying' salt to other pupils). The result is that many pupils choose to go off site at lunchtimes – a substantial twenty-minute walk – to the local sweet shop and fast-food outlets. The school has shifted its curriculum from food design and technology to cooking skills, so that more children get the chance of hands-on experience. A recent session involved pupils bringing ingredients from home to cook curry. While some brought chicken and jars of curry sauce, others brought prawns, lemongrass and more 'exotic' items such as mangetout. This episode reveals rather different approaches to food and the way food culture is linked to social class within the school. This is the place where food is discussed most explicitly in the formal curriculum.

This sketch of the school food culture is related to broader social and economic changes. In many ways, pupils' food preferences seem to conform to what a senior teacher described as the 'south Bristol diet' (chips with everything). As in many places, there has been a shift from a manual to largely service-based economy, characterised by sedentary work patterns and a car culture. Generally, both parents are in paid employment, and food procurement is through the two large supermarkets located within the catchment area of the school, which increasingly dominate the food retail landscape. There are few butchers or greengrocers in the area now, though gentrification of parts of the catchment area has led to the opening of a number of high-end coffee shops and restaurants, and there are a number of 'ethnic' restaurants reflecting the movement of people from the New Commonwealth and Pakistan. These changes in the nature of food provision interact in complex ways with the food behaviours of a predominantly white, working-class community. The school is attempting to focus on the idea of a healthy lifestyle, and cycling has been encouraged for both staff and students.

However, broader forces shaping the city seem to work against these developments. The locality of the school is best described as highly urbanised; in recent years, it seems that every scrap of spare land has been taken for housing development, and the school grounds (though extensive) are used mainly for team sport. Though the city makes claims to be a 'sustainable city', much development is geared to car-based transportation and high-end retailing. The city boasts organic restaurants that have featured in the weekend sections of quality national newspapers, but few of the children and families from the school have visited these. Like many schools, children in Bedford Park are addressed through a predominantly urban-based, commercial culture that is divorced from the rich agricultural history of the region. Spending any amount of time in the school reveals that children are spoken to by a global culture. As among many children, there is an expressed preference for fast food, even though some children will express their knowledge and understanding of the question of food politics ('we know McDonald's is bad, but [...]'). At the same time, teachers in the school encourage pupils to be aware of the lives of children and communities in the developing world, through its links with schools in Kenya, and through the formal curriculum in geography and citizenship. These point to the existence of a putative global awareness of the links between the choices we make as individuals concerning food and the wider networks of food production.

For further study

1. Using the scalar analysis tool in Table 5.1, undertake an analysis of the food culture of your school. What might be the implications of this analysis for (a) your geography department and (b) your school?

Conclusion

This chapter sketches an agenda for geography education that entails a shift from teaching about the geography of agriculture to teaching about the cultural geographies of food. In the predominantly urban cultures that developed in the Fordist period, many of us were cut off from knowledge and understanding of where our food came from and how it got there. Geography lessons that offered a descriptive account of regions of agricultural production seemed remote from experience, and, as the agricultural crisis developed, more and more geography lessons focused on the question of rural land use in a more leisure-oriented society. The emergence of food as a central concern of cultural studies and cultural geography offers real opportunities to engage young people in knowledge and understanding of the centrality of food cultures in everyday life, and to help them examine where the food they eat comes from, how it was produced, by whom, and under what conditions. These developments also offer the possibility for geography teachers to play a significant role in whole-school and community policies towards food in schools. The framework for analysis offered in the final part of this chapter aims to ensure that geography teachers can help students learn about the uneven geographies of food production and consumption, and how they might be redesigned to reflect goals of social and environmental justice.

Activities

1. What does it mean to teach about rural geography in a society that is 90 per cent urban?

2. What are the implications of the arguments in this chapter for a geography teacher seeking to develop cultural approaches to teaching the geographies of food?

6

The nature of cities

Cities are fundamental ecological features in themselves and the processes that build cities are ecological processes. The world of ecology and that of cities are part and parcel of each other; what we have to do is link them together much more strongly, in a more programmatic way.

(Harvey, 1996: 27)

Introduction

This chapter seeks to take seriously David Harvey's injunction that we should link the worlds of ecology and cities more strongly in our geography teaching. In the past few years I have watched a number of geography lessons in schools which have as their starting point scenes from the film *The Day After Tomorrow* (2004). The film was consciously launched to a public exposed to the controversy about global warming, and the plot revolves around a scientific theory that global warming will lead not to a steady warming and gradual melting of glaciers, but rather will force a tipping point, causing sharp cooling and the rapid onset of an ice age. The climax of the destruction is a fifteen-minute disaster spree that begins with the flooding of New York. The waves sweep into Manhattan and pour down the avenues. Then, suddenly, temperatures drop and everything enters a deep freeze. Despite the destruction, the ending is upbeat: tens of thousands of New Yorkers escape to the rooftops of the skyscrapers and are saved. The movie ends with a rescue and the flight southwards to the warmth of Mexico. New York is left behind.

There are other images of the imagined impact of global warming on cities. Hurricane Katrina, which in 2004 destroyed parts of New Orleans, raised the fear of more frequent and violent hurricanes, which could devastate coastal cities. The up-market magazine *Vanity Fair* included in its second annual 'green issue' an image of a flooded New York, and the same image reappeared in Al Gore's 2006 movie *An Inconvenient Truth*. These images of the destruction of large US cities by environmental disasters are difficult to separate from the wider '9/11 culture' that has persisted since 2001. Indeed, it might be argued that the significance of such representations is that they serve less as accurate geographical texts, and more as responses to a deep-seated human need to cope with the fears of a runaway and uncertain world. This point is developed in Max Page's (2008) book *The city's end*. Page draws on a 1966 essay by the cultural commentator Susan Sontag, called 'The imagination of disaster', which argued that humans live under the shadow of two equally fearful destinies: unremitting banality and inconceivable terror. Page suggests that we destroy New York (and other cities) on film and on paper to contain the fear of natural and man-made disaster:

> [...] to escape the sense of inevitable and incomprehensible economic transformations, by telling stories of clear and present dangers, with causes and effects, villains and heroes, to make our world more comprehensible than it has become.
>
> (Page, 2008: 9)

While Page seeks to persuade us that these disasters are rooted in wider concerns about economic and social life, the fact is that they tap into an emergent feeling that large cities have grown and developed in ways that fail to recognise the forces of nature and are liable to 'act back' on society, in sometimes alarming and occasionally disastrous ways. This view finds expression in Mike Davis' (1998) *Ecology of fear: Los Angeles and the imagination of disaster*, which is the latest sequel to his analysis of Los Angeles. Davis explores the dystopian side of life in a city that is seen as paradigmatic of what is variously called postmodern urbanism or post-metropolis. In *Ecology of fear*, Davis explores the natural disasters that continually threaten the city. These include the storms that sweep across the Los Angeles basin from the Pacific, the wildfires of summer, and the landslides that push expensive homes into the valley or sea below. As John Rennie Short (2008) points out, *Ecology of fear* is 'enormously exaggerated' and 'marvellously overwritten'. This is perhaps true, but more importantly, what it signals is the end of any pretence that it is possible to separate the social and physical aspects of cities. Urban nature is political. This is reflected in the emergence of the perspective of urban political ecology, which is discussed later in this chapter.

Davis' (2006) most recent work sees him shift his sights to urban dystopia on a global scale. *Planet of slums* is a tour of the horizon of what Davis calls 'urbanization without industrialization'. His analysis is based on two observations. First, for the first time in human history, there are now more people living in cities than in the countryside. Second, because the global hinterland has reached its maximum population, all future growth in the number of humans will happen in cities, and '95 percent of this final buildout of humanity will occur in the urban areas of developing countries'. In the past, the growth of mega-cities was prevented by the mass migration of people to the settler societies of the new world. Today, hardened borders make large-scale migration impossible; slums become sinks of surplus humanity. The result is a large reserve army who live legally and semi-legally in the informal economy. While those of us who studied and taught geography in the 1980s were encouraged to see slums as places of hope rather than despair, as resourceful urban dwellers found creative ways to make a living, Davis is not so positive, referring to the 'illusions of self-help'. Davis' book has divided critics. In an extended review, Angotti (2006) accuses him of a form of 'apocalyptic urbanism'. His main concern is that Davis adopts a negative (Western) outsider's view with regard to the cities of the South, and lumps together a wide variety of urban forms under the title 'slums'. This prevents him from seeing the positive and progressive ways of living in cities that characterise 'slums'. The danger, he thinks, is that it is this type of thinking that justifies governments' bulldozing of the homes of the poor, replacing them with hyper-modern residential and retail developments.

Despite the controversial reception of Davis' writing, there is little doubt that he is seeking to develop important insights into the relationship between urbanism as a way of life and the forces of nature, and is thus a useful departure point for this chapter.

The industrial city

The onset of the industrial revolution profoundly and irrevocably shifted human relationships with their physical environments. The great surge of economic activity that took place at the end of the eighteenth century and continued during the nineteenth century saw a tremendous concentration of people and capital in cities. In 1760, Manchester had a population of 17,000; by 1830 it had increased to 180,000, and by the time of the 1851 Census it had reached 303,382. The structure and nature of the early capitalist city is brilliantly recorded in Friedrich Engels' *The condition of the Working Class in England in 1844*. The book is a record of the appalling housing conditions of workers in the great cities:

> If anyone wishes to see in how little a space a human being can move, how little air – and such air! – he can breath, how little of civilization he may share and yet live, it is only necessary to travel hither. Everything which here arouses horror and indignation is of recent origin, belongs to the industrial epoch.
>
> (Engels 1849/2005: 92)

The influential urban planner Peter Hall refers to this period as 'The City of Dreadful Night' (a reference to James Thomson's 1880 poem). However, these 'shock cities' (e.g. Chicago, Manchester) of the industrial revolution eventually created the context for government intervention in the organisation of cities. A sensationalist report on the conditions of urban life in London, *The bitter cry of outcast London* (Preston, 1883) proved to be one of the most influential writings in the whole history of British social reform. It led to the establishment of the Royal Commission of 1885, which sought to encourage local authorities to make provision for the poorer sections of society. Middle-class shock and outrage about the conditions of the 'strangers in their midst' was in part linked to fears of social disorder and political insurrection (the 1884 Reform Act had just enfranchised the urban male working class). This was a period in which there were concerns to map 'darkest London' and develop reliable statistics that could inform policies of social reform.

It was this context of middle-class concern that gave rise to ambitious plans to solve the problems of cities. In 1898, Ebenezer Howard published his book *Garden cities of to-morrow*. For Howard, cities in Europe and America had become too densely populated and suffered from 'foul air, murky skies, slums and gin palaces'. Howard proposed the establishment of Garden Cities or new, self-contained settlements of around 500,000 inhabitants spread over 12,000 acres. These would combine the best of what the city could offer (economic and social opportunities, well-lit streets) with the fresh air, bright sunshine and space of the countryside. In England, two Garden Cities were established: Letchworth (1903) and Welwyn (1920). These were bold attempts to forge a new relationship between the urban and rural. Elizabeth Outka (2009) has argued that these types of settlement can be seen as the cultural products of a society experiencing a transition to modernity, which welcomed the products of urban society, yet sought to maintain the 'authenticity' of the rural past and its association with nature.

The invisibility of nature in urban geography

Twentieth-century ideas about cities were rooted in a deeply ingrained dualism between city and wilderness, nature and culture. Urban geographers shared this outlook. For example, Chicago School human ecologists predicated their theories of the city on ecological metaphors but they were not concerned with nonhuman natures per se: they counted hobos and juvenile delinquents and women who voted but they did not count prairie grasses or hedgehogs. Later versions of urban geography were very different, but their objects of analysis were thoroughly humanized cities and suburbs from which nature was excluded. Exactly how cities got built and used, and their impacts, depended on who was talking. For urbanists grounded in neoclassical theory, cities were built by rational producers and consumers had orderly, quantifiable bid-rent curves, predictable land-use patterns [...] But regardless of stripe, most twentieth-century urban geographers did not think about urban rivers or oak trees or red-legged frogs.

(Wolch, 2007: 373)

As Jennifer Wolch suggests, the field of urban geography has operated on an assumed separation between nature and society. A survey of recent introductory texts in the field confirms that this is still largely the case. This is also true of how the subject is taught in school geography. This section summarises the various traditions of urban geography as taught in UK schools.

There is one sense in which urban geography teaching since the 1970s has been influenced by ecological thinking. The most famous diagram in geography is Park and Burgess's (1967) model of urban structure based on fieldwork in Chicago in the first quarter of the twentieth century. As many have pointed out, this portrayed the city as an organism which grew by processes of accretion. The language of the model is steeped in ecological terms, such as invasion and succession, competition and the emergence of niches. The model has its roots in nineteenth-century social science, which relied heavily on biological metaphors, and which imagined societies as integrated, functional wholes. One effect of this language, it has been argued, is to suggest that social relations (between individuals and groups) can be explained in terms of natural processes (as in the idea of the law of the jungle operating in cities). It suggests that human societies are structured and can be explained through ecological laws.

A second influential strand of urban geography teaching in cities has been the use of models of land use derived from neoclassical economics. In these models, cities are seen as economic spaces in which the laws of profit maximisation and 'least-cost location' are obeyed by self-interested individuals, or 'rational economic man'. These models of spatial science rely upon universal explanations of processes, and are ahistorical. There is little room here for the consideration of nature in cities.

A third approach found in urban geography emerged out of the calls for 'relevance' that followed the 'rediscovery of poverty' in North American and Western Europe in the late 1960s. In his introductory text *Urban geography*, David Herbert (1972) stated that 'The most basic problems of cities are those posed by the process of urbanisation itself, a process by which the world is becoming a more urban society with the shift from more rural and agricultural forms of living'. Subsequently, the 1970s and 1980s saw the publication of a large number of geographical texts that focused on the social problems of cities. Herbert noted that 'the theme of relevance is becoming explicit in geographical research to a far greater extent'. The development of a 'welfare approach' is strongly associated with the work of David Smith (1974), who posed the question about the allocation of resources: 'who gets what, where and how?' Geographers such as David Harvey pointed to the conflicts that were generated in cities over the allocation of resources, and the subsequent development of social geography highlighted how divisions existed in cities along the lines of gender, ethnicity, and (less remarked) income. From the early 1970s, feminist geographers raised awareness of how urban space was organised in ways that marginalised and discriminated against women. There was a concern with women's place in the domestic division of labour, their limited access to urban space, and issues of access to childcare, leisure and other facilities. With hindsight, it is possible to see how this concern with access to economic resources could provide the basis for the emergence of a focus on the production and consumption of urban nature discussed in this chapter.

School geography's engagement with urban nature was most developed in the emergence of what, in chapter two, was termed environmental geography. This tradition emerged as an attempt to teach children about their environment in the light of the physical changes that took place in the post-war period. According to this narrative, Britain entered the post-war period with a huge legacy of old Victorian terraced housing in the inner areas of its industrial cities. The appalling condition of much of this housing led whole areas to be declared unfit for human habitation and designated as 'comprehensive development areas'. The 1950s saw the beginning of massive inner-city 'slum clearance'. Whole communities were uprooted in this process, and by the end of the 1950s this 'clean sweep' physical planning was being criticised for its social insensitivity.

While there is little sustained discussion of the role of nature in urban environments in present approaches to school geography, this chapter suggests that this should be an important area for development in any agenda concerned to teach geography as if the planet matters. As Susan Smith (1994) reminds us, the interpretation of urbanism is 'essentially a political rather than an ontological question. Urban geography is as much a contest of ideas as a quest for reality; as much a statement of how things ought to be as an account of how things are'. This is the basis on which this chapter proceeds.

For further study

1.   To what extent does the study of towns and cities in your school geography include or exclude the natural world? What would an urban geography that took nature seriously look like?

Bringing nature back in

It is in practice, hard to see where society begins and nature ends […] In a fundamental sense, there is in the final analysis nothing unnatural about New York City.

(Harvey, 1996)

As argued in the previous section, urban geography as taught in schools has tended to present cities and towns as essentially separate from nature. As the material discussed in this section shows, however, this is beginning to change. As a prelude to more recent developments, we first consider two texts published in 1984 that deal with the relationship between cities and nature. Michael Hough's *City form and natural process* argues that:

the traditional design values that have shaped the physical landscape of our cities have contributed little to their environmental health, or to their success as civilizing, enriching places to live in […] There is an urgent need for urban landscape form that is in tune with the growing awareness of, and concern for, the issues of energy, environment and natural resource conservation.

(Hough, 1984: 1)

Hough is concerned that urban society is alienated from environmental values and cultural connections with the land, and that in the development of cities, little attention has been paid to understanding the natural processes that they rely on. In the presence of apparently abundant and cheap energy, the urban environment has been shaped by a technology 'whose goals are economic rather than environmental or social'. The chapters in his book trace how cities create an artificial climate, and how they could be designed to create more pleasant places to live; the way in which the aesthetic preference for manicured parks and recreations leads to a loss of variety of biodiversity; how cities tend to seek to preserve the boundaries between human and animal life, with the result that people's need for a relationship with the animal world is diminished; and the potential for cities to become sources of food production. These themes resonate with more recent discussions of urban sustainability, and Hough's book can be seen as a relatively early account of the relationship between cities and nature:

The food that appears in the shops has little connection any more with the fields adjacent to the city. Rather it is dependent on world-wide marketing and distribution networks operating on fossil fuels. But increasing fuel and food costs and shrinking farmlands will, over time, influence current patterns of consumption and priorities.

(Houghton, 1984: 201–202)

Also published in 1984 was Ian Douglas' book *The urban environment*. Douglas argues that:

By the year 2000 more than half the world's people will be living in cities and throughout the twenty-first century the urban population will continue to grow steadily […] For the future survival of cities, understanding of the character of the physical and biological environments within cities and around cities will be essential. The schools and universities of the future will have to orient their teaching of the biological and earth sciences towards the conditions the bulk of the world's people experience every day. Physical geography will become that of the city first and that of the mountains, forests, coasts, ice-caps and oceans second.

(Douglas, 1984: vii)

The urban environment attempts to develop an integrated bio-social-physical approach to cities. Chapter 2 is called 'The city as an economic system and as an ecosystem'. As economic systems, cities are flows of money, goods, services and materials. As ecosystems, cities are flows of energy, water and chemical elements, and organisms. The book successfully puts the physical geography of cities back on the agenda of urban studies. There are limits to this approach, though. At times it seems as if we are talking about 'first nature' – with the sense of physical geography as a force 'acting back' on cities. There is an assumption that the disciplines of management and engineering will overcome the effects of nature. Better coordination and planning are required. The social geography depicted in Douglas' book is not as complex as his treatment of physical processes, although there are occasional hints about the uneven effects of urban development:

[…] modern cities, with democratically elected governments, provide basic services for all, but face dilemmas over who wins and who loses from the effects of service provision or environmental improvements. If a new freeway into the city centre reduces traffic jams and perhaps the rate of discharge of exhaust fumes in some suburbs, yet at the same time cuts inner city communities in two and causes the removal of shops and community facilities, perhaps the possibly wealthier inhabitants of outer suburbs will gain easier access to the city as the price of disruption for the inner city community.

(Douglas, 1984: 203–204)

Writing less than a decade after the financial crisis of New York City of 1975, Douglas comments that capitalism places many of the real costs of production, including environmental ones, on the public sector:

> The financial crises of New York City in the 1970s can thus be interpreted in terms of attempts to make the city the world corporate capital, of decisions based on private profit calculations and of the failure of society through the political process to place social needs ahead of the imperatives of the market.
>
> (Douglas, 1984: 7)

Prior to this, Douglas suggests, New York had been a compassionate city, providing welfare, housing and education at little or no cost. However, the reassessment led to reductions in manpower and maintenance. With hindsight, the example of New York City is prescient, since the crisis (famously encapsulated in President Ford's blunt message in response to the city administrators' calls for a financial bail-out: 'Ford to City: drop dead') precipitated a rebranding of New York and an aggressive neoliberal economic restructuring (see Greenberg, 2009). What Douglas' approach is unable to do is to explore how nature was enlisted as a very part of that process of industrial restructuring. So decisions about the retrenchment of welfare or the privatisation of water resources were intimately concerned with the social use of nature. It is impossible to separate them.

An example from Douglas' book that reflects the need to think about how nature is in fact inextricably linked to cycles of economic growth is the example of suburbs. He discusses the nature of suburbs in a chapter on 'The biogeography of the city', and is careful to differentiate between different types of suburban nature. Thus the inner suburbs of cities are rarely devoid of gardens with mature trees; gardens are a rich habitat with a combination of mown grass, open grown trees and patches of flowers, shrubs and vegetables. This 'intra-urban savanna' receives artificial increments of water and nutrients as people cultivate their gardens; though, being at the whim of gardeners, productivity is spatially and temporally variable. Insects exploit the variety of the garden, being both food for birds and pests for the gardener. Like weeds, insects are the target of chemical sprays. Douglas describes how, in mature suburban areas, trees have grown to a substantial height and shade large parts of gardens for much of the day. In some mature suburbs there is substantial cover, and this acts as a noise barrier and a green corridor. The new suburbs of cities built on former farmland have a smaller number and lower height of trees, and a greater proportion of mown grass. The total biomass is much lower and there is a less abundant and varied fauna.

While this account of suburban nature is informative, it is necessary to understand how it is linked with broader economic and political processes. In their discussion of the 'suburban gothic' (the dark side of the suburban dream) in the USA, Hanlon et al. (2010) note that in the USA, from 1982 to 1997, 1.4 million acres were converted into developed land each year. Developers favoured building larger houses at lower densities, thus requiring more land and increasing the effects on ecosystems. This type of development is too diffuse to support public transport or easy walking, and therefore encourages a reliance on private auto transport, which in turn relies on fossil fuel consumption. It hardly needs pointing out that the development of a suburban lifestyle is part of a broader political–economic system, albeit one that, in the wake of the financial crisis of 2008, seems unsustainable:

> Low-density US suburban sprawl was only possible with relatively cheap fuel and lack of accountancy for the environmental impacts. It is unlikely that the cheap gasoline that literally lubricated suburbanization will ever return. The suburbs were built on gas costs to the order of $27 a barrel (at 2007 prices). In one month in the summer of 2008, prices reached over $140 a barrel with OPEC officials suggesting that an ideal price, for them, was between $60 and $70. Prices will remain deflated during recessions, but they will then tend to rise as the economy improves. There are few large oil reserves left, and the price will inevitably rise when the global economy ticks upwards. Where does that leave low-density urban sprawl, which is so reliant on large-scale private car usage?
>
> (Hanlon et al., 2010: 166)

This example illustrates the importance of thinking about the way in which nature is socially produced, which is an important insight of recent studies of urban political ecology. In the next section, we briefly discuss some examples of how geographers have developed historical accounts of the co-evolution of cities and nature.

Environmental histories of urbanisation

An important aspect of recent study in environmental history, which has clear links with the concerns of geographers, is the study of urban environmental history. William Cronon's (1991) *Nature's metropolis* is widely regarded as a central text in the development of an understanding of the relationship between cities and nature. Cronon starts by showing how, during the second half of the nineteenth century, the American landscape was transformed. It was in this period that the great cities were built, the fertile farmlands, the transport systems that linked the large cities and their regions into an integrated world market. Yet Americans have tended to see cities and country as separate places, more isolated from each other than connected. Cronon explains how, through his attempt to tell the environmental history of a single city, he came to understand that the city's history cannot be separated from the countryside that surrounds it. In the case of Chicago, the meatpacking industry drew a net over a vast geography (1500 miles east to west, 1000 miles north to south). Wherever corn could be converted into more profitable pigs, or where otherwise useless prairie grass could be used to raise cattle and then moved in railcars, became part of the vast hinterland of the city. Life in these areas, though apparently rural and part of 'nature', was closely linked to the fortunes of the commodity markets in wheat futures and pork bellies. Where animal slaughtering had been done seasonally by local farmers, it was now continuous. For Cronon, the appearance of the livestock industry was 'another manifestation of second nature [...] a new animal landscape governed as much by economics as by ecology'.

Matthew Gandy's (2002) *Concrete and clay* examines the urbanisation of New York City and explores a series of relationships between the city, nature and social power in the creation of the city's water supply, Central Park, urban parkways, and an anti-waste campaign in Brooklyn. He explores questions of environmental justice in a city where toxic facilities and land use are consistently concentrated in minority-dominated areas of the city, and the Cross-Bronx expressway destroyed viable neighbourhoods. An important part of this analysis is the way in which processes of privatisation of the city's water supplies have led to conflicts over water supply and waste disposal. Gandy argues that New York contains a multitude of 'urban natures', including its verdant parks and gardens, its landscaped parkways, and its 'magnificent' water technologies, which 'have harnessed a regional hydrological cycle to serve the needs of nine million people'. He argues that the design, use and meaning of urban space involve the 'transformation of nature into a new synthesis'. These transformations did not occur without conflicts and tensions, and were often prompted by problems of public health.

This sense of conflict about how urban nature is to be shaped, and in whose interest, is strongly evident in Matthew Klingle's (2007) study *Emerald City*. He explores how Seattle's boosters imagined themselves as completing 'the work that nature had left undone' by draining the city's waterfront and making stable sites for the growth of the city. This immediately raised questions about the balance of private property rights and the need for communal public space, which continue to animate politics in the city. He explores the role of engineers in harnessing nature, and the cultural arguments over wild and tamed nature linked to the landscape architect Frederic Olmstead's projects to build public parks. A common theme in Klingle's account is the way that nature has been used to promote social order and to create a divided geography, something that has led to an individualistic and car-centred society that prioritises private property over shared nature. This is the source of his title, the *Emerald City*, which refers to the film *The Wizard of Oz*. Just as Dorothy and friends found a darker reality when they entered the Emerald City, the same is true of those who look more closely at Seattle's environment.

Finally, Maria Kaika's (2005) *City of flows* seeks to understand the production of urban nature with particular reference to water supply in Athens. She deciphers the historical–geographical process through which modernity discursively constructed the modern city and the modern home as autonomous 'space envelopes', independent from natural processes. She argues that, although the conceived ideas of planned modernity attempted to separate these, in the realisation of these plans there was a creative destruction in which networks of flows of natural elements, social power relations and capital shaped the city. Her empirical chapters, based around the development of water management in Athens, seek to reveal these 'fetishised' social relations of production and the hidden material networks of flows that urbanise nature. In doing so, she talks about the notion of a hybrid nature, one in which cities, people and natural processes are inextricably linked. One of the strengths of Kaika's book is the way it seeks a more general periodisation of modernity's relationship to nature in cities, as follows.

■ Modernity's nascent promethean project (early nineteenth century) – in this period, the industrial city experiences deteriorating social and environmental conditions and becomes the 'city of dreadful death'. Urban rivers become a source of disease and death.

- The heroic moment of modernity's promethean project (1880–1975) – this period sees the development of large-scale urban sanitation projects (water supply and sewerage) as well as the construction of impressive transport and communications networks. It is a time when technology is admired and nature is tamed and controlled as the prerequisite for urban and industrial development.

- Modernity's promethean project discredited (1975–2010) – in the most recent period, the increasing demand for resources in Western societies, coupled with a crisis in public funding, impedes further improvement of urban infrastructure. Environmental disasters around the world discredit modernity's Promethean project and question the logic and practice of continuous development – nature is now cast as a potential source of crisis (Kaika, 2005).

Kaika's book makes use of theories associated with the field of urban political ecology, which draws inspiration from the work of Neil Smith and David Harvey to insist that capitalist development has increasingly incorporated nature in its circuits of accumulation. This means that, in seeking to understand nature, we should no longer imagine a pristine or 'first nature' that exists outside human schemes of value, but must recognise how 'second nature' is always linked with wider social systems. This political ecology perspective is discussed in the following section.

The political ecology of urbanisation

Taking on this argument about 'second nature' suggests that, in seeking to incorporate environmental themes into the study of urban geography, we cannot explain changes in physical systems without close attention to the changing political economy (see Heynen et al., 2006 for a collection of essays that reflect this perspective). Keil and Graham (1998) argue that the Fordist cities developed in the post-Second World War period were characterised by intensive accumulation, which introduced a cycle of mass production and mass consumption regulated by the economic policies of the Keynesian state. During this period, human relationships with nature in the city continued to be incorporated into the circuits of capital. As a result, nature was taken for granted in urban spaces. For instance, in an age of manicured front lawns, nature becomes materially unimportant. Instead, it is viewed as a separate entity reflected in the separation of town and country. Agriculture happens elsewhere, tourism opens up nature in foreign and exotic places, and children come to think that milk comes from plastic cartons. The automobile as the key commodity of Fordist production and consumption enables the urban field to be expanded, and villages and hamlets to be overrun by endless subdivisions, thereby losing their 'rural' character:

> How people eat, what their food contains, where the waste and the sewage go are questions of rather minor technical detail – as long as the stream of oil from the well into the gasoline of our petrol tank of our automobile is not interrupted.
>
> (Keil and Graham, 1998: 105)

This separation of society and nature is perhaps most vividly realised in the residential suburbs, where, through networked supplies of goods, residents are more closely linked to industrial natures or agriculture on far distant continents than they are to their nearest city.

However, for Keil and Graham, the collapse of the Fordist consensus from the mid-1970s has led to changes in how we understand cities. One of the effects of the restructuring of urban space has been to allow for the re-emergence of nature as a part of cities. This is part of an ongoing critique of the modernist visions of planning and order. Western societies are increasingly suspicious of large-scale developments that are polluting and consume large amounts of the world's resources. The Club of Rome's report *The limits to growth* in the early 1970s fuelled the fire of critique of Fordist modernity. It argued that resource-intensive economic development could not continue indefinitely, and sparked the emergence of environmental movements that sought to offer alternative forms of social development. For instance, this was the period that saw the emergence of green parties in Europe. However, of more importance, Keil and Graham suggest, was the political resolution that came with the Brundtland Report (World Commission on Environment and Development, 1987). Keil and Graham argue that this was effectively a way of shifting responsibility for the planet's health from the workings of the global capitalist economy to individuals, their communities, their bodies and personal metabolisms. Instead of radically challenging the workings of the capitalist economy, sustainability was redefined as a means of renewal of the capitalist accumulation process.

The trend towards eco-modernisation means that plans and policies for urban restructuring and new urban developments invariably have a green or urban sustainability element, based on the widely accepted idea that environmental concerns should be integrated into all aspects of human society. Thus we should ensure that measures of societal progress are based not simply on income or wealth, but on aspects of well-being, health and welfare. A second aspect is the use of smart solutions or the development of technologies that allow for cleaner, greener cities. The third aspect is to pay attention the idea of the convivial or liveable city. This is the optimistic assessment of Benton-Short and Short's (2008) recognition that 'There are emerging discourses that attempt to redesign, recreate and rethink cities within a larger framework of liveability and sustainability.' These new urban environmental discourses include slow growth, new urbanism and smart growth.

Benton-Short and Short's observation is in line with Keil and Graham's argument that, in the post-Fordist city, nature has been 'creeping back in'. However, Keil and Graham insist that it is important to remember that despite its post-industrial narratives, industry – mass production and consumption – has not disappeared but has merely been shifted to new zones of production. It is not a coincidence that, just when industry has been expunged from cities, nature is increasingly 'welcomed back' into urban space, notably as a way of 'selling' the city and realising profit. Thus, in the post-Fordist era, urbanisation is now conceptualised and achieved through nature and ecology, rather than against it. Nature in effect adds value to post-Fordist urban environments.

For further study

1. Using the idea of 'second nature' and analysis of suburbs as an example, develop an urban political ecology analysis of one of the following: (a) sprawl; (b) gentrification; (c) new urbanism; (d) the urban–rural fringe.

Case study – The urban nature of Bristol

Bristol is a medium-sized city with a population of approximately half a million, located in the south-west of England. By 1700, Bristol had become the largest city and port outside London. Wealth from the slave trade and other mercantile ventures was invested in the city's infrastructure. In the 1800s, the city expanded in size and population. This growth transformed the city. It acquired a modern transport system, a commercial centre, and eastern industrial district and suburbs. The Great Western Railway reached Bristol in 1841. This growth divided the city's population along class lines, with the rich creating and gravitating to the north and west of the city. The growth of the city in the nineteenth century led to the aggravation of problems of public health, housing and congestion. In 1850, Bristol was the third most unhealthy city in Britain, with a death rate of one in twenty-eight per year. The city was slow to improve public health. An inadequate system of sewerage was built in the 1850s, but a new one had be paid for at the end of the century. The adoption of the 1848 Public Health Act led to setting up of a Sanitary Authority in 1851, and this led to moves to clean, light, pave and surface the streets. In terms of housing, there were moves on the part of philanthropists to improve the dwellings of the working classes. By the end of the century, the city had a network of services designed to counter the worst health hazards of large-scale urbanisation and to improve the condition of the physical environment.

Fordist cities generally consist of a central business district, surrounded by zones of industry and housing, linked together with roads and other infrastructure. Roads, electricity and telecommunications concentrate flows of energy, materials and commuters through large factories and offices. Fast and efficient transport also allows for the decentralisation of industry and services, suburban living and lower urban densities. The key technology of the Fordist city is the motor car. For much of the post-war period, Bristol displayed the characteristics of a classic Keynesian–Fordist city, which was reflected in its built environment. For example, the industrial landscape was dominated by the docks, and industries associated with tobacco (Wills and Imperial), confectionery (Fry's), paper and packaging (Robinson, DRG) and aerospace (Rolls-Royce, British Aerospace). There were high levels of state investment in road infrastructure, education and health, as well as large council estates built to alleviate housing problems. While these developments brought wealth to the city and the general levelling of incomes, the nature of the built environment caused problems. Industries were polluting of air and water courses, and the large estates were criticised for being monolithic and alienating.

Furthermore, the tendency to build horizontally fuelled the need for longer commutes and traffic congestion. Most people are alienated from nature and the natural resources and services that sustain their lives. People are less aware of the sources of energy, food and other products that they consume, and of the destination of their waste. They have less direct contact with plants, animals and green landscapes, and are protected from extremes of weather and climate. In the post-war period, Bristol developed in ways that saw nature as a resource to be exploited. Much of the city was rebuilt for commercial purposes; urban motorways were built to transport people from their homes on the edge of the city to the centre; and Bristol became increasingly hooked into national networks of supplies of food and manufactured goods. The city's water supplies were increased by the flooding, in the 1960s, of a series of valleys to the south of the city.

From the mid-1970s, Bristol underwent a transformation from an industrial city based on manufacturing to a post-industrial city based on services. The recession of the early 1980s saw the loss of employment in tobacco, confectionery, paper and packaging, and aerospace, as well as the slow decline of the city's docks. The economic recovery of the mid-1980s saw a major economic restructuring, with employment growth in financial services, education and medicine-related activities, and the service economy of food and drink, office cleaning, entertainment and leisure. These changes were accompanied by an occupational shift away from manual and semi-skilled jobs to white-collar work. This led to the regeneration of parts of the city, with new, gleaming office towers to house banking and insurance companies and, fittingly, the demolishing of old tobacco warehouses to make way for the Lloyds building. By the late 1980s, it was apparent that Bristol had weathered the economic recession better than many cities in the north, and there were signs of urban renaissance. In 1985, the Environment Secretary, Kenneth Baker, declared Bristol to be 'the shining buckle on Britain's silicon belt'. This renewed prosperity meant that Bristol underwent a cultural renaissance too, fuelled by the sheer purchasing power of white-collar professionals. If anything, these trends were exacerbated through the 1990s and early 2000s, to the extent that the Work Foundation posited the idea that Bristol should be considered an 'ideopolis' or 'a sustainable knowledge intensive city that drives growth in the wider city-region. It gives cities a framework for developing knowledge-intensive industries that will be economically successful and improve quality of life' (Work Foundation, 2006). A crucial part of an ideopolis is the existence of creative industries which, according to the economic geographer turned 'city booster' Richard Florida, makes cities attractive to the talented, tolerant and technologically minded groups who are seen to be crucial to economic growth.

Part of this narrative of transformation is the 'greening' of Bristol as a city. The city promotes itself as a sustainable city, and has won awards for the relatively high lengths of cycle paths provided by the council, general provision for the recycling of domestic waste and high-profile organic food festivals. At the same time, these initiatives are undercut by a lack of investment in public transport, the promotion of high-end luxury consumption (based on the assumption that people will travel by car), and the continued growth of new house-building on the northern fringe and on areas of green-belt land to the south west of the city. These developments are all predicated on assumptions of private transport to and from work in the city (a recent report named Bristol the seventh most congested city in Britain). In addition, the growth of the city in the 1990s and 2000s has been uneven, and high levels of social deprivation and economic instability continue in some parts of the city.

In sum, there is little doubt that current growth strategies seek to 'bring nature back into the city'. However, the broader policies of pursuing growth through the mechanism of property-led housing developments and the provision of high-status shopping opportunities looks doubtful from the perspective of 2010, and in the wake of the economic downturn.

Beyond urban political ecology: reasons to be cheerful?

The discussion of urban political ecology (along with the case study of the development of Bristol) highlighted the importance of placing attempts to bring about the greening of cities in a broader economic context. From this perspective, it is tempting to conclude that there is little escape from the grip of economic forces, and that even attempts to bring nature back in are part of a process of capital accumulation (represented by Neil Smith's argument, referred to in chapter three, that nature is increasingly used as an accumulation strategy). Against this, there are those who are more optimistic about the possibility of improving the nature of towns and cities. An example of this is found in the work of the urban geographer Paul Knox, one of the most influential and prolific writers on the world economy and urbanism. In *Small town sustainability*, Knox and Mayer (2009) discuss the ways in which a movement of 'small towns' (defined as urban places with no more than 50,000 residents) offers examples of escaping the grip of the forces of globalisation in order to develop distinctive and local economies and ways of life. These small towns, say Knox and Mayer, represent a significant fraction of the total population in many regions of Europe, North America, Australia, New Zealand and Japan. For example, in Europe, small towns are home to 20 per cent of the population. These towns are places that can have their own identity and provide a sociable and enjoyable way of life for their inhabitants:

They can be havens in a fast world, places whose inhabitants think globally but act locally.

(Knox and Mayer, 2009: 1).

Knox and Mayer seek to find examples of how small towns are finding ways to resist the forces of globalisation that undermine towns' liveability and sustainability. This is a 'reaction against the consequences of the far-reaching economic, environmental, and socio-cultural forces associated with globalisation and the work-spend lifestyle that dominates the economic and social dynamics of contemporary society' (Ibid.). The keys to this resistance are attempts to live lives that are 'local', 'organic', 'authentic' and 'slow'. There is a focus in these towns of ensuring the local distinctiveness is preserved, especially in the realm of food and eating, and in vernacular architecture. Knox and Mayer make much of the Slow Food and Cittaslow movements. The Cittaslow movement (www.cittaslow.org.uk) began in 1999 in Greve in Chianti, a Tuscan hill town. The mayors of four municipalities committed themselves to a set of principles that included working towards calmer and less polluted physical environments, conserving local aesthetic traditions, and fostering local crafts, produce and cuisine. They also pledged to use technology to create healthier environments, to make people aware of the value of more leisurely rhythms of life, and to share their expertise in devising creative solutions to urban problems. The Cittaslow movement is mirrored in Britain by the emergence of transition towns (www.transitionnetwork.org). Knox and Mayer provide a wealth of examples of small towns that are going some way towards making liveable and sustainable environments. However, at the end of their book, the question is raised as to how far these towns can begin to shape economic regions that are in some sense 'de-linked' from the broader flows of the 'fast' global economy; and how far these developments are a new form of lifestyle for the relatively wealthy and privileged, who are able to afford a 'slower' way of life.

Knox's most recent book, *Cities and design* (2011), concludes with a chapter titled 'Toward liveability and sustainability'. It documents a range of concepts and ideas that seek to move towards more sustainable forms of urban development. These include 'true urbanism', which aims to recognise the variety of actors in urban systems and the need for flexibility and diversity in guiding urban development; 'integral urbanism', which stresses the need for joined-up thinking about the different elements that make up urban systems; moves for convivial public spaces; and movements for green design. These are, in many ways, compelling visions of urban development more aligned with nature. However, they come at the end of a book that convincingly explains how the design of cities has been shaped by the various phases of capitalist modernity, culminating in the dominance of neoliberal ideas about the economy that favour private wealth over the public good, and consumption-led regeneration. Indeed, the optimistic tone of Knox's chapter is undermined by his citation of a commentary by Leslie Sklair, which highlights the dominance of the paradigm of the 'oppressive/consumerist city' – one in which consumerism 'inevitably exacerbates the twin crises of capitalist globalization – namely, class polarization and ecological unsustainability' (Sklair, 2009).

The tenets of green urbanism

Timothy Beatley (2000), in his book *Green urbanism*, details the progress and policies of twenty-five of the most innovative cities in eleven European countries. He identifies the following tenets of green urbanism.

- Cities that strive to live within their ecological limits, fundamentally reduce their ecological footprints, and acknowledge their connections with, and impacts on, other cities and communities and the larger planet.

- Cities that are green and that are designed for, and function in, ways analogous to nature.

- Cities that strive to achieve a circular rather than a linear metabolism, which nurtures and develops positive symbiotic relationships with and between its hinterland.

- Cities that strive towards local and regional self-sufficiency and take full advantage of, and nurture, local/regional food production, economy, power production, and many other activities that sustain and support their populations.

- Cities that facilitate (and encourage) more sustainable, healthful lifestyles.

- Cities that emphasise a high quality of life and the creation of highly liveable neighbourhoods and communities.

For further study

1. Undertake a study of your nearest town or city to understand what policies and initiatives are in place to bring about its 'greening'. Re-read the case study of Bristol. How far do the developments you have studied confirm or challenge the urban political ecology view that nature is increasingly used as a means of increasing economic value?

Conclusion

This chapter argues that, given the fact that we live in an urban world (whether we call this a 'planet of slums' or the 'third urban revolution'), it is important to recognise the complexity of the relations between urbanisation and nature. The fundamental argument of those working in environmental urban history and urban political ecology is that we cannot view nature as separate from the wider circuits of power and money that shape the development of cities. The two are closely related. The pedagogical challenges in teaching geography in this way are great, not least because it requires that students should be introduced to ideals in political economy. As the material discussed in this chapter suggests, this may best be achieved through a detailed focus on case studies that are attentive to the historical and economic contexts of urban development. This is important because it provides geography lessons with a sense of reality about the potential for the greening of cities, and about the powerful structures that make any change difficult.[1]

Activities

1. Urban geography is an important part of many school geography syllabuses and schemes of work. Review the schemes of work in your school geography department. How might they be rewritten to include the ideas about urban nature discussed in this chapter?

7

Changing economic geographies

Introduction

On 10 February 2010, *BBC Breakfast* carried a news item that showed how, in the wake of the credit crunch and economic recession, many planned developments in large UK cities were being delayed (http://news.bbc.co.uk/1/hi/england/8507598.stm). The report showed footage of boarded-up sites, and members of the public were interviewed and expressed their concern that these sites were an eyesore and were not great adverts for the towns and cities. In light of this, the report went on to show how these sites are being reclaimed for other uses – including urban gardens (allotments), football pitches and walkways, with seats and public art. While these were heralded as a positive development by many, the report ended by stating, 'But these alternatives to rubble-strewn holes are all just temporary. The sport, greenery and gardening will all go when the economy picks up.' The first time the report was shown, one of the presenters commented that it was a pity that these things would be lost. However, she was quickly corrected by her co-presenter that, of course, it was more important to get the economy back to normal. When the report was repeated an hour later, the presenters made no comment. This is an interesting moment, since it represents a moment when it became obvious that the drive to get the economy back to 'normal' would invariably lead to the replacement of something people wanted, needed and valued (green space, conviviality, engagement with nature) by something they already feel they have enough of (retail outlets, expensive city-centre flats). At the same time, it is this common sense that could never be allowed to challenge the rational discourse of economics. As Jim Stanford states at the start of his book *Economics for everyone*:

> Most people think economics is a technical, confusing, and even mysterious subject. It's a field best left to the experts: namely, the economists.
> But in reality, economics should be quite straightforward. After all, economics is simply about how we work. What we produce. And how we distribute and ultimately use what we've produced. Economics is about who does what, who gets what, and what they do with it.
>
> (Stanford, 2008: 1)

Geographers, of course, would want to stress the importance of where we work, where we produce. Economic geography is about who does what, who gets what, and what they do with it *where*. As Benko and Scott, in their review of the development of the field of economic geography, state:

> The central concerns of economic geography revolve around the ways in which space – in its various manifestations as distance, separation, proximity, location, place etc. – dictates the shape and form of economic outcomes. In more concrete terms, we can say that the task of modern economic geography is to provide a reasoned description of the spatial organization of the economy and, in particular, to elucidate the ways in which geography influences the economic performance of capitalism.
>
> (Benko and Scott, 2004: 47)

The final clause in this definition – 'to elucidate the ways in which geography influences the economic performance of capitalism' – is central to the argument in this chapter, which is that economic geography can be a resource for teachers to develop pupils' understanding of the spatial manifestations of economic systems. However, this implies that geography teaching should pay close attention to the nature of these economic systems. The chapter starts with a discussion of the models of economic location that were introduced into school geography in the 1970s. These are still commonly taught in school geography, especially at higher levels. However, these models and theories should be recognised as the product of, and a reflection of, a particular moment in the development of advanced Western economies. They drew upon a particular version of neoclassical economics and sought to apply spatial insights to these. These models were questioned in the 1980s as the result of a breakdown in the consensus about how economies should be organised. The emergence of new 'spatial divisions of labour' and attempts to resolve the crisis of profitability through industrial restructuring led geographers to engage with arguments and concepts from political economy, especially those inspired by Marxism. The 1980s were marked by a divided society and a divided geography. However, as the advanced Western economies emerged into a period of economic growth and expansion, economic geographers turned their attention to the cultural aspects of economic activity. In particular, there was a focus on processes of consumption. This so-called 'cultural turn' had many advantages, not least because it focused on the meanings and practices involved in the production of economic space and activity. However, it can be argued that it perhaps adopted a rather optimistic assessment of consumption, and was rather sanguine about the ability of the capitalist–consumption nexus to continue unimpeded. Political economy approaches continued to highlight the active production of globalised space and drew attention to the uneven development that this entailed. Throughout the 1990s and 2000s there developed an approach that focused on the possibilities for the emergence of 'alternative economic spaces' and ways of thinking and acting outside capitalism. These questions have become increasingly salient in light of the spectacular collapse, in the financial crisis of 2008, of the most recent economic settlement. In particular, the questions of what some have called 'alternative hedonism', based on lower levels of consumption, and the possibilities for the greening of capitalism are addressed in the final section of the chapter.

Economics for all?

Since the 1970s, cohorts of geography students in schools have been exposed to the neat and clean lines of Christaller's central place theory; Weber's locational triangle and 'isodapanes'; Alonso's bid rent curves; and Von Thünen's rings of agricultural intensity. These models were 'discovered' by economic geographers in the 1950s, who were concerned to develop more rigorous, 'scientific' approaches to the subject to supersede atheoretical descriptions of the location of economic activity. The search was for general explanatory statements about the spatial structure of the economy. The development of these models was a deliberate attempt on the part of economic geographers to 'move away from a regional-synthetic to a more systematic-analytic approach and self-consciously to identify itself as a theory-building and hypothesis-testing enterprise' (Benko and Scott, 2004). In Britain, these ideas were disseminated by two geographers, Peter Haggett and Richard Chorley, who organised a series of conferences for geography teachers from the mid-1960s to the early 1970s. These conferences deliberately chose 'rising young star' teachers, largely working in private schools, and led to an important period of curriculum development in school geography. The conditions for these developments were favourable in that the advent of a more scientific approach to geography allowed a higher status for the subject and thus for greater prestige and resources. This was also a time when there were strong moves to modernise the school curriculum through the infusion of rational curriculum planning, and the systematic and scientific approach dovetailed with this.

Almost as soon as these models started to be taught in schools, economic geographers rejected them on the grounds that the models did not 'fit' the real world, and that this was because of the unreal nature of the assumptions on which they were based. One difficulty was the lack of human agency that underpinned these models. An attempted solution was to develop ideas in behavioural geography, which paid attention to the cognitive processes that operated in decision-makers' heads. Thus it was suggested that rather than seeking to maximise profits, people may be content to satisfy their needs. This idea led to the modification of models such as David Smith's (1971) 'spatial margins of profitability', in which it was recognised that entrepreneurs might locate at 'sub-optimal locations' as long as production was profitable. While behavioural geography added a complicating set of restrictions to the landscapes of the new economic geography, it did not significantly challenge its operating assumptions.[1] In particular, the models were unable adequately to explain the changing economic landscape, especially as the economic performance of capitalism worsened in the 1970s and 1980s.

For some readers, this section on the models of economic geography may seem heavy going, and this is certainly the experience of many pupils in schools (and probably in undergraduate classes, too). To many students, these models seem overly abstract and unworkable. The question is, why were they taught for so long? To understand this, we need to consider wider developments in the discipline of economics.

Economics remains a high-status subject in schools, taught at the higher age levels. However, it is dominated by one particular form of economic analysis – that associated with neoclassical economics. This was not always the case. In their study *From political economy to economics*, Milanokis and Fine (2009) relate the story of how economics was once a rich, diverse and pluralistic area of study, but gradually shifted from political economy to economics through the 'dehistoricisation' and 'desocialisation' of the subject as it separated from sociology and history. Milanokis and Fine argue that classical political economy was concerned with explaining the capitalist economy, drawing upon whatever historical and social factors were deemed to be relevant. This meant that, despite differences between key figures such as Adam Smith, Karl Marx and David Ricardo, the economy was treated as part of a wider historical milieu, with political economy as a unified social science. However, this pluralism was threatened by the 'marginalist' revolution out of which economics was established as a discipline. The disputes over method concerned the relative merits of abstract, theoretical analysis versus the historical method. The neoclassical approach won the day, and established three characteristics of orthodoxy that remain to the present (and are reflected in the models of location taught in school geography). First is the idea of methodological individualism, which takes the individual (rather than collectives or social classes) as the basic unit of analysis. The economy is treated as if it were simply the aggregation of its individual elements. Second, the economy is defined as market supply and demand, and all the other factors are considered to be non-economic or social factors. Third, economic analysis is based on principles that have no attachment to history.

Far from being an abstract set of intellectual debates, these developments have had important implications for how we understand 'the economy', for, as Fine and Milanokis (2009) demonstrate, this purification of the discipline of economics paved the way for 'economics imperialism' or the process whereby economics seeks to explain areas of social life that are beyond its remit. For them, this culminates in best-selling books such as *Freakonomics* (Levitt and Dubner, 2006) and *The economic naturalist: why economics explains almost everything* (Frank, 2008), in which economists claim to be able to explain almost *all* aspects of human behaviour (such as the names parents give to their children) according to a few simple economic principles. In recent years, economic geography as a field of study has been subject to this process of 'economics imperialism', notably in the attack of the award-winning economist Paul Krugman, who has argued for a 'new economic geography' based on the recovery of five 'lost traditions' in geography – location theory, gravity and potential models, cumulative causation, land use and land rent models, and local external economies. However, as Martin (1999) argues, it is important to remember that these traditions were not lost, but were positively rejected by economic geographers:

> They were deliberately abandoned on philosophical and epistemological grounds, as part of the large-scale movement away from logical positivism that occurred in geography at that time. The location-theoretic, regional science models were cast aside not because the mathematics of maximization-and-equilibrium had (temporarily) reached their limits, nor because geographers were unable intellectually

to elaborate those mathematical tools, but precisely because of the realisation that formal mathematical models impose severe limits on our understanding. Geographers became more interested in real economic landscapes, with all their complex histories, local contexts and particularities, and less entranced by abstract models of hypothetical space economies.

(Martin, 1999: 81)

In this context, it becomes easier to see why people who dare to suggest that land might better be used to provide the things people need in towns and cities are reminded that, 'it's the economy, stupid'. A major task of teaching economic geography in schools is to suggest to students that there are other possibilities for organising economic space.

For further study

1.   Undertake a week-long study of how the economy is represented in the popular media. Read newspapers (quality and popular), and watch the television news, and any programmes that discuss economics. What models of economic reality are provided? From which perspective are economic issues addressed – the government's, businesses, workers? What are the implications of your findings for geography teaching in schools?

The models don't work

Although the types of location analysis and behavioural geography discussed in the previous section continued to influence the teaching of geography in schools, they became increasingly outdated and anachronistic in the 1980s and 1990s. Their ascendancy in geography as a whole was short-lived as, according to Hudson (2000), economic geographers sought 'more powerful conceptualisations of the processes that generated geographies of economies'. This entailed geography becoming more closely aligned with the social sciences, which were themselves undergoing significant changes. The turmoil of the 1960s and the 'rediscovery of poverty' meant that social theories based on ideas of gradual improvement and consensus were challenged. Faced with this, the social sciences began to rediscover the Marxian heritage, as well as exploring other positions.

The mid-1970s and early 1980s were a period of de-industrialisation and restructuring, and geographers sought to develop accounts of these changes that stressed the importance of social structures in shaping geographical landscapes. A landmark text in this respect was Doreen Massey's (1984) *Spatial divisions of labour*. Massey was writing in the midst of a restructuring of the UK economy away from manufacturing into services, and the production of an uneven geography which meant that people in different places and localities experienced these changes in different ways. Massey insisted that the spatial patterns observed by economic geographers could not be explained by spatial processes, but required an understanding of the social processes of production.

The 1980s saw the publication of texts by geographers that mapped the geography of a 'divided nation'. A series of locality studies, which paid close attention to how economic restructuring was having an impact on specific places, were in many ways a response to the deterministic account of economic change, which held that declining regions and localities are the victims of a global shift in economic production. Against this, localities studies sought to recognise the ways in which local authorities may respond to boost economic production. A typical example of a text that recognised an increasingly divided nation was Hudson and William's (1986) *The United Kingdom*, written in the aftermath of the miners' strike of 1984–85. It explicitly drew attention to the aspirations for social consensus in the post-war period and the reality of an economically, socially and politically divided society in the 1980s. Hudson and Williams stressed the long-term decline of Britain's economic power in the post-war period, which meant that national governments were often seeking to implement policies that were at odds with the direction of Britain's economy. This led to the problem of 'stop–go' or 'boom-and-bust', whereby governments sought to increase overall demand in the economy through fiscal policy and were then required to dampen demand lest growth becomes inflationary and leads to increased imports of overseas goods. There were goals of full employment in the first half of this period, along with goals of economic modernisation throughout the 1960s and early 1970s. The changing social and occupational structure led to changes in the class composition of the population, with the growth of affluent middle classes and the de-traditionalisation of gender and class. The economic crisis of the 1970s led to important challenges to the idea of social consensus and ushered in a period of conflicting politics. Hudson and Williams raise the question of how far it was possible to speak of a national economy in a context where events at the international or global scale impinged on activity within the national borders. Overall, the 1980s was a period of important geographical change. The decline of traditional manufacturing in the northern regions and large cities changed the shape of the landscape, and saw a population drift to the south; a movement to new mortgaged estates in the suburbs and beyond; and the re-emergence of the north–south divide, which has been a recurrent feature of national economic development.

Approaches in economic geography that were based on political–economic models that stressed the structural causes of economic change did not find much expression in school geography. One reason may be the perception that these ideas are too difficult for students to understand (Bale, 1985). Another is that these approaches invariably focus on the way geography is made in ways that divide social groups (along lines of class, ethnicity and gender), and geography teachers generally seek to avoid controversy and stress consensus (Machon 1987). In a period when it was clear that spatial patterns could not be explained without reference to questions of politics, it was perhaps easier for geography teachers to stick to the 'facts'. A good example of this tendency is found in Townsend's (1993) book for sixth-formers, *Uneven regional change in Britain*. The book aimed to help students 'understand how the geography of today's British regions arises from change':

> It is the task of this book to *measure regional economic differences in a precise way* and to explain past and present regional change in terms of increasing levels of detail.
>
> (Townsend, 1993: 6; emphasis added)

The approach is historical; patterns of economic activity in the present are seen to have their roots in the past. Townsend starts with an account of how dispersed patterns of industry in the nineteenth century were replaced by concentrated patterns as a result of 'agglomeration economies'. The growth and decline of regions is explained with reference to Kondratieff's 'long-waves' of economic development. In practice, it is considered more important for students to measure and describe patterns of uneven development rather than be provided with theories that might help them to explain the changes. This is clear in a chapter entitled 'De-industrialisation and the "north–south" divide'. Much of the chapter is devoted to describing the changes, and the explanation tends to focus on the investment decisions made by individual firms, emphasising the fact that it was not so much the location of factories that explained closure, but the role of the factory in the overall 'spatial division of labour'. While this is an important factor, it tends to downplay or sideline other, more structural explanations of economic change.

Economic geographies in context (1)

So far, this chapter has discussed two approaches – location theory and political–economic theory – to the teaching of economic geography in schools. At this point, it will be useful to put them in context. The quarter century from immediate post-war construction until the mid-1970s was one of unique growth and stability. On a world basis, every year from 1947 to 1974 was one of growth. Although inequalities remained, on its own terms, the capitalist system seemed to be working well. Dunn (2009) suggests that there were three elements to this. First was the consensus that existed between labour, capital and the state. Second was the Cold War, which ensured high levels of military spending. Third was the dominance of the USA, which allowed for new patterns of accumulation.

This period of economic and social stability meant that the social sciences were called to act as technical 'problem-solvers' for the capitalist system. It is this that allowed for ideas of spatial equilibrium, for the design of regional and urban policies to alleviate poverty and equalise income. From the mid-1970s, this period of economic growth and stability faltered. Economic historians and analysts are divided about the exact causes of the failure of the post-war system. The immediate trigger was the oil price increases orchestrated by OPEC in 1973–74, but this cannot explain the onset of economic recession prior to that date. Another explanation is that of worker militancy leading to reduced productivity. A third is that the high levels of state expenditure that had sustained consumption and supported the reproduction of the system became increasingly unproductive, thus cutting into corporate profits. Whatever the exact cause, this crisis of profitability led to an extended period of reduced economic output and consequent unemployment and increased poverty. The impacts of these events were spatially selective and led to a divided economic geography. In retrospect, we now see this period as one in which a particular economic settlement was in the process of breaking up, and it was not at the time clear what would replace it. In retrospect, economic geographers now see this period as part of an epochal shift in the organisation of economy, society and culture. Ash Amin announced these developments in the following terms:

Though not uncontroversial, there is an emerging consensus in the social sciences that the period since the mid-1970s represents a transition from one distinct phase of capitalist development to a new phase. Thus, there is a sense that these are times of epoch-making transformation in the very forces which drive, stabilize and reproduce the capitalist world. Terms such as 'structural crisis', 'transformation' and 'transition' have become common descriptors of the present, while new epithets such as 'post-Fordist', 'post-industrial', 'post-modern', 'fifth Kondratiev' and 'post-collective' have been coined by the academic prophets of our times to describe the emerging new age of capitalism.

(Amin, 1994: 1)

While there are evident differences in conceptualisation, there is generally broad agreement among social analysts about the nature of the changes taking place in the economic sphere. It is widely touted that the economic regime of mass industrial production and capital accumulation faltered in the 1970s, and that out of this crisis there emerged a new and invigorated global capitalism. Three factors underpinned this revival. The first was the development of new information and communications technologies that began to transform manufacturing and distribution systems. The second was the influence on economic policy of neoliberal ideas, which emphasised the primacy of markets and (in theory at least) posited a less interventionist role for the state. The third was the emergence of counter-cultural values among the middle classes that gave rise to post-materialist values associated with identity, ethics and belonging. Taken together, these developments led to the emergence of a new set of economic geographies. These are discussed in the next section.

New times and the geographies of consumption

The economic restructuring of the 1970s and 1980s gave way to a very different set of landscapes and practices – a new economic geography. Accounts of the 1980s and 1990s stress the emergence of a society characterised by new forms of consumption. Whereas previously geographers had tended to see consumption as a distraction from the 'real' geographies of work and production, many began to recognise that consumption was a site where individuals could define their identities and forge new political projects. The de-traditionalisation of society meant that previously fixed identities around gender, class, sexuality, age and ethnicity were being loosened. Identities were in flux, and consumption was one of the means through which people could fashion their identities. For some commentators, this choice meant that consuming was a means of distinction, a way of being an individual, and this chimed with the political messages of Thatcherism that stressed the primacy of the market over uniform and inferior state provision.

The idea that consumption was a active process that carried a wide variety of meanings became the common sense of academic research in the 1990s. Human geography was one of the most important areas where this developed, making links with the field of cultural studies. It is impossible to review all these in the space available, other than pointing to important contributions. Peter Jackson's (1989) *Maps of meaning* was attentive to the practices of consumption and the idea that there existed dominant and subordinate cultures, and that consumption could become a place of resistance. Rob Sack's (1992) *Place, modernity and the consumer's world* was an important study of how consumption spaces tend to abstract from the natural and social worlds. Sack's book was one of the first to treat the spaces of consumption seriously, though he is critical of the ways in which commodities hide from us the real relations of production and are thus 'immoral'. Throughout the 1990s, geographers became more involved in the study of consumption. This was part of a wider shift in the social sciences and was associated with postmodernism. Rob Shields' (1991) *Places on the margins* explored the alternative spaces of modernity, and later his edited collection *Lifestyle shopping* explored new spaces for the subject of consumption:

> Lifestyle shopping is not intended as another celebration of the triumph of an ideology of lifestyles and marketing but a critical marking of the interdependence of the private spaces of subjectivity, media and commodity consumption, and the changing spatial contexts of everyday public life.
>
> (Shields, 1994: 1)

These new, broadly positive assessments of cultures of consumption rejected what Alan Tomlinson (1990) called the 'sad, dislocated, elitist, perhaps menopausal' critiques of consumer culture, in favour of an approach that treats consumption as 'an active, committed production of self and of society which, rather than assimilating individuals to styles, appropriates codes and fashions, which are made into one's own'. Indeed, Shields appears to argue that there were new ways of being and acting in the new consumer spaces:

> Many consumers are now ironic, knowing shoppers, conscious of the inequalities of exchange and the arbitrary nature of exchange value. As social actors, they attempt to consume the symbolic values of objects and the mall environment while avoiding the inequalities of exchange. They resort to browsing through stores as a leisure practice, shoplifting, the purchase of cheaper imitations and look-alikes, and by reclaiming the sites of consumption through a crowd practice which returns the (usually private) spaces to the public sphere of market square and street behaviour.
>
> (Shields, 1994: 99)

Apart from the shopping mall, geographers studied the new retail spaces that emerged in the light of the expansion of credit, and the new cultures of consumption linked to ideas about gender and ethnicity, the cultures of leisure and tourism, the transformation of city centres as they shifted to post-industrial economies, and the impacts of consumption on rural spaces. Urban geographers became interested in the new sites of consumption and heritage that were rising – phoenix-like – in the derelict spaces of inner cities; rural geographers became interested in how the lifestyles of the professional middle classes were reflected in the post-productivist countryside; economic geographers became interested in the cultures of organisations and the performance of work. In general, over time, geographical accounts of consumption have become increasingly wary of making claims about the potential for progressive politics. Instead, there is more focus on what might be called the exclusionary nature of consumption; for example, May's (1996) study of consumption in a multicultural city stresses how middle-class gentrifiers use consumption as a means of distinction; and Jarvis draws attention to the experience of more mundane aspects of everyday life (Jarvis *et al.*, 2001; Jarvis, 2005).

These developments have some important implications for geography educators, not least because, as young people are actively involved in these practices of consumption, there may be a mismatch between the worlds described in school geography and the worlds consumed by students. It has become less common for geography teachers to adopt a 'Relphian' view of the modern landscape as 'placeless', which seeks simply to criticise the 'blandscapes' associated with mass tourism and mass consumption (following the work of the humanistic geographer Edward Relph, whose book *Place and placelessness* (1976) remains a classic statement of the argument that modern 'mass' culture has led to the loss of character and authenticity in the built environment). Instead, there might be attempts to deconstruct the meanings that are encoded in postmodern landscapes of consumption. In other words, landscapes can be read as texts. In general, geography teachers in schools are encouraged to take seriously and respect the consumption and leisure choices made by children and young people. Perhaps the paradigmatic text that reflects this approach (and one that is frequently referenced in the literature of geography education) is Tracy Skelton and Gill Valentine's (1998) edited collection, *Cool places: the geographies of youth cultures*. This book was strongly influenced by research in cultural studies which focused on the agency and active consciousness of young people. It sought out places that were rarely studied by geographers, and showed how, in these spaces and places, children and young people were actively involved in the construction of space and identities. This was not a simply celebratory account, since at times there is attention to the structures that limit young people's agency and control of their own lives, but it is in general positive about the notion of young people as consumers.

The essays in *Cool places* cover a wide range of geographical spaces (the home, the street, the club) and identities. The collection as a whole tends to adopt the arguments of cultural studies that stress how young people actively construct their identities. Identities here are treated in a quite post-structural way, as malleable and flexible (as the cultural theorist and sociologist Stuart Hall put it in a memorable metaphor, identities are like bus tickets, in that they enable you to get from one place to another, but beyond that can be discarded). This way of thinking about geographies and identities is attractive in that it stresses that young people are the 'co-constructors' of their personal geographies. However, there is a tendency to downplay the role of structure in shaping and moulding young people's identities. For example, in Dwyer's (1998) essay on the representations of young British Muslim women, we learn a lot about the girls' practices of dress and style, but little about their family backgrounds and status, or their economic position in relation to production and consumption. Their identities may be said to be 'in flux', and it is implied that this postmodern practice of 'pick-and-mix' is in many ways in the girls' control.

For further study

1.   To what extent has the geography you studied at university and/or now teach in schools been influenced by the cultural turn and ideas about spaces of consumption? What do you see as the strengths and limits of these developments?

2.   How do you respond to the idea that young people possess their own personal geographies and are actively involved in the creation of places and spaces? What are the implications of this view for your work as a geography teacher?

Economic geographies in context (2)

The spaces and places of consumption studied by geographers are inextricably connected to the globalisation of the economy, which is imagined by neoliberal economics. The new economic landscapes appeared to offer the prospect for a new politics beyond that of the older forms of class conflict. In particular, they drew attention to the new identities that were being shaped as the older settlements broke down. These seemed to chime with a more 'modern' Britain that was emerging in the spaces of leisure and consumption, as economic growth returned and the expansion of credit allowed for more and more people to join in the 'brave new world' of late capitalism (see, for example, Mort, 1996). Although there is no simple connection between economic realities and academic ideas, it is possible to argue that the study of places became increasingly informed by the optimistic mood of cultural transformation in the 1990s. It is surely no coincidence that geography took a distinctive cultural turn during this period. As Shurmer-Smith noted:

> Not only in the universities, but also in the media and in private encounters, virtually everyone, everywhere, became increasingly conscious of the problem of creating meaning in situations in which so many of the parameters of economic, political and social life had shifted.
>
> (Shurmer-Smith, 2002: 1)

In all of this, geographers were in step with the *zeitgeist*, a growing consensus that Britain has become a different place in light of these economic transformations, and this is reflected in the lifestyles, values and attitudes of the population. This is seen in the 'flagship' new sites of consumption that are transforming cities, and the new suburban estates in which people spend larger proportions of their leisure time; it is also seen in patterns of leisure and travel – the rise of budget airlines enabling most of us to escape to the sun for at least part of the year, and in new forms of work. The changes have been cultural too – some talk of a dramatic shift in gender relations and sexuality (Weeks, 2007) and of the decline of Christian Britain (Brown, 2008); and, apparently, we are less deferent and more open to new experiences (see, for example, Weight, 2002; Marr, 2007). Cultural geographers have mapped these patterns and new developments. They have not done so uncritically, as they have been concerned to understand how the categories of social life are constructed and to draw attention to the processes of inclusion and exclusion, but much of this work is concerned to describe what it means to live in a post-manufacturing, consumer society.

The economic context in which this focus on culture has occurred is important, with geographers arguing that there has been a fundamental shift in the nature of economic organisation which means that the *what*, the *how*, and the *where* of production shifted. The crisis of profitability of the early to mid-1970s required a new mode of regulation, a new means of realising profits. This readjustment required a change in how the relationships between governments, businesses and labour were managed. David Harvey (2005) uses the term 'embedded liberalism' to describe the relative stability of the Fordist period, from the end of the Second World War to the mid-1970s. Markets were surrounded by a web of social and political constraints and a regulatory environment that set the parameters for economic development. The goal of neoliberalism has been to disembed markets from these regimes in order to enable capital to circulate more quickly and over increasing distances. The upshot is that the fast world of the global economy is characterised by an intense connectedness that ties together a billion or so people through global networks of communication and knowledge, production and consumption. The competitive drive of capitalism leads to an endless drive to seek out new markets and reduce the turnover time of capital. As countless advertisements remind us, time costs money, and the inevitable result is the acceleration of everyday life. At the same time, more of our daily encounters and relationships (e.g. childcare, schooling) are based on the mechanism of the market. The commodification thesis holds that more and more of the things that people do are bought and sold, so that it becomes necessary to have employment to earn money to purchase the goods and services advertised. In order to secure access to the 'good life', there is a lengthening of the working day, and households depend on more than one income, with resulting stresses on domestic life and the emergence of the work–life balance as personal and policy problem.

The effects on people's everyday lives are profound. People's notions of self-worth are increasingly organised around consumption. The work–spend cycle has become fundamental to the economic and social dynamics of contemporary society. Speed has become a hallmark of many aspects of consumption – as reflected and prompted by advertising. Speed and busy-ness of schedules are transformed from negatives into symptoms of laudable, well adjusted and fulfilling lifestyles. As Knox and Mayer put it, capitalism literally delivers:

> speed of delivery, speed of service, speed of cook time, speed of bill-paying, speed of opening-cans, speed of gratification.
>
> (Knox and Mayer, 2009: 15)

Or it did. The financial crisis of 2008 rapidly turned into an economic crisis, and it is widely argued that there is a need for a fundamental shift in the ways in which capitalism is regulated. This will invariably be accompanied by a new set of economic geographies, since – to return to the definition of economic geography set out at the start of this chapter – 'the task of modern economic geography is to provide a reasoned description of the spatial organization of the economy and, in particular, to elucidate the ways in which geography influences the economic performance of capitalism' (Benko and Scott, 2004).

Contested economic geographies

> Writing now, at the end of the first decade of a new millennium, it is difficult for those of us who lived through it not to think back to another decade when much of what is now crashing to the ground was first established in its dominance. The 1980s, that epochal decade of Thatcherism and Ronald Reagan, of the establishment of a new dispensation in which individualism and competition, finance and financialisation, privatisation and commercialisation were hammered home as the only possible ways of being in a 'modern' economy and society.
>
> (Massey, 2009: 136)

The final part of this chapter considers the types of economic geographies that might be developed in the future and their implications for school geography. In the same way as the crisis of the 1970s and 1980s led to the development of what Tim Edensor (2005) called 'industrial ruins', which then emerged as sites for speculative investment, the latest financial crises and its attendant economic recession will see the emergence of new economic landscapes. In what follows, I discuss a series of alternative futures for economic geography. These are not meant as predictions, but to set out the types of debates and arguments about economic geographies that could form the basis for teaching.

Farewell to cool capitalism?

In *Cool capitalism*, Jim McGuigan (2010) explains how, in response to the need to realise profits, capitalism in its later phase appropriated aspects of the counter-cultures associated with young people and incorporated them into its own culture. It did so by persuading people that having the latest mobile phone, and changing fashions every season, was about not merely buying more things, but developing a lifestyle profile. Many academics, too, McGuigan claims, were taken in by the 'cool' stance of neoliberal capitalism, adopting at times a rather celebratory notion of consumption as empowering, as a site in which individuals were able to undertake 'identity work'. In the light of the economic crisis, this optimistic stance has increasingly been challenged. Whereas in the mid-1990s Daniel Miller (1995) could write (perhaps tongue-in-cheek) of consumption as the 'vanguard of history', and there was a celebration of the complex uses of objects, recent studies have marked a return to more evaluative work on consumption. In *Excess*, Kim Humphery explores the new politics of anti-consumerism in advanced Western economies:

> While there is much about material culture and our relationship with things that can be understood as constructive we cannot escape the need also to reflect on and question market systems, consumption decisions, and the ultimate value of particular kinds of objects. It is the preparedness to tackle this latter imperative that has indelibly shaped contemporary anti-consumerist critique.
>
> (Humphery, 2008: 16–17)

There are signs that there is a more general acceptance of the costs of consumerism. This is reflected Neal Lawson's (2009) *All consuming*, which provides an accessible and thought-provoking account of the costs of consumerism for individuals and society. In *Radical consumption*, Jo Littler (2008) discusses the potential for radical consumption in bringing about progressive change. Her book is one of the most astute and complex analyses of the politics of consumption. She starts off by providing evidence of how the call to consume in 'progressive' ways has become almost central to consumer capitalism. A glance around supermarkets and adverts in magazines urges forms of green and ethical consumption, and large corporations such as Marks & Spencer and McDonald's present themselves and their products as caring and environmentally friendly. She traces the rise of ethical consumption as a moralistic response to the contradictions of a consumer society, and examines forms of cosmopolitan caring through which consumers are encouraged to be 'activists', making links with people and environments in distant places; the emergence of 'corporate social responsibility'; and different forms of anti-consumerism which reflect, to varying degrees, on our position in an unequal world and the ecologies of green consumption. This focus on consumption, she argues, should be situated in the shift from Fordism to post-Fordism, and the notion that the state is no longer effective as an agent of social change and that consumers and private corporations are the site of power and control. Littler argues that ethical consumption can be used to shore up existing inequalities of wealth, help corporations mislead the public, facilitate snobbery and one-upmanship, and distract people from the work that needs to be done to create more equal and environmentally sustainable societies. However, it can also help people to 'share the wealth' through consumer cooperatives; put pressure on companies to pay attention to the social and environmental impacts of their products and supply chains; offer people an alternative to products produced through exploitation; and focus our need for social, psychological and environmental sustainability. The essays in Lewis and Potter's (2010) *Ethical consumption* provide a rich source of ideas for developing geography lessons based around ideas of ethical consumption, and a useful set of papers that explore the pedagogy of consumption can be found in Sandlin and McLaren (2010).

Barry Smart (2010) is not optimistic about the possibilities for changing direction. He concludes that in 2009, governments around the world faced two interconnected crises: one economic, the other environmental. The first appeared suddenly, while the second had been developing for a number of decades:

> Whether as a consequence of a lack of political will, imagination, or understanding, for the most part consuming futures have continued to be presented as simple linear extrapolations from the present. Governments have continued to extol the virtues of economic growth and have proceeded to introduce various measures designed to revive it through a regeneration of consumer demand.
>
> (Smart, 2010: 184)

Whether or not this is sustainable is an open question.

The 'greening of capitalism'?

An alternative set of arguments can be found in texts such as *Factor four* (von Weizsacker *et al.*, 1997), *Natural capitalism* (Hawken *et al.*, 2010) and *Factor five* (von Weizsacker *et al.*, 2007). *Factor four* appeared in 1997 as an update of the report to the Club of Rome, *The limits to growth* (Meadows *et al.*, 1972). While that report was extremely pessimistic, *Factor four* was decidedly upbeat, asserting that, 'if resource productivity was increased by a factor of four, the world would enjoy twice the wealth that is currently available, whilst simultaneously halving the stress placed on our natural environment'. Published a year later, and with two endorsements from former US President Bill Clinton, *Natural capitalism* offers a new agenda for capitalism based on new energy and resource-efficiency technologies, waste elimination and clean production facilities. The messages of these books are relentlessly upbeat and challenge the idea that we need to abandon affluence. Capitalism as an economic system will be transformed in ways that are ecologically sustainable and profitable.

Factor four and *Natural capitalism* are geared towards appealing to elite policy-makers, corporate managers and investors. They provide a wealth of examples of innovation that could improve energy, materials and transport productivity. But there are some fairly obvious weaknesses with this approach, not least that its faith in science and technology can serve to detract attention from the social and political roots of social and ecological problems. Complex relations and entities are lumped together as natural or human capital, to be accessed and managed. The politics that accompany this are distinctly managerial. This tends to reflect a lack of historical and geographical specificity.

Challenging injustice

A remarkable feature in the aftermath of the financial crisis of 2008 has been the outpouring of articles and books that claim to map the contours of an acquisitive and divided society, and that call for greater justice and equality. After years of edging around the topic, there is an increased willingness to 'name and shame' capitalism as the cause of social division, injustice and environmental degradation. The psychologist Oliver James explains the new affliction of *Affluenza* (2007) and in a companion volume (2008) collates the evidence on 'selfish capitalism', and in 2010 republished an earlier book, *Britain on the couch*, which explains rising levels of stress and depression as due to the breakdown in social bonds since the 1950s. Another psychologist, Sue Gerhardt (2010) has weighed in with her book *The selfish society*. An economist at the London School of Economics, Richard Layard, has amassed evidence to show that wealthier societies have not led to higher levels of happiness and contentment, and has led an influential enquiry into the state of childhood in Britain. In a book that has caused a heated debate in the aftermath of the UK General Election in May 2010, Richard Wilkinson and Kate Pickett (2009) argue that more equal societies invariably have higher levels of social cohesion; and Daniel Dorling's (2010) *Injustice* is a major statement from a geographer documenting in detail the five new tenets of injustice – elitism, exclusion, prejudice, greed and despair. Dorling's arguments are provocative and draw attention to the multiple hurts piled on the poorest sections of society. He adopts a historical approach, which relates growing inequalities to moves in the 1970s to reverse programmes designed to equalise society.

The end of capitalism (as we know it)?

As I completed this book, the UK was bracing itself for the announcement of a wide-ranging series of cuts in public expenditure, which were explained as necessary for restoring investors' confidence in the market, and popularly conceived as pay-back time for a society that had been living beyond its means. There were important economic arguments about whether these austerity measures would lead to a reduction in demand and precipitate a double-dip recession, or whether they would lead to a surge in private-sector job creation. In any case, both the Conservative–Liberal Democrat coalition government and the Labour opposition shared the view that there was no alternative to drastically cutting the public debt. In this scenario, capitalism is presented as an all-powerful force. It seems that There is No Alternative. However, within economic geography, Kathy Gibson and Julie Graham (writing as J.K. Gibson-Graham, 1996) have argued that it does not help to conceive of global capitalism as a coherent and all-powerful entity. In reality, much of the real work of economic production and social reproduction is done in ways that do not rely on monetary exchange. Once we begin to think in these terms, it becomes possible to imagine all manner of ways of making the economy. Colin Williams (2005) makes a similar point, backing this up with careful empirical evidence to show that economic life is becoming less, rather than more dependent on formal employment and cash trading. In their book *Alternative economic spaces*, Leyshon *et al.* (2003) discuss a variety of alternative economies. The political importance of this task is clearly identified. We live in a time when the rich and powerful routinely announce the hegemony and dominance of capitalism. Leyshon *et al.*'s edited collection, like that of Gibson and Graham, seeks to show that contrary to Mrs Thatcher's claim, there are always alternatives to the mainstream of global neoliberalism. The book consists of a series of empirical studies of 'actually existing' alternative economies. These include: credit unions, local exchange trading systems, 'retro-retailing', informal work, employee-ownership, the social economy, and 'back-to-the-land' migration.

The possibility that there may be spaces to develop socially and ecologically sustainable ways of living outside of the relations of capitalism has been explored by John Holloway (2010) in *Crack capitalism*. Holloway argues that capitalism exists and survives only through individuals contributing their labour to produce 'exchange value' (i.e. producing value that is skimmed off by capitalists). The challenge is for people to realise 'use-value', to undertake work and activity that is pleasurable and meaningful to them. In so doing, this creates the spaces which undermine the logic of private ownership, and allows for individual needs to be met collectively. Similar arguments are made by Chris Carlson (2010), who has coined the phrase 'Nowtopia'; and Chatterton (2010), who argues that, 'We are likely to see an increase in this community-directed resourcefulness as people begin to reassemble the scraps of the neoliberal economy.'

For further study

1.	Devise a scheme of work that encourages pupils to consider future economic geographies.

Conclusion

Economic processes are central to the future life chances of pupils in schools. At present there is much talk of a 'lost generation', who have diligently taken the advice of their teachers, studied hard to gain their qualifications, and are set to leave higher education with the prospect of unemployment and/or significant debt. The provision of economic understanding in the school curriculum is minimal. Economic geography offers the potential to help pupils develop an understanding of the spatial dynamics of capitalism. This would be really useful knowledge. However, there is very little theoretically informed teaching of economic geography in schools. The aim of this chapter is to provide a context that may enable teachers to develop curricula that reflect the workings of capitalist economies. There are no quick and final answers to what such curricula will look like, but the materials and references provided here are starting points, along with the newspapers, which report daily on the remaking of economic space.

Activities

1. Analyse the economic geography that is taught to pupils in your geography department (Key Stage 3, GCSE, AS level). What concepts and ideas are taught? How do these relate to the discussion of economic geography in this chapter?

2. How far do you think school geography lessons should seek to help pupils become aware of the costs and benefits of consumption? What should be the main elements of teaching about the geographies of consumption?

3. In a world where economic geographies are being dramatically restructured, what should geography lessons teach students about the economy?

8

Climate change, mobile lives and Anthropocene geographies

It may seem hard to believe today, but there was once a time that business denied there was such a thing as climate change. Vast amounts of money and effort went into discrediting the scientific basis on which the case for action was made.

(Newell and Paterson, 2010: 36)

The 'once a time' that Peter Newell and Matthew Paterson refer to was little more than two decades ago. From the mid-1990s, many businesses sensed that regulation of greenhouse gases was on its way, and 'that they were better off preparing to compete and survive in this new environment' (Ibid.). Government attitudes shifted, too. In her book *The green state*, Robyn Eckersley (2004) argues that we are witnessing the emergence of a new form of environmental politics. Eckersley argues that there have been three principal elements in global politics that have engendered ecological unsustainability. These are competition between nation-states, global capitalism, and the weak character of democracy. These have led to patterns of development that are unsustainable, and also act as constraints to responding to the problems caused by these forms of development. However, Eckersley thinks that there are promising signs for the 'greening' of society in all three areas. First, there are moves towards 'environmental lateralism' as nation-states seek to join together collectively to fight climate change. Second, capitalism is being greened by processes of ecological modernisation. Finally, there are new experiments in democratic practice that offer models for alternative ways of organising economy and society. The emergence of the green state provides an explanation of why our schools are now required to promote pupils' awareness and understanding of issues of climate change and sustainable development, and to become sustainable schools by 2020.

It is tempting to leave it at that, and to end this book on a very optimistic note, looking forward to the day when these collective efforts by corporations, governments and individuals lead to the greening of economy and society. However, the final chapter in this section of the book attempts to explore the challenges and dilemmas in teaching about climate change in school geography, and then broadens the discussion to include recent concepts of mobility and Anthropocene geographies. In line with the perspective of critical geography education argued for in this book, I suggest that it is important to examine carefully the knowledge and understanding that is available to pupils in school.

Geography teachers' climate problem

A couple of years ago, I attended a meeting of geography teachers who were considering the question of how to teach about sustainable communities. During the discussions, one of the teachers exclaimed that he was angry with the TV broadcaster Channel 4, as it had broadcast a documentary programme that challenged the accepted 'scientific' consensus about global warming. This, he said, had undone all the 'good work' he had done with his students. The problem that this geography teacher was describing should, I suggest, be understood as the result of the ways in which geography teaching has evolved historically. Geography teaching has tended to be separated into physical and human aspects of the subject, and teaching in physical geography has been strongly influenced by the scientific approach, which seeks to observe and measure physical processes. This faith in the methods and approaches of positivist science has influenced how human geography is taught in schools. In the 1970s and 1980s, the new geography that informed curriculum development was based on the search for laws, rules and models that were seen to be capable of generalisation. This belief in an actually existing, observable real world has continued to influence geography teaching in schools, even though it is recognised that human beings may attach meanings or values to the things that exist. The geography teacher at the meeting was concerned about what he regarded as an unacceptable gap between the accepted 'facts' about climate change and those who would seek to 'distort' this picture of reality.

In the first seven chapters of this book, I have attempted to challenge this view of the relationship between physical and human aspects of geography teaching by drawing on perspectives in human geography that accept the materiality of non-human entities (nature), but I argue that we cannot separate their material existence from our knowledge of them. This approach stresses the ways in which discourses on nature create their own truths. As suggested in chapter three, this does not necessarily lead towards pointless relativism. Instead, it requires a disciplined educational approach that explores the construction of ideas about nature and environments, and relates these to the implications for human action.

This social nature perspective challenges the widely accepted 'neutral-chair' approach to teaching about a controversial topic such as climate change, which stresses the importance of teaching the known scientific facts about the topic. In the neutral-chair approach, the teacher's role is to frame the topic and to teach the 'facts', and students are left to decide for themselves what to do with this knowledge. Within the teaching of this topic may be some recognition of alternative perspectives or arguments, but it is stressed that these stand outside the scientific consensus. This approach underpins the Defra pack about climate change (discussed in chapter one), in which Al Gore's film *An Inconvenient Truth* is presented alongside a set of activities for science, geography and citizenship teachers. But there is another element to this pedagogy, and it is concerned with values. After all, what is the point of having this knowledge if it is not to be used or acted upon? Irwin and Michael say that 'Scientific literacy (or scientific ignorance) is equated with the capacity to act as a citizen in a democracy. In sum, to have improved scientific literacy is to be intellectually better equipped to contribute to the processes of a liberal democracy within which scientific knowledge has become fundamental' (Irwin and Michael, 2003). From this perspective, then, the geography teacher's concern to ensure the scientific consensus about global warming is taught and learned is linked to a broader aim of global citizenship, which ensures that students are equipped to become involved in political choices or to make sensible choices about how to live their lives. In reality, that is the point where the geography lesson (literally) ends, and students are left to decide what to do with that knowledge.

This approach is derived from a scientific model of the curriculum, and it is a particular model of science that separates 'fact' from 'values'. This is not to say that values are not considered, but that they are always to be assessed in the light of the evidence.

From the social nature perspective, there are problems with this model of teaching about climate change. The first task of any critical geography teaching is to *problematise* the knowledge that forms the school geography curriculum. This involves asking the questions: Why am I teaching about climate change in my geography lessons now? Who decided? Was this taught before? What types of 'knowledge' about climate change are included in representation of this topic? Which perspectives are excluded?

For further study

1.   How is climate change (or global warming) taught in your school? What models or approaches are used? How are issues of scientific authority and climate change denial addressed?

The teaching of climate change (especially global warming) in schools is a relatively recent phenomenon. In the 1970s to mid-1980s, geography students may have been taught about theories of global cooling.[1] But then, in the early 1990s, geography textbooks and teachers began to speak about the greenhouse effect, or, as we learned to call it, the 'enhanced greenhouse effect'. Climate change began to be found on exam specifications. Who decided that this was an important issue to be taught in schools is more difficult to answer. There are complex relationships between the media and school curricula, as curricula are part of the wider culture. Simon Cottle (2009) has described the rise of global crisis reporting, and explains how certain events are labelled as global even though their effects may be relatively localised or have a regional aspect. Also, there is a more formal answer that may accept the idea that the school curriculum is a public sphere in which issues of public import are aired and debated.[2] Another argument is that the school curriculum represents the 'official knowledge' that the state thinks it is important for all children to learn (Apple, 2000). There is evidence for this in the official guidance on teaching about climate change that is available to teachers. The questions here are linked to critical theories of curriculum knowledge. They do not accept that school knowledge is neutral or objective, but may reflect the interests of powerful social groups. This raises some interesting questions about what are the powerful interests that underpin the official curriculum. Here it is useful to explore the difference between the view of ecological modernisers who have influenced government thinking since the mid-1990s, and those who reject moves to intervene in the economy. As we have noted at various points in the book:

> The idea [of ecological modernization] is that a clean environment is actually good for business, for it connotes happy and healthy workers, profits for companies developing conservation technologies or selling green products, high quality material inputs in to production (e.g. clean air and water), and efficiency in materials usage. Pollution, on the other hand, indicates wasteful use of materials […] it is cheaper to tackle environmental problems before they get out of hand and require expensive remedial action.
>
> (Dryzek and Schlosberg, 2001: 299)

Ecological modernisation is discussed by Mark Whitehead (2007) in *Spaces of sustainability*. He argues that successive UK governments' attitudes towards the environment have been paradoxical. In the 1970s and for much of the 1980s, the notion that governments should seek to intervene in the activities of firms was eschewed. This was due to a concern about loss of competitiveness, and meant that the British government 'was only willing to intervene within economic practices where there was a burden of scientific proof to support the validity of state intervention' (Ibid.). A change was signalled by Prime Minister Thatcher's 1988 speech to the Royal Society, in which she argued that Conservatives were the 'true friends of the earth'. In 1990, the government published its first White Paper, *Our common inheritance*, and in 1994 this was followed up by its response to the Rio Earth Summit, *Sustainable development – the UK strategy*. Whitehead notes that although new policies for ecological modernisation were being developed throughout the 1990s, 'it was not until 1997, and the election of the New Labour government, that ecological modernization became a widespread principle of UK policy'. It was at this moment that those working in the field of environmental education and education for sustainability were increasingly recognised, and education for sustainable development became part of the panoply of concerns within which the government looked to develop its brand of social democracy, which sought to balance economic growth through the market with a concern for social and environmental justice. As pointed out in chapter one, this form of 'green governance' and its influence on education is challenged by those who argue that this concern with climate change is part of a broader corruption of the curriculum, whereby schools are being asked to teach about 'good causes'.

A focus on climate change in education therefore reflects a broader societal recognition of its importance, and its inclusion in the curriculum is part of a vision of the wider purposes of education to promote environmental citizenship. Invariably, this means that certain types of knowledge of climate change are favoured. It is interesting to reflect on why Al Gore's film *An Inconvenient Truth* is seen as an acceptable resource for classroom use, to the extent that a copy was distributed to all state schools in England and Wales (which itself is an interesting example of state-sponsored knowledge).

It is easy to see why *An Inconvenient Truth* might be a popular teaching resource in schools. It has high production values, contains a hard-hitting and dramatic narrative, and Gore himself is a charismatic figure. However, a more critical perspective suggests that *An Inconvenient Truth* is seductive in the way it provides just enough sensation to appeal to the ideal that there is a need for change, while at the same time suggesting that the solution lies in reform of the system rather than transformation. In addition, Gore provides a list of things that individuals 'can do to save the planet', which is appealing to schools seeking to encourage future environmentally aware and responsible citizens. This, it might be argued, is ideology masquerading as education. In *The enemy of nature* Joel Kovel argues that:

> [...] An *Inconvenient Truth* fails to mention the word 'capitalism', [...] it oozes with technological determinism, does not take into sufficient account the global South, never questions the industrial model, promises his approach will generate a lot of wealth, and offers no way out beyond voting the proper people, i.e. people like himself into office. Thus neither capital, nor the capitalist state, is at all questioned, nor is any authentic democratization offered.
>
> (Kovel, 2007: 166)

Gore's film presents the ideology that we are all part of the problem, and that it is individuals who hold the key to reducing greenhouse gas emissions. Kovel admits that pointing to the things we can do is understandably popular, as 'they comprise a risk-free way of feeling good about oneself in the face of over-whelming crisis'. However, these strategies offer no real solution. His analysis suggests that geography teachers would be better off helping school students understand the principles of how capitalism works in order to recognise the link between economic expansion and climate change. This is the terrain that geography teachers should occupy, and in the next section I set out an agenda for this.

For further study

1. Get hold of a copy of Al Gore's *An Inconvenient Truth*. Having watched the film, assess the arguments it makes about the causes of, and solutions to, global warming. How might this resource be used in a unit that takes a critical approach to understanding climate change?

Teaching climate capitalism

Beyond voluntarism

According to the New Economics Foundation's Andrew Simms (2008), we have 100 months to save the planet. What this means is that we have 100 months to reduce greenhouse gas concentrations so as to maintain the global average temperature within +2°C of their pre-industrial levels. Evidence such as this gives a sense of the need for human societies to make rapid and radical changes in how they organise themselves. Over the past few years, there has been a deluge of books that seek to popularise issues of climate change and offer advice on what individuals can do to help the fight against it. These include *The climate diet*, *The hot topic*, and 'anti-environmental environmental' treatments such as *Crap at the environment*. However, like Gore's film, these solutions are based at the individual level, whereas what is required is a collective response to climate change. As Newell and Paterson argue:

> Dealing successfully with climate change entails a wholesale transformation so that the economy can be 'decarbonised'.
>
> (Newell and Paterson, 2010: 7)

As individuals, we can each analyse aspects of our lives in order to understand how we are implicated in the carbon economy, and measure our carbon footprints. And we may even accept the argument made by some politicians that we should all have a set 'personal carbon allowance'. However,

> […] if decarbonisation of the economy is really to take off, the challenge has to be addressed at many more scales. The suppliers of our energy have to have incentives to switch to renewable options. We have to have transport systems that do not create incentives for individual and unnecessary car use, which in turn implies changes in planning systems for a carbon-constrained world.
>
> (Newell and Paterson, 2010: 8)

This is why it is so difficult to 'decarbonise the economy', since virtually all aspects of how we live our lives are wrapped up with it. The economic system depends for its expansion on carbon, and if it doesn't continue growing, it implodes in crisis as we saw in the 1930s, and more recently in the aftermath of the 2008 financial crash.

The geography of carboniferous capitalism

Newell and Paterson's insistence on the need to use the term 'climate capitalism' in order to remember how economy and environment are closely related suggests that, in school geography lessons, teachers need to relate the emergence of climate change to a broader history of historical–geographical development. Generations of school geography students growing up in the 1970s were taught about the geography of 'carboniferous capitalism'. This was reflected in maps of resources such as coal and the main coalfields, and how the manufacturing industry of the large conurbations was linked to their proximity to coalfields. In many ways, this geography was transformed by the change to the use of oil and gas, aided by the discovery and development of North Sea resources from the 1960s. These were the resources that have spurred economic development and growth in the global economy. Even with the oil price-rise shocks of the early 1970s, which raised the spectre of breaks in supplies of cheap energy, the general pattern has been one of optimism and belief in the inevitability of finding new supplies or technological solutions. Indeed, these earlier shocks themselves produced an interesting geography. For the UK and Norway, they stimulated the search for energy resources within their own territories (North Sea oil and gas). Other nations did not have this option, and developed alternative approaches. France, for example, developed its nuclear production, while Denmark developed alternative sources in its promotion of wind energy.

At the same time as this trajectory of fossil-fuelled economic growth was occurring, scientists were in the process of 'discovering' global warming. It had been established by the early 1960s that CO_2 levels were rising. Even as knowledge of human-induced climate change was developing, this was largely decoupled from economic growth, which had taken a particular form in the period since the mid-1970s. As pointed out in chapter seven, neoliberalism was based on a number of key features, including belief in the efficacy of markets; relaxation of controls on banking and finance so as to speed up the rate of transactions and investment; and belief that higher levels of wealth inequality could be tolerated so long as average prosperity was increasing (i.e. the economy was growing).

Newell and Paterson argue that these dominant ways of thinking about the economy have led to distinctive ways of seeking to decarbonise the economy, and this is based on the idea of markets. Rather than seeking to reduce use of fossil fuels, the response has been to create markets for emissions, new or expanding markets for renewable energy technologies, and new investment opportunities. This is reflected in the idea of the 'carbon market'. What these approaches have in common is that they turn carbon into a commodity that can be traded. Newell and Paterson outline a series of scenarios as to how the decarbonisation of capitalism may occur in the next twenty to thirty years. These scenarios, developed and taught as part of a wider unit of work, could be the basis for analysis and discussion in school geography.

Newell and Paterson's scenarios for carbon capitalist futures

A: Carbon capitalist utopia

The introduction of markets for the exchange of carbon emissions leads to a process of investment in renewable energy, energy efficiency, carbon capture and storage, advanced public transport, and renewed green urban infrastructure reform. Together, these lead to rapid shifts away from fossil fuel use. The regulators of financial markets force companies to disclose their use of CO_2 and ensure that imposed carbon allowances are adhered to. The World Bank decarbonises its lending policies to ensure it does not sponsor fossil fuel-led development projects. Tax-payers in the advanced Western economies are no longer willing to allow their money to underwrite financial backing for fossil fuel projects at a time when they are seeking to reduce their own consumption through personal carbon allowances.

As a result of these market innovations, over a period of twenty to thirty years, the overall demand for energy stabilises, and the energy mix shifts from 90 per cent use of coal, oil and gas to 70 per cent reliance on renewable energy. The remainder of fossil fuel use is extracted and used in the most energy-efficient ways available.

B: Stagnation

Carbon markets come to be seen as just the latest in a series of financial scams operated by the financial and banking sector to make money. Carbon markets lose their legitimacy, and the continuing economic crises leads firms to seek to maximise their profits in the short term. Corporations such as BP and Shell reduce their investments in renewable energy. National governments apply forms of weak regulation of the carbon market, allowing corporations to persuade them to set weak targets for carbon reduction and a voluntary code to monitor compliance. Governments, fearing high unemployment, continue to support the old manufacturing giants such as oil and gas.

Internationally, agreements on reduced carbon emissions are hampered by inter-state rivalry and an unwillingness to cooperate. Periodic crises related to ongoing climate change, such as hurricanes, flooding and drought, ensure that climate change remains high on the public agenda, but the lack of progress leads to cynicism and despair. Insurance companies respond by refusing to provide cover for people living in vulnerable areas. Affluent but concerned individuals feel powerless to do much, and are increasingly worried about the possibility of influxes of environmental refugees.

C: Decarbonised dystopia

As carbon prices begin to have an effect on behaviour, investment is drawn to series of quick fixes, techno-fixes, and drastic measures that have the effect of realising profits for investors, but leading to uneven and unjust impacts. In the face of growing evidence of the impact of climate change, there is a rush to embrace scientists' schemes (such as spreading iron filings on the ocean floor to accelerate the rate at which CO_2 is absorbed) and geo-engineering 'solutions'. Investment pours into biofuel production, which results in the creation of large monocrop plantations with appalling labour conditions. The high price of carbon leads to investment in nuclear power, with plants being located in remote areas populated by poorer and marginal populations.

In the drive to reduce carbon emissions, governments shift the burden onto individuals and go to great lengths to monitor and police compliance, leading to the rise of a surveillance culture. The rich are easily able to buy up extra credits from poorer people, who are increasingly forced into fuel poverty, reducing their carbon consumption through consuming less of everything.

D: Climate Keynesianism

Critics of laissez-faire approaches to carbon markets begin to win political arguments, and governments act to ensure markets are geared towards the goal of decarbonisation rather than speculation. There are stringent targets, and loopholes in trading rules are closed, with the result that there is transparency about use of CO_2. Governments realise that markets alone are insufficient to bring about

> desired levels of decarbonisation and thus embark on a large-scale programme of public investment to make homes energy-efficient, and to improve transport infrastructure in towns and cities to encourage people out of their cars. These investments have the effect of stabilising the construction industry and preventing speculative house-building schemes that require car use.

It is significant that Newell and Paterson's book does not set out to examine post-capitalist futures. They argue that it is important to recognise that responses to climate change have 'so far been organised for the most part around the construction of markets in carbon emissions'. The aim has been to put a price on carbon and thus make explicit the costs to those polluting. Although Newell and Paterson have serious doubts about whether capitalism is capable of solving the problem, they argue that it sets the political and social context in which it will need to be resolved. They recognise that there will be conflicts, and in the aftermath of the financial crisis of 2008, financiers have resisted calls for greater regulation of their activity. There are also doubts about whether agreements can be put in place in time to make significant moves to 'decarbon' the economy. For Newell and Paterson, there will be winners and losers in this process, and they argue for administering these changes in ways that recognise ideas of fairness and social justice. However, they are clear that:

> To be effective, to be coherent, the global system will need to engage, enrol, and change the actors that govern the global economy at the moment.
>
> (Newell and Paterson, 2010: 187)

These actors are powerful government leaders, global entrepreneurs and business leaders, and those whose actions determine the flow of global finance and wealth. They are those who operate in what Peet (2008) terms the 'geography of power'. This suggests that geography lessons that urge students to do their bit by behaving as good environmental citizens will fall short of their goals of helping students to understand the forces that are shaping current and future social and environmental relations.

Mobile lives and climate change

Another perspective on the issue of climate change is offered by the sociologist John Urry, who argues that climate change:

> [...] is a legacy of the 20th century, when powerful high carbon path dependent systems were set in place, locked in through various economic and social institutions. And as the century unfolded those lock-ins meant that the world was left a high and growing carbon legacy. Electricity, steel-and-petroleum cars, and suburban living and associated consumption are three of those locked-in legacies.
>
> (Urry, 2010: 198)

This is a powerful statement, since it implies that slowing down (let alone reversing) increasing carbon emissions requires 'the reorganization of social life, nothing more and nothing less'. Urry argues that these high-carbon systems have developed in tandem with the rise of mobile forms of life. The ability to move becomes central to how people in the 'rich' world define success and happiness. Life is less tied to the local, as people have a 'supermarket' of choice about who are their friends and acquaintants. People's desire to be connoisseurs and collectors of places means that they seek to travel to many different places. Contemporary capitalism presupposes that people will be relatively free of local constraints, at least periodically, as they travel to new places in search of the experiences that help them define their identities.

Echoing Newell and Paterson's analysis, Urry argues that the rate of expansion of this high-carbon mobility complex has been accelerated in the past few decades by the dominance of a neoliberal view of the economy, which assumes the right of capital, goods and people to move at will. The idea of the free market resists attempts by states to halt these processes of mobility. One result of this has been the emergence of 'places of consumption excess'. The classic example in recent years is the transformation of Dubai, a centre of oil production, to a site of elite and excess consumption, with its human-made island archipelago 'The World', the world's only seven-star hotel, a domed ski resort, the world's tallest building, and carnivorous dinosaurs (Davis, 2006). Urry concludes on an ominous note:

> 20th century capitalism generated the most striking of contradictions. Its pervasive, mobile and promiscuous commodification involved utterly unprecedented levels of energy production and consumption, a high carbon society whose dark legacy we are beginning to reap. This contradiction could result in a widespread reversal of many of the systems that constitute capitalism as it turns into its own gravedigger.
>
> (Urry, 2010: 208)

These discussions of climate capitalism may require a more concrete link with the everyday places and spaces of pupils' lives. The box on 'Mobile geographies' focuses on how climate change is linked to the system of mobilities that characterises late-capitalist societies.

Mobile geographies

John Urry is a sociologist at the University of Lancaster. Since the mid-1980s he has published a large amount of work that explores the changing nature of space and society. His most recent work raises important questions about environmental sustainability.

In 1987, Scott Lash and John Urry published *The end of organized capitalism*, in which they argued that that the final decades of the twentieth century were characterised by a shift from 'organised' to 'disorganised' capitalism. Lash and Urry's starting point is Marx and Engels' (1848) *Manifesto of the Communist Party* and its characterisation of capitalism as a revolutionary force, sweeping away older social relations and replacing them new ways of producing and working, new ways of living. They see Marx and Engels as prophets of modernity, where 'all that is solid melts into air'. *The end of organized capitalism* examines the claim that, towards the end of the twentieth century, the capitalism that Marx and Engels were describing has, 'in certain societies, come to an end'. They propose a periodisation that starts with nineteenth-century liberal capitalism, in which the circuits of capital more or less operated at the level of the locality or region. In the twentieth century, the rise of organised capitalism meant that money, the means of production, consumer commodities and labour power came to flow most significantly on a national scale. At the end of the twentieth century, circuits of capital, commodities and money took place on an international scale. In this sense, capitalism is disorganised because 'the flows of subjects and objects are progressively less synchronised within national boundaries'. *The end of organized capitalism* examined the economic development of the USA, Britain, Germany and Sweden, and argued that all these nations were in the process of shifting from organised to disorganised capitalism.

Lash and Urry subsequently developed their analysis in *Economies of signs and space* (1994), which depicts a world characterised by the process of time–space compression, with capital, goods, images and people moving ever greater distances at increasing speed. There is a dissolution of social structures based on age, class, family and gender, which means that individuals are left with few secure signposts with which to make sense of their lives. Many commentators see this as a negative development, leading to degrees of 'ontological insecurity' and a loss of identity. However, in *Economies of signs and space*, Lash and Urry stress the potential for new forms of subjectivity associated with the increased velocity of flows of goods, images and people:

> In our view this spatialization and semioticization of contemporary political economies is less damaging in its implications than many of these writers suggest. [...] these changes also encourage the development of reflexivity [...] a growing reflexivity of subjects that accompanies the end of organized capitalism opens up many positive possibilities for social relations – for intimate relations, for friendship, for work relations, for leisure and for consumption.
>
> (Lash and Urry, 1994: 31)

Since the publication of *Economies of signs and space*, John Urry has developed these ideas in a series of books concerned with the theme of mobilities. In *Sociology beyond societies* (2000), he presented a manifesto for a sociology that 'examines the diverse mobilities of peoples, objects, images, information and wastes; and of the complex interdependencies between, and social consequences of, these diverse mobilities'. Urry wants to consider how the development of various global networks and flows undermines endogenous social structures, which have generally been taken within sociological discourse to possess the power to reproduce themselves. This concept of societies which has been at the heart of sociology no longer adequately describes how the world works, and thus he calls for a 'sociology beyond societies'. These arguments have implications for geography, which has tended to be underpinned by a particular view of space as settled and relatively stable. Space is the backdrop to social action, and there is little sense of the ways in which these patterns have been produced through various mobilities. Urry's 2007 book *Mobilities* presents evidence for what he calls the 'mobilities turn':

> From SARS to plane crashes, from airport expansion controversies to SMS texting, from slave trading to global terrorism, from obesity caused by the 'school run' to oil wars in the Middle East [...] issues of what I term 'mobility' are centre-stage on many policy and academic agendas.
>
> (Urry, 2007: 6)

This mobility turn is, according to Urry, spreading in and through the social sciences, 'mobilizing analyses that have been historically static, fixed and concerned with predominantly a-spatial "social structures"'.

This analysis has the advantage of helping us to combine knowledge and understanding of physical systems with knowledge and understanding of economic and social systems. Urry has recently developed these ideas in a book with Anthony Elliott called *Mobile lives*, which takes as its starting point the fact that:

> People today are 'on the move', and arguably as never before. Massive social changes – globalization, mobile technologies, intensive consumerism and climate change – are implicated in the ever-increasing movement of people, things, capital, information and ideas around the globe.
>
> (Elliott and Urry, 2010: ix)

In this context, Elliott and Urry are concerned with how these movements affect the ways in which 'lives are lived, experienced and understood'. They are particularly interested in the impact of mobile lives on people's personal relationships, their social lives, their working practices and their patterns of consumption. They recognise that there are both advantages and perils involved in living mobile lives:

> On an institutional level, fast-track mobile lives (the privileged, gated worlds of those we call 'globals') involve endless organizational remodelling, corporate downsizing, just-in-time production, carbon crises and electronic offshoring. On an individual level, today's acceleration of mobile lives has come to signify, among other practices, cosmetic surgery, cyber-therapy, speed dating and multiple careers.
>
> (Elliott and Urry, 2010: x)

Mobile lives is an exhilarating journey through the 'economies of signs and space' of early twenty-first-century capitalism. The penultimate chapter is called 'Consuming to excess', and charts the emergence of extraordinary new places built on elite consumption, the most notorious example of which is Dubai. Such places of hyper-consumerism have a number of features: their exclusivity, their reliance on an invisible labour force, their appeal to the spectacular dreamworlds and fantasies of consumption; but, ultimately, their most significant feature may be that they take to extremes the hyper-high-carbon societies of the twentieth century. This occurs through their gigantic building, their profligate use of energy and water, and the vast use of oil to transport people in and out. Finally, in *Mobile lives*, Elliott and Urry countenance the environmental limits to disorganised capitalism, and suggest that their book is a contribution not to postmodern social science (or postmodern geography), but to post-carbon social theory. In the light of the possibility of reduced fossil fuel consumption and an uncertain world of climate change, Elliott and Urry discuss scenarios for a contested future (see box).

Elliott and Urry's scenarios for a contested future

A: Local sustainability

As a result of the politics of climate change, peak oil and economic crises, travel is substantially reduced and far more local. Cars no longer monopolise the roads. The global population will be lower as a result of poorer healthcare and reduced food supplies. There is a shift to lifestyles that are more local and smaller in scale. Friends are chosen who are more local, families will not move away as they grow, employment will be found close to home, and education sought in local schools, college and universities. Foodstuffs will be seasonal as food miles are reduced, and most goods and services will be locally sourced.

B: Regional warlordism

In this future there are oil, gas and water shortages and intermittent wars. There is a falling standard of living and much reduced movement, and local 'warlords' controlling recycled forms of mobility and weaponry. There are frequent resource wars over control of water, oil and gas. This is the *Mad Max 2* scenario.

C: Hypermobility

The resource shortages and effects of climate change turn out to be less significant, especially for those in the rich North. Movement becomes more extensive and frequent with the development of new kinds of vehicles and fuels, which overcome the limits of space and time. Personalised air travel will be common, with cars becoming a rather second-rate way of getting around.

D: The 'digital nexus' future

New software intelligently works out the best means of doing tasks, whether this involves meeting up, travelling or staying in place. There is more use of 'face-to-face' meeting through virtual communications. On the street, there are small, smart, ultra-light, battery-based vehicles that are hired rather than owned. There are on-demand minibuses, bicycles and hybrid vehicles, all designed to provide joined-up travel from home, to work, to places of leisure. Neighbourhoods are redesigned to reduce sprawl. Personalised carbon allowances lead to rationing of movement to reduce overall energy demand.

For further study

1. To what extent do you think a focus on mobilities – in which societies are characterised by movement and flows of capital, goods, people and information – represents a challenge to traditional ways in which geography is taught in schools? What would a geography curriculum organised around the concept of mobilities look like?

Anthropocene geographies

This chapter focuses on questions of how to develop approaches to teaching about climate change that allow students to explore the relationship between climate change and wider economic systems of mobility. It is important to remember that this is only one approach to the topic, and that in the realm of climate change there is genuine controversy about how to understand these developments, usefully explained in Mick Hulme's (2009) *Why we disagree about climate change?*

The larger point that is implied in this chapter is that it is clear that human beings are now living in an environment that is increasingly a matter of their own making. The assumption of an external environment that somehow influences human activity is not a useful starting point for thinking about environmental change. To emphasise the role of the 'human factor' in shaping the biosphere, Paul Crutzen (2002), who won a Nobel Prize in chemistry for his work on the ozone layer, and other scientists have proposed that we designate current times as a distinct geological era – the Anthropocene – which emphasises the new human 'forcing mechanisms' that are driving change in the biosphere. In 2008, the Stratigraphy Commission of the Geological Society of London asked the question, 'Are we now living in the Anthropocene?' The twenty-one members of the Commission unanimously answered 'yes', based on their assessment of evidence to support the hypothesis that the Holocene epoch (the interglacial period of stable climate that allowed for the development of agriculture and urban growth) has ended. They reported:

> The combination of extinctions, global species migrations and the widespread replacement of natural vegetation with agricultural monocultures is producing a

distinctive contemporary biostratigraphic signal. These effects are permanent, as future evolution will take place from surviving (and frequently anthropogenically relocated) stocks.

(Zalasiewicz *et al.*, 2008: 6)

Environmental historians debate the question of when the Anthropocene started, but the key development is often seen as the emergence of wide-scale use of fossil fuels in the industrial revolution. This started a worldwide transformation of rocks into air, a geological reversal of hundreds of millions of years of carbon sequestration from the atmosphere by living processes. Steffen *et al.* (2007) track atmospheric carbon dioxide concentration since 1750. From a pre-industrial value of 270–75 parts per million (ppm), atmospheric CO_2 had risen to about 310 ppm by 1950. They identify a great acceleration, in which atmospheric CO_2 concentration has risen from 310 to 380 ppm since 1950, with about half of the total rise since the pre-industrial era occurring in just the past thirty years.

Simon Dalby puts these developments in terms which render them meaningful to everyday life:

The economic phenomena we talk about in terms of globalization are physical phenomena; global trade is moving stuff round the planet and turning rocks into air in ways that mean humanity has become a geomorphic and climatological agent, even if that is not quite what we think we are doing when we stop to fill our car's fuel tank on the way to the shopping mall to buy things made on the other side of the world. The sheer scale of human activity is novel, and we have begun a major transformation of the biosphere.

(Dalby, 2009: 105)

This globalisation is in fact global urbanisation, since we increasingly live in an interconnected global urban economic system – and Dalby proposes the term 'glurbanisation' to acknowledge this. Dalby's analysis points to the need for new geographical imaginations and concepts that can help us understand Anthropocene geographies. This means challenging the traditional geographical urge to draw boundaries around spaces and give them labels (urban, rural, wilderness, tourist zone, conservation area, etc.). The consumer identities of being a tourist, or a car driver, are essentially about urban ways of living that use up global resources. The geographical concern with mapping sits uneasily with the question of how to understand flows that do not stay within the static categories of nations, states and regions. At present, much hope is placed in extraordinary developments in visualisation associated with geographical information systems, but much of this suffers from the tendency to want to gaze upon and capture the world as whole, rather than developing the sense of impermanence, connection and contingency required to make sense of the precarious relationships between people and planet. There are significant challenges in developing a geographical education that is appropriate to the Anthropocene.

For further study

1. Simon Dalby proposes the term 'glurbanisation' to help us recognise that urban life is part of a global economic system. He also suggests that geography as a subject has been guilty of 'terrestrocentrism' due to its focus on the land as opposed to humanity's relation to the biosphere and atmosphere. To what extent might such new concepts be useful in teaching Anthropocene geographies?

Activities

1. The environmental educator David Selby (2008) recently argued that:

    > an 'adequate responsiveness' on the part of schools to climate change would require a cultural shift on significant, even seismic proportions. It would require a culture of uncertainty, systems consciousness, a dynamic sharing of subjectivities and multiple voices, and action-oriented learning. However, the compartmentalised nature of the curriculum means that climate change is seen as a topic in the science curriculum. Teacher training courses exacerbate this division, with little chance to bridge the 'two cultures'.
    >
    > (Selby, 2008: 254)

    To what extent to you agree or disagree with Selby's argument? Does your school have a whole-school policy on teaching climate change? What would it look like?

2. What are the advantages and disadvantages of using scenarios such as the ones included in this chapter in teaching about complex environmental issues?

Section three:
Practices

9

Teaching geography as if the planet matters: let's be realistic

Introduction

Geography teachers are idealistic. They tend to choose to teach geography in schools because they believe the subject can have a transformative effect on how young people view the world. Some geography teachers want to enable young people to experience the 'awe and wonder' they themselves feel when they come across (often through their own travel experiences) a magnificent landscape. Other geography teachers are motivated by a desire to help young people become 'global citizens', able to play a part in maintaining and sharing the planet. For yet other geography teachers, there is a desire to pass on what they have learned through geographical study. In general, there is a shared narrative about why geography matters, expressed succinctly in the Geographical Association's manifesto, *A different view*:

> Geography fascinates and inspires: the beauty of the earth, the terrible power of earth-shaping forces – these things can take us out of ourselves. Geographical investigation both satisfies and nourishes curiosity. Geography deepens understanding: many contemporary challenges – climate change, food security, energy choices – cannot be understood without a geographical perspective.
>
> Geography serves vital educational goals; thinking and decision-making with geography helps us to live our lives as knowledgeable citizens, aware of our own local communities in a global setting.
>
> (GA, 2009: 5)

This is a strong statement, and captures something of the geographical imagination that informs the argument in this book. As *A different view* goes on to explain, there is a need for teaching that is strongly informed by the concepts and perspectives offered by geography as a discipline. Geography teachers play a central role in this process, as they are actively involved in constructing the curriculum. It is important to recognise that *A different view* is making this argument within the context where many geography teachers are finding it hard to develop this rigorous approach to the subject in schools. Increasingly, geography teachers are encouraged to plan lessons in line with a prescribed script, with objectives, starter activity and the obligatory plenary. They are urged to ensure all lessons are planned with 'assessment for learning' in mind, and to incorporate thinking skills and personalised learning. They sometimes work in schools where 'learning' is publicly valued over 'teaching', where it is held that how pupils learn is more important than what they learn, and where there is a concern to develop competence and transferable skills. With all this going on, it is perhaps unsurprising that geography teachers report they have little time to engage in curriculum planning that develops their own geographical knowledge and understanding.

This is the (unpromising) context in which *Teaching geography as if the planet matters* was written. This final substantive chapter addresses the question of how far it is possible to develop the type of geographical education advocated in this book.

In what follows, I want to start by clarifying the perspectives developed in *Teaching geography as if the planet matters*. The chapters in section one provide an analysis of the content of school geography and its relation to ideas from the wider discipline. These chapters can be understood as a form of ecocritique, which examines representations of society and nature in school geography. This critique suggests that dominant forms of school geography have promoted ideological understandings of society and environment, and that, to enable students to understand how geographies are made and remade, there is a need to develop forms of geographical knowledge that are rooted in political economy and social construction. These would enable teachers and students to deconstruct representations of environmental issues and develop alternative readings of landscapes and environments.

It is important to stress that this part of a tradition of critical geography education. What is now often called critical geography had its roots in the 1960s, when geographers such as Richard Peet and David Harvey responded to geographical inequalities in cities and at the global scale. Radical geography was characterised by critique of the imperialist and sexist nature of geographical knowledge. From this perspective, geography as an academic discipline was seen to represent the interests of the powerful. Feminist geographers developed these insights, showing how geography served to exclude the perspectives of half the world's population. These critiques gained increasing influence as geographers began to develop theories about the relationship between society and space. Rather than seeking to explain spatial patterns in terms of spatial processes, it was recognised that society and space are mutually constitutive. From that moment, it became possible to argue that geography matters. This paved the way for a stronger relationship between geography and the broader social sciences. For much of the 1980s, the new models in geography were those linked to political economy, though these approaches, which stressed the economic forces shaping space and place, were joined by ideas about the importance of culture and meaning. More and more, geographers paid attention to the importance of representations in shaping and mediating people's understanding of the world. Again, this was part of a broader shift in the social sciences associated with the cultural turn. Landscapes, places and environments could be seen as texts that were authored and needed to be interpreted. Following ideas in literary theory, it became possible to read texts for what they included and excluded. At times, this concern with texts could be interpreted as suggesting that there was no final and singular reading of the landscape, and that there was a sense of multiple geographies and a tendency to indulge in ever-decreasing circles of word play; but at its best, the critical approach in geography has sought to place representations of places and environments in material processes that recognise the role of power and economy.

It is important to recognise that 'education' has been quite marginal to the broader project of critical geography, although there have been some useful and challenging articles written from this perspective.

A place in the margins

It should be clear that the language and approach of critical geography (with its strong emphasis on political–economic theory and ideas of social construction) is not easily reconciled with dominant ways of teaching and learning geography in schools, with the result that many commentators have recognised the widening gap between school and university geography. This section provides an account of the changing nature of geographical education in schools, set within the wider context of changes in the nature of teachers' work.

In his book *Geography in education*, Norman Graves (1975) remarks that, when he began teaching in 1950, he does not remember the staff discussing the curriculum operating in the school, other than what to do with the fifth and upper sixth forms after the examinations were over. It is important to understand the context of this 'curriculum inertia'. Grace argues that, arising from the political, economic and social crises of the 1920s:

> the autonomy of English state schooling in curriculum, assessment and pedagogic approaches steadily increased and by the 1960s the autonomy of English schools from external prescriptive agencies was considerable.
>
> (Grace, 1995: 13)

This situation began to change during the 1960s. The development of a modern, technologically minded society raised questions about the types of curriculum and learning that were on offer to pupils in schools. The expansion of schooling for all children after the Second World War, along with the cultural changes associated with increasing levels of affluence and personal consumption, led many teachers in schools to find ways to adapt to pupils' needs, and a gap opened up in schools between those younger teachers impatient for change and the more traditional teachers. These developments were given a boost with the formation of the Schools Council in 1964, which was prompted by a comment from Minister of Education David Eccles in 1960 that the government should pay more attention to 'the secret garden of the curriculum'. Though some feared the Schools Council might impinge on the autonomy of schools and teachers regarding curriculum, in practice the Schools Council's whole ethos overtly stressed the responsibility of individual schools and teachers in evolving their own curriculum. This paved the way for what Rawling (2000) described as the 'golden age of curriculum development' in school geography. Significantly, it led to the development of a 'new professionalism' for geography teachers. The three Schools Council curriculum projects in geography allowed for the development of a new language of curriculum and pedagogy. It offered new ways of understanding the relationship between university and school geography, and important changes in approaches to teaching and learning. Curriculum development was more than simply developing new teaching materials and writing new syllabuses; it was about changing the very nature of what it meant to be a geography teacher. As Hickman *et al.* (1973), discussing the work of the Geography 14–18 Project, stated:

1. Teachers need more opportunities to discuss and evaluate new ideas if they are to be used more effectively to provide 'intellectually exacting study in geography'.

2. The abilities to adopt and to adapt new ideas, and to re-design curricula, are becoming key skills in geography teaching because changes in the subject will continue.

3. Teacher-based curriculum renewal is practical and rewarding when teachers have adequate incentive, support and feedback, and can influence the form, pace and assessment of their use of new ideas.

(Hickman *et al.*, 1973: 1)

These developments were linked to university education departments, which were involved in the initial training of geography teachers and their continuing professional development. Geography educators such as Norman Graves (1979), Bill Marsden (1976) and David Hall (1976) all wrote books that introduced to teachers the tenets of 'rational curriculum planning', which appeared to promise a logical and rational justification for the choices about what to teach in school geography. Thus we see the incorporation of the models of rational curriculum planning in discussions of school geography. At around the same time, geography was being redefined in universities away from a descriptive (regional) discipline to a normative (systematic) discipline. The new models provided important new content that could inform rational curriculum planning. One of the results of these changes was that geography in schools could present itself as a scientific subject and thus gain greater status as resources.

This view of curriculum planning in geography accorded with a view of geographical knowledge that assumed the existence of an objective world to which we can gain access. It is also suited to the belief that we can search for generalisations and key ideas, discover simple, orderly causal processes, and represent reality in unproblematic ways. With this view of geographical knowledge, planning becomes an essentially technical exercise of deciding what to study, and how to organise that study to maximum effect.

Beyond rational curriculum planning

At this point it is important to recognise that these moves to develop rational approaches to curriculum planning in schools were challenged by those who argued that they reflected a technocratic tendency to deny human meaning and creativity, and to reduce the educational process to a system of inputs and outputs. This argument is well expressed in Fred Inglis' (1975) *Ideology and imagination*, which critiqued the narrow version of human relations that was reflected in rational curriculum planning. At the same time, writers associated with the new sociology of education explored the ways in which the organisation of school knowledge itself (the official curriculum) worked to sort students. This new sociology of education focused on the content and the form of knowledge. By focusing on school curriculum and knowledge, it sought to explain how social reproduction was enacted at the everyday level of school practice. In doing so, it challenged the idea that knowledge is 'above' politics. The contributors to Michael Young's (1971) edited collection *Knowledge and control* discussed the ways in which particular kinds of knowledge are validated in the academy – knowledge that is pure, general and academic. In contrast, knowledge that is applied, specific and vocational is marginalised. Though these distinctions are arbitrary, they serve to keep particular elite groups in control of the official school curriculum. More radical perspectives were offered by writers such as Michael Apple (1979), who argued that the content and organisation of the school curriculum was ideological and served to legitimise existing inequalities in society. Schools were places where you learned to accept your role in a class-divided society. Madeleine Arnot explains the context in which these ideas were developed. It was one in which liberal ideology represented schooling as contributing to progressive social change, providing personnel to 'push back the frontiers of technical knowledge and to consolidate these advances and bring them into our everyday lives' (Arnot, 2006). Second, there was an assumption that education is capable of redressing social inequalities – as providing a ladder and an avenue for social mobility. Finally, education and the culture it both produces and transmits were viewed as independent and autonomous features of our society. Educational policies were directed towards the production of both knowledge and knowledgeable individuals through the sponsoring of academic research and curriculum reform. The idealism within the liberal tradition presented both culture and schooling as politically neutral forces for social change.

These arguments did not have much impact on those who were busy designing rational approaches to curriculum planning. For example, while Graves (1975) acknowledged that the new sociologists of education offered an 'illuminating' account of the relationship between the curriculum and powerful interests, he rejected it 'because it does not answer the normative question as to the criteria which ought to be used to plan curriculum'. Graves' solution was to start with the assumption that geographical knowledge was neutral, and the curriculum problem simply involved personal and collective choices about what to teach, how to teach it and how to deliver it.

An alternative account of the development of school geography teaching in Britain, one which forms the starting point for the analysis in this book, is found in an essay by John Huckle entitled 'Geography and schooling'. In this article, Huckle (1985) reversed the assumptions on which rational curriculum planning was based. The curriculum is not something that geography teachers control, but is the product of larger social and economic forces:

> Contrary to the beliefs of many geography teachers, changes in the nature of schooling, curriculum content, and methodology are not then simply a response to the growth of knowledge or the changing preoccupations of geographers and educationalists.
>
> (Huckle, 1985: 294)

Huckle stressed how the geography curriculum is a reflection of economic structures. One of the major roles of education is to transmit ideology. Thus, for Huckle, the majority of geography lessons 'cultivate a voluntary submission to existing social, spatial and environmental relations'. He sought to show how the success of geography as a school subject was achieved through it adopting forms more or less acceptable to the needs of capital and the state. Huckle was particularly critical of the development of geography in the post-war period, offering a different view of the 'golden age'. He argues that it was an elitist exercise and an attempt to render the schooling of a minority of pupils more 'technocratic and vocationally relevant'. This agenda was supported by the co-option of examinations boards, the Geographical Association, Her Majesty's Inspectors of Schools and textbook publishers. Teachers were brought in line with the promise of a 'new professionalism'. The new geography was advocated by educationists in university education departments, who combined rational curriculum theory with positivist geography. These were then the basis for dissemination and professional development. From this perspective, the curriculum projects, rather than being progressive educational developments, were concerned largely with the management of change as the state sought to restructure in the face of new challenges, and with the sectional interests of a community of educators.

However, at the same time, the mounting crises of capitalism were requiring new educational thinking, and Huckle describes how some geographers were using humanistic and structuralist philosophies to design lessons on such topics as environmental degradation, global inequalities and urban redevelopment. These were a direct response to the 'crisis in education' precipitated by economic recession and capital's attempts to restore profitability. This went along with the break-up of social democracy and the decline of political consensus. The immediate concern was to find ways to promote the attitudes and values needed to produce willing and disciplined workers at a time when there was high youth unemployment. Huckle detected the reassertion of the traditional academic curriculum. He noted that this would lead to a 'tighter control over the curriculum', a stronger role for inspectors, and changes to teacher education. These were designed to seek a stronger correspondence between schooling and the economy and erode the autonomy that teachers had enjoyed. Huckle argued that, in response to this, geography teachers became more aware of the developments taking place in universities, and in educational theory that offered humanistic and radical alternatives.

A flavour of these alternatives can be seen in the issues of the journal *Contemporary Issues in Geography and Education* published by the Association for Curriculum

Development between 1984 and 1987. The journal published themed issues on racism, sexism, wealth and poverty, environmental degradation, and war and conflict. In participating in these debates, geography teachers were engaging in wider debates about the nature of schooling and how it differed from broader notions of education. The aims of the journal were:

> [...] to promote an emancipatory geography; it seeks, in other words, to promote the idea that the future is ours to create – or to destroy – and to demonstrate that education bears some responsibility for building a world responsive to human needs, diversity and capabilities.

(ACDG, 1983: 1)

More specific objectives included:

- to develop a critique of current curricula

- to explore the assumptions underlying much of geographical education and to make these assumptions explicit

- to examine the ideological content of geographical education in relation to its political content.

(Ibid.)

So far I have presented two distinctive traditions of geography teaching, which offer different interpretations of geography teachers' work. The first comes from a liberal humanist perspective, and is rooted in the idea of education as contributing to social progress and technological development. The second regards education as distinct from schooling, and sees geography teaching as means of transmitting overt and hidden curriculum. In the first version, knowledge is neutral; in the second, knowledge is produced in support of the economic interests of capital. A central feature of school geography's development since the late 1980s has been the loss of teachers' ability to select, define and develop the school curriculum in line with changes in geographical understanding.

The narrowing of teachers' work

In his book *The death of progressive education: how teachers lost control of the classroom*, the educational historian Roy Lowe (2007) provides an account of the way in which teachers' work has increasingly come under the control of the state. In the post-war period, teachers enjoyed what Grace called 'licensed autonomy'. In effect, this meant that teachers had the space to interpret the curriculum and to develop approaches to teaching and learning in ways that they thought best for their pupils. Of course, this led to variable practice, and in reality the power of the public examination largely defined what teachers taught. Throughout the 1970s, the Conservative party was clear that, if elected, it would move to implement a National Curriculum, which would ensure that all children were taught the same material. It was also a subject-centred curriculum, designed to ensure the end of 'trendy' or progressive teaching approaches. The National Curriculum was sold to teachers as an 'entitlement' for all students, though teaching unions lamented their members' loss of professional autonomy over what was taught.

The election of a New Labour government in 1997 ushered in further changes to the nature of schooling and teachers' work. The 1997 White Paper *Excellence in schools* set challenging targets in performance for schools. New Labour was strongly influenced by the idea of 'school effectiveness' research. Researchers at the Institute of Education produced results that claimed to identify eleven factors that seemed to correlate with high-performing schools. These were managerial, organisational and communication factors. Ministers leapt on these ideas to claim that they should be the basis for school improvement, proclaiming that it was no longer acceptable for schools to explain their performance based on factors such as social class ('poverty is no excuse').

With the question of curriculum content no longer seen as a central concern of geography teachers, more attention was focused on the processes of teaching, in particular, making sure all pupils were achieving to their 'limits'. There were moves to ensure common approaches to 'good practice' shared across the teaching profession. These National Strategies were very effective in communicating 'what works' in classrooms. There was a Secondary Literacy Strategy that sought to encourage geography teachers to adopt particular approaches to reading and writing, and a Numeracy Strategy with a geographical component. More influential was the Key Stage 3 Strategy, which provided advice on techniques such as 'thinking skills', 'objectives-led teaching' and 'assessment for learning'. Though many teachers may have felt the satisfaction and rewards that accompanied improvements in measured pupil performance, it is important to note that these developments had the effective of marginalising the types of subject-specific pedagogy that had been developed over time. Crucially, teaching was considered a technical, rather than an intellectual or creative, activity and practitioners (as they were often called) were expected to comply with national guidelines for 'lesson delivery' and be seen to adopt strategies supposed to maximise 'learning outputs'. These teaching methods are inculcated during postgraduate training courses, which are based on a competence model with Professional Standards for Qualified Teacher Status set by external bodies such as the Training and Development Agency for Schools. Ainley and Allen (2010) summarise the effects of these policies:

> The reality for teachers has been an iron-cage of micro-management with teachers doing what they are told when, following lesson plans and delivering centrally-determined learning objectives while having to justify how they spend their time in schools.[1]

> (Ainley and Allen, 2010: 66)

Though recent years have seen moves to recognise the autonomy and creativity of teachers, a focus on developing teachers' knowledge and understanding of their subject has been notably missing. A typical (and influential) example of this is David Hargreaves'

(1999) call for 'knowledge-creating schools' which, he claims, should be open to the outside world beyond the classroom; develop a culture of commitment and enthusiasm for continual improvement; encourage informal, task-relevant, rather than hierarchical relationships; and demonstrate a readiness to experiment with new ideas in a spirit that sees mistakes as 'paths to learning'.

In general, literature about changes in teachers' work points to the way in which teachers have less autonomy over the direction of their work and are subject to increased accountability. In Britain, key events include the establishment of the National Curriculum in 1990, and its associated regimes of testing and assessment, which have led to the publication of school league tables and the introduction of performance-related pay, which is in part based on the value added by individual teachers. In their longitudinal research on teachers' career paths, Day *et al.* (2007) suggest that the performativity agenda promoted in the period 2001–05 had five consequences:

- implicitly encouraged teachers to comply uncritically (teach to the test)

- challenged teachers' substantive identities

- reduced the time teachers have to connect with, care for and attend to the needs of individual students

- threatened teachers' sense of agency and resilience

- challenged teachers' capacity to maintain motivation, efficacy and thus commitment.

(Day *et al.*, 2007: 8)

They note that, although recent reforms have sought to provide teachers with additional resources and time to manage their workload and undertake professional development activity, and to increase the range of leadership roles linked to teaching and learning, there is as yet little evidence that 'levels of morale and commitment have been raised'. None of these is conducive to the disciplined intellectual commitment to developing a deeper understanding of geographical knowledge and ideas, as advocated in this book.

Additional insights into the changes that have taken place in teachers' work are provided by Moore (2004), who documents important shifts in the discourses of what constitutes a good teacher. In the 1980s, Moore argues, teacher education was based on the charismatic or 'ready-made' teacher model, in which it was the personal qualities of individual teachers that determined their success or failure (for example, qualities of caring or personal commitment). In the early 1990s, an educational discourse became more influential, based around notions of the reflective practitioner, which saw the teacher as both learner and theorist. This was replaced as the decade developed by a training discourse, which saw teaching as essentially a form of craft that required particular skills. Finally, Moore notes the emergence of a pragmatic discourse, based on notions of the effective teacher who draws eclectically on a range of things that are perceived to work. This pragmatic discourse has been promoted by government strategies that purport to offer evidence-based accounts of what makes effective teaching. Importantly, for Moore, this pragmatic approach tends to view the role of the teacher as non-political, and his research noted the unwillingness of teachers to debate important educational and social issues such as the balance between basic literacy and numeracy skills and social, creative and thinking skills; the choice of content in curriculum areas; and the pros and cons of school uniforms.

The overall picture is one of the gradual decline in geography teachers' capacity to act as curriculum-makers. Even though progressive revisions of the National Curriculum have provided teachers with more room to develop their own local curriculum responses, to the point where the most recent version of the curriculum is concept-based and provides minimal guidance on the content to be covered, it is doubtful whether teachers in schools have the time and space to rethink the principles of curriculum construction.

What is to be done?

In *Lost generation? New strategies for youth and education*, Patrick Ainley and Martin Allen argue that, rather than focusing on stimulating students' curiosity to develop the self-confidence that young people need to change the world, the schools, colleges and universities have become little more than 'exam factories', turning out batches of certificated students for employers to select or reject:

> As a consequence, students at all levels of learning are alienated from learning and adopt a largely instrumental approach to their studies. They memorise particular pieces that are required and devote large amounts of time to improving their exam technique through the endless practice of past papers and the unquestioned construction of 'model answers'.
>
> (Ainley and Allen, 2010: 133)

My argument in this book has been that this strategy is perhaps unsurprising, given the types of knowledge that students are offered as curriculum content in geography lessons. Rather than offering them historically grounded accounts of the economic and social processes that are shaping human and physical environments, geography lessons routinely offer mystification and simple models (e.g. push-and-pull factors, gains and losses, and sanitised versions of complex concepts such as regeneration or gentrification). Where alternatives are offered, these are often handled in a superficial way. This situation is not helped by moves towards learning based on internet searches, which often encourages a 'supermarket' approach to information retrieval and reproduction (Brabazon, 2008).

As geographer John Pickles wrote in 1986, society gets the kind of geography education it deserves. In the 1980s, education became linked to the needs of the economy. While this was initially concerned with social control (as Clarke and Willis, 1984 suggested, this was about 'schooling for the dole'), as the 1990s wore on it was about preparing people for life in the global knowledge economy. The fact that capitalist economies could no longer guarantee future workers a job for life meant that education had to be 'lifelong', and students were required to learn the skills to teach themselves – to 'learn how to learn'. This is the basis of the idea that what we learn is less significant than how we learn it. As realisation of the precarious nature of life in the global economy dawned, schools became places where it was necessary to learn the skills of citizenship and self-care, leading to a distinctly therapeutic ethos (Ecclestone and Hayes, 2008). Most significantly, schools, rather than being a place where we learned the disciplines of work, became 'cool places' where we learned how to play, to be creative, and to be optimistic.

There is a correspondence between the type of education that young people are offered and the ways in which economic and social life is organised. A society geared towards ever-higher levels of consumption and the work ethic that allows people to work longer and harder in order to finance this lifestyle invariably relies on an education that prioritises those values and attitudes. Yet schools are reflective of society, and there is some space for an alternative 'imaginary'. As Kate Soper argued in her submission to the UK Sustainable Development Commission:

> In school and university, young people are encouraged to develop an altruistic and citizenly ethics, and to reflect on social ends and values, at the same time as they are prepared for a work-world where competitive self-interest and an uncritical commitment to profit win the highest esteem and reward.
>
> (Soper, 2007: 5)

Assuming the dialectical relationship between schooling and the economy, it is likely that the near-to-medium term will see a developing tension between the narrow goals of current education policy based on 'more, faster and better' learning, and the broader need to engage in a proper debate about how to develop sustainable ways of organising production and consumption. Geographers who wish to teach geography as if the planet matters can make an important contribution to these developments.

Activities

1. To what extent do you agree with the argument in this chapter that geography teachers have, over time, lost control of the curriculum?

2. Why do you think that critical approaches to school geography (which draw on aspects of social and political theory) have struggled to find a place in the curriculum?

3. Write a short account of how you see the relationship between schooling and the wider society. In your experience, do you agree that school geography tends to promote ideas and values that support powerful forces in society?

Conclusion

From modern to real postmodern school geography

Always the towns have remained fundamentally the same in character, for they have existed to serve the little-changing needs of generation after generation of little-changing people. But now, suddenly as it were, a startling new habit has developed. A single invention, in the course of a few years' development, has placed within the grasp of every man and woman a means of rapid personal movement ten to twenty times faster than walking. It is not a matter of building a few roads, it is a matter of dealing with a new social situation. New urban arrangements are needed if the killing and the wounding, the noise and the stink and the confusion are to be avoided. Alternatively, the old arrangements may yet suffice if the new mobility is surrendered, or at least drastically restrained. It is certain that there has never been a choice so significant to the future of our towns.

(Buchanan, 1958: 207)

This statement, from Colin Buchanan's *Mixed blessing: the motor car in Britain*, seems to me to capture the essence of what it meant to teach geography in schools until around the mid-1970s. On the one hand, geography teaching in schools was about describing to the next generation the face of the land, a face that had been etched out of a mixture of physical processes and culture – the geographies of a little-changing people. On the other hand, beyond the school gates was a world that was in the process of transforming itself – a vibrant, modern geography, where new ways of thinking, feeling and acting were emerging. The motor car and the freedom it appeared to promise, Buchanan grasped, was not just changing the face of the land, but was creating new types of people. School geography, no doubt imperfectly at times, served to mediate between landscapes of tradition and landscapes of modernity.

Modernity's promise was that it would result in more wealth, more satisfaction, more freedom, and these were sold in the advertisements and television programmes that accompanied the expansion of consumption. Modern geography's contribution to this project was to play at least some part in ensuring that the process was rational and ordered. This modern geography is reflected in a little book called *Resources for Britain's future* (Chisholm, 1972), which comprises a series of articles that appeared in *The*

Geographical Magazine in 1969 and 1970. The back cover summarises the book's concerns:

> Modern technology is causing the spoliation and destruction of our country on a gigantic and irrevocable scale that would not previously have been thought remotely possible.
>
> Exploitation of natural resources, whether in the felling of trees or the mining of coal, has, up till recently, been carried out for the further material well-being of the exploiters. But now it is vital to consider all our resources in their relation to one another and to ourselves so that we may be in a position to make the right decisions.

There is a hint of criticism here about the direction in which modern society is travelling, but the belief is that there are logical and rational solutions to the problems, and geographers are on hand to help. Michael Chisholm, who edited the series of articles, wrote an introduction with the title, 'The geographical task ahead'. The authors were acclaimed experts in their field, they wrote with authority, and appeared to believe their voices would be heard by those in power.

I first encountered *Resources for Britain's future* as an A-level student in 1983. By this time, it was becoming clear that the ordered and rational plans contained in its pages were being disrupted by economic recession and social conflict. As the 1980s wore on – with its industrial conflicts, its politics of division and the unravelling of the post-war social consensus – this tension became ever more apparent. The modern geographical project – with its promise to provide order – rang hollow.

This is where postmodern geographies appeared. Postmodern geographies seemed to offer a less strident, less monolithic way of thinking about the subject. They clarified what we already knew, that geography tended to be dominated by white, middle-class men. Geographers hid their values behind the cloak of science, and were fascinated by the promises of technology. Few people were prepared for very long to proclaim themselves as postmodern geographers, but the influence of postmodern ways of researching, writing and thinking continued. As postmodernism permeated the wider culture, schools, too, were influenced by its insistence that we see truth as provisional, recognise the equal importance of feelings, and make room for as many voices and narratives as possible.

As Stuart Sim (2010) argues in *The end of modernity*, postmodernity was really a continuation of modernity. It critiqued the over-blown claims of modernity's metanarratives, and pointed out how it excluded the perspectives of different groups of people and non-human nature, but it did so essentially in order to make sure that everybody enjoyed the benefits of modernity (greater wealth, more freedom). Postmodern geography alerted us to the existence of multiple geographies. For Sim, the collision of the slow-burning environmental crisis that has unfolded over the past half-century, and the rapid collapse of the economic settlement which has dominated the past three decades, means that we are living in the 'real postmodern', where ever-increasing rates of growth and progress can no longer be sustained. We are faced, he suggests, with the prospect of a post-progress world, where we are mindful of the limits of nature. This is the context in which this book has been written, and my aim has been to provide some provisional 'road maps' that can inform the construction, in schools, of a *real postmodern geography* which takes seriously questions of sustainability. Perhaps this will be the challenge of teaching geography in the twenty-first century.

Notes

Chapter 1

1 The manuscript for this book was completed in the first month (May 2010) of the formation of a Conservative–Liberal Democrat coalition. At that point it was unclear how the new government would view 'education for sustainable development'.

2 Readers of this book may be familiar with the writings of Alex Standish, a former geography teacher who, in a series of short articles and a recent book (Standish, 2009), has argued that school geography is being undermined by a concern for teaching about values and moral issues. His position should be seen as one example of this wider analysis of how the idea of progress and development is being challenged.

3 Donald *et al.* (2008). ManTownHuman is a forum for critical architecture and design: www.mantownhuman.org/who.html

4 Indeed, some people have argued that the group of writers discussed in this section represent a form of 'entryism' into political circles to advance the interests of pro-market and pro-development organisations.

5 Readers may have spotted Porritt's title as the inspiration for the title of this series of books. This is partly true, although Porritt's title itself is derived from the subtitle of E.F. Schumacher's (1973) classic book *Small is beautiful: economics as if the planet mattered*.

6 See, for example, James Gustave Speth's (2008) *The bridge at the end of the world*. Speth seems to have travelled in the opposite direction from Porritt, as he was deeply embroiled in capitalist corporations and has now concluded that capitalism is the problem, not the solution.

Chapter 2

1 Denys Thompson went on to become headteacher at Yeovil School in Somerset. He was influential in the teaching of English, founding the journal *The Use of English*. In his voluminous writing he continued to expound the themes found in culture and environment.

Chapter 3

1 A glance at any inter-war text on physical geography or geomorphology will quickly reveal the influence of one of the founders of modern physical geography, W.M. Davis. Davis worked mainly on the eastern part of the USA, and absorbed and developed evolutionary and unformitarian ideas into his explanation of landforms and the cycle of erosion.

The ideas of evolutionary theory became hugely influential and have had an impact on other branches of physical geography. Teachers will be familiar with them. For example, in biogeography, Clements (1928) explained that the distribution of plant species in space and time was the result of succession as the plant community adapted to sets of environmental conditions or controls, ultimately producing a climax community subject to a main control – climate. In climatology, Bjerknes and Solberg (1922) discussed the life cycle of mid-latitude depressions using the concepts of cyclogenesis and frontogenesis.

The impact of Davis' work on modern physical geography should not be underestimated. His work became established teaching until well into the 1950s, and as late as the 1970s school texts such as R.J. Small's (1970) *The study of landforms* and B.W. Sparks' (1972) *Geomorphology* still testified to his influence. However, a criticism of work in physical geography influenced by Davis was that it lacked sufficient knowledge of environmental processes. For instance, in geomorphology it was pointed out that although the Davisian cycle of erosion embraced structure, process and stage or time, the emphasis had invariably been on stage, with very little upon process. Sims (2003) notes that 'Process studies became very much "The Holy Grail" of geomorphology from the late 60s onwards.' In geomorphology, the developing science of hydrology gained importance, focusing on drainage basins and catchments. The predominant interest in fluvial processes came from a recognition that many geomorphologists had studied humid temperate landforms without explaining the processes involved, and that techniques were becoming available to establish short-, medium- and longer-term field experiments in which processes and detailed changes in the environment could be studied at a range of scales. There were studies of fluvial processes on hill slopes in small catchments, a renewed interest in channel form and pattern, the solute and sediment loads in rivers, and so on. This is the approach to physical geography that tends to be found in schools at higher levels of study.

2 That these ideas are no longer held by the majority of geography educators can perhaps be seen in the critical response to the writings of Alex Standish, particularly in his 2009 book *Global perspectives in the geography curriculum*. Echoing the ideas of writers such as Frank Furedi (discussed in chapter one), he argues that geography has become informed by an anti-development stance that seeks to turn the clock back on human progress.

3 It has become common to identify a strong social constructivism. An example is Keith Tester's (1991) *Animals and society: the humanity of animal rights*. Another example is William Cronon's (1996) edited collection *Uncommon ground: rethinking the human place in nature*. Macnaghten and Urry's (1998) *Contested natures* and John Hannigan's (2006) *Environmental sociology* see nature as a social construction.

Chapter 6

1 In developing such curriculum materials, geography teachers will be supported by Lisa Benton-Short and John Rennie Short's (2008) *Cities and nature*, which provides a comprehensive introduction to the literature. They survey a wide range of environmental issues in cities, and are attentive to what they call the 'current wave of urban transformation', which includes the impact of giant urban regions and megacities, post-industrial cities and brownfields, urban sprawl, new industrial spaces and shanty towns. Also, Roberts *et al.*'s (2009) *Environment and the city* offers a useful overview of attempts to manage urban environments in sustainable ways.

Chapter 7

1 These were its commitment to individual methodism, its acceptance of Marshallian marginal economics, and its lack of attention to historical context.

Chapter 8

1 At school in the 1980s, I remember learning about the coming 'ice age', which was popularised by the science writer John Gribbin. We were all intrigued by the line in The Clash's song *London Calling* that went 'The ice age is coming/the sun's zooming in/engines stop running/the wheat is growing thin', though I imagine we mixed all this up in our minds with fears of a 'nuclear winter' triggered by nuclear war. When I started teaching, there was a growing sense of global crisis linked to the environment that was expressed in terms of acid rain and the hole in the ozone layer.

2 In chapter four, we noted how the Edexcel AS specification has a unit called Global Challenges, which is intended to teach students about 'headline global issues'.

Chapter 9

1 In writing this account, I have had to think very carefully about the evidence for this. I have worked as a teacher educator for the past ten years, which has entailed roughly 500 visits to student teachers in schools, where I have observed lessons and discussed with mentors. I have examined PGCE courses and held numerous conversations with other teacher educators. I have worked on a PGCE course where there has been a gradual increase in demands to provide evidence that students (or trainees, as we are urged to call them) are meeting the Standards. Increasingly, in talking to teachers I get myself into trouble by even gently raising questions about what is seen as 'good' practice across departments and schools. I read assignments from student teachers that are full of the jargon of gifted and talented, strategies, and the obligatory references to assessment for learning. The one thing I find that nobody wants to talk about is the nature of the geography that is being taught to pupils in schools.

References

ACDG (1983) 'Editorial: An introduction to contemporary issues in geography and education', *Contemporary Issues in Geography and Education* 1 (1): 1–4.

Adair, G. (1986) *Myths and memories*. London: Fontana.

Ainley, P. and Allen, M. (2010) *Lost generation? New strategies for youth and education*. London: Continuum.

Amin, A. (1994) *Post-Fordism: a reader*. Oxford: Blackwell.

Angotti, T. (2006) 'Apocolyptic antiurbanism: Mike Davis and his planet of slums', *International Journal of Urban and Regional Research*, 30 (4): 961–7.

Apple, M. (1979) *Ideology and curriculum*. London: Routledge.

Apple, M. (2000) *Official knowledge: democratic education in a Conservative age*. London: Routledge.

Arnot, M. (2006) 'Retrieving the ideological past: critical sociology, gender theory, and the school curriculum', in L. Weis, C. McCarthy and G. Dimitriadis (eds) *Ideology, curriculum, and the new sociology of education*. London: Routledge, 17–36.

Ashley, B., Hollows, J., Jones, S. and Taylor, B. (2004) *Food and cultural studies*. London: Routledge.

Bale, J. (1985) 'Industrial geography 11–19' in G. Corney (ed.) *Geography, schools and industry*. Sheffield: Geographical Association, pp.28–36.

Beatley, T. (2000) *Green urbanism*. Washington DC: Island Press.

Beck, U. (1992) *The risk society*. London: Sage.

Belasco, W. (2008) *Food: the key concepts*. Oxford: Berg Publishers.

Bell, D. and Valentine, G. (1997) *Consuming geographies: we are where we eat*. London: Routledge.

Benko, G. and Scott, A. (2004) 'Economic geography: tradition and turbulence', in G. Benko and U. Strohmayer (eds), pp.47–63 *Human geography: a history for the 21st century*. London: Arnold.

Benton-Short, L. and Short, J.R. (2008) *Cities and nature*. London: Routledge.

Bjerknes, J. and Solberg, H. (1922) 'The life cycle of cyclones and the polar front theory of atmospheric circulation', *Geofysiske Publikationer* 3 (1): 3–18.

Blaikie, P., Cannon, T., Davis, I. and Wisner, B. (2004) *At risk: natural hazards, people's vulnerability, and disasters*. London: Routledge.

Boserup, E. (1965) *Conditions of agricultural growth: the economics of agrarian change under population pressure*. Chicago, IL: Aldine.

Bowers, J.K. and Cheshire, P. (1983) *Agriculture, the countryside and land use: an economic critique*. London: Methuen.

Brabazon, T. (2008) *The University of Google: education in the (post) information age*. Aldershot, UK: Ashgate.

Brown, C. (2008) *The death of Christian Britain*, 2nd edn. London: Routledge.

Buchanan, C. (1958) *Mixed blessing: the motor car in Britain*. London: Leonard Hill Books.

Buchanan, C. (1964) *Traffic in towns*. London: HMSO.

Burke, G. (1976) *Townscapes*. London: Penguin.

Butcher, J. (2003) *The moralisation of tourism: sun, sand – and saving the world?* London: Routledge.

Capra, F. (1982) *The turning point*. London: Fontana.

Carlson, C. (2010) *Nowtopia*. New York: AK Press.

Carson, R. (1962) *Silent spring*. Boston, MA: Houghton Mifflin.

Castree, N. (2005) *Nature*. London: Routledge.

Castree, N. (2009) 'The environmental wedge: neoliberalism, democracy and the prospects for a new British left', in P. Devine, A. Pearmain and D. Purdy (eds) *Feelbad Britain: how to make it better*. London: Lawrence & Wishart, 222–33.

Castree, N. and Braun, B. (eds) (2001) *Social nature: theory, practice and politics*. Oxford: Blackwell.

Castree, N., Coe, N., Ward, K. and Samers, M. (2003) *Spaces of work: global capitalism and geographies of labour*. London: Sage.

Castree, N., Demeritt, D., Liverman, D. and Rhoads, B. (eds) (2009) *A companion to environmental geography*. London: Sage.

Chatterton, P. (2010) 'Do it yourself: a politics for changing our world', in K. Birch and V. Mykhenko (eds) pp.188–205, *The rise and fall of neoliberalism. The collapse of an economic order?* London: Zed Books.

Chisholm, M. (ed.) (1972) *Resources for Britain's future: a series from the* Geographical Magazine. Harmondsworth, UK: Penguin.

Christian, G. (1966) 'Education for the environment', *The Quarterly Review*, April.

Clarke, J. and Willis, P. (1984) 'Introduction', in I. Bates., J. Clarke, P. Cohen, D. Finn, R. Moore and P. Willis (eds) pp.1–16 *Schooling for the dole? The new vocationalism*. Basingstoke, UK: Macmillan.

Clements, D., Donald, A., Earnshaw, M. and Williams, A. (eds) (2008). *The future of community (reports of a death greatly exaggerated)*. London: Pluto Press.

Clements, R.E. (1928) *Plant succession and indicators*. New York: H.W. Wilson.

Colls, R. (2002) *Identity of England*. Oxford: Oxford University Press.

Commoner, B. (1970) *Science and survival*. New York: Ballantine Books.

Cons, G. J. and Fletcher, C. (1938) *Actuality in school: an experiment in social education*. London: Methuen.

Cottle, S. (2009) *Global crisis reporting: journalism in the global age*. Buckingham: Open University Press.

Cronon, W. (1991) *Nature's metropolis: Chicago and the Great West*. New York: W.W. Norton.

Cronon, W. (ed.) (1996) *Uncommon ground: rethinking the human place in nature*. New York: Norton.

Crutzen, P. (2002) 'Geology of mankind', *Nature* 415: 23.

Dalby, S. (2009) *Security and environmental change*. Cambridge: Polity Press.

Davis, M. (1998) *Ecology of fear: Los Angeles and the imagination of disaster*. London: Picador.

Davis, M. (2006) *Planet of slums*. London: Verso.

Day, C., Sammons, P., Stobart, G., Kington, A. and Qing Gu (2007) *Teachers matter: connecting lives, work and effectiveness*. Maidenhead, UK: Open University Press.

Department for the Environment (1972) *How do you want to live? A report on the human habitat*. London: HMSO.

Devine, P., Pearmain, A. and Purdy, D. (eds) (2009) *Feelbad Britain: how to make it better*. London: Lawrence & Wishart.

Diamond, J. (2005) *Collapse: how societies choose to fail or succeed*. London: Penguin.

Dobson, A. and Bell, D. (eds) (2005) *Environmental citizenship: getting from here to there*. Cambridge, MA: MIT Press.

Doddington, C. and Hilton, M. (2007) *Child-centred education: reviving the creative tradition.* London: Sage.

Donald, A. (2008) 'A green unpleasant land', in D. Clements, A. Donald, M. Earnshaw and A. Williams (eds) *The future of community (reports of a death greatly exaggerated).* London: Pluto Press.

Donald, A., Williams, R., Sharro, K., Farlie, A., Kuypers, D. and Williams, A. (2008) *Mantownhuman: towards a new humanism in architecture.* London: ManTownhuman. www. futurecities.org.uk/images/mantownhuman.pdf

Donnelly, M. (2005) *Sixties Britain: culture, society and politics.* London: Pearson.

Dorling, D. (2010) *Injustice: why social inequality persists.* Bristol: Policy Press.

Douglas, I. (1984) *The urban environment.* London: Edward Arnold.

Dryzek, J. and Schlosberg, D. (2001) *Debating the Earth.* Oxford: Oxford University Press.

Dunn, B. (2009) *Global political economy: a Marxist critique.* London: Pluto Press.

Dwyer, C. (1998) 'Contested idenitites: challenging dominant representations of young British Muslim women', in T. Skelton and G. Valentine (eds) *Cool places: geographies of youth cultures.* London: Routledge, 50–65.

Ecclestone, K. and Hayes, D. (2008) *The dangerous rise of therapeutic education.* London: Routledge.

Eckersley, R. (2004) *The green state: rethinking democracy and sovereignty.* Cambridge, MA: MIT Press.

Edensor, T. (2005) *Industrial ruins: spaces, aesthetics and materiality.* London: Berg.

Ehrlich, P. and Ehrlich, A. (1968) *The population bomb.* New York: Ballantine Books.

Elkington, J. and Hailes, J. (1988) *The green consumer guide.* London: Gollancz.

Elliott, A. and Urry, J. (2010) *Mobile lives.* London and New York: Routledge.

Engels, F. (1849, 2005) *The condition of the working class in England in 1844.* London: Penguin.

Ferguson, M. (1980) *The Aquarian conspiracy.* Los Angeles: J.P. Tarcher.

Fien, J. and Gerber, R. (eds) (1988) *Teaching geography for a better world.* London: Oliver & Boyd.

Fine, B. and Milonakis, D. (2009) *From economics imperialism to freakonomics: the shifting boundary between economics and other social sciences.* London: Routledge.

Forsyth, T. (2003) *Critical political ecology: the politics of environmental science.* London: Routledge.

Foster, J. (2009) *The sustainability mirage: illusion and reality in the coming war on climate change.* London: Earthscan.

Frank, R.H. (2008) *The economic naturalist: why economics explains almost everything.* London: Virgin Books.

Frankel, B. (1987) *The post-industrial utopians.* Cambridge: Polity Press.

Friedan, B. (1963) *The feminine mystique.* New York: Norton.

Furedi, F. (2009) 'What happened to radical humanism?' in J. Pugh (ed.) *What is radical politics today?* Basingstoke: Palgrave Macmillan 27–35.

GA (2009) *A different view: a manifesto from the Geographical Association.* Sheffield: Geographical Association.

Gandy, M. (2002) *Concrete and clay: re-working nature in New York City.* Cambridge, MA: MIT Press.

Gerhardt, S. (2010) *The selfish society: how we all forgot to love one another and made money instead.* London: Simon & Schuster.

Gibson-Graham, J.-K. (1996) *The end of capitalism (as we knew it).* Oxford: Blackwell.

Goldsmith, E., Allen, Pz., Allaby, M., Davoll, J., and Lawrence, S. *A Blueprint for Survival.* London: Penguin.

Goodman, D. and Redclift, M. (1991) *Refashioning nature: food, ecology and culture.* London: Routledge.

Grace, G. (1995) *School leadership: beyond education management.* Brighton, UK: Falmer Press.

Graves, N. (1975) *Geography in education.* London: Heinemann.

Graves, N. (1979) *Curriculum planning in geography*. London: Heinemann

Gray-Donald, J. and Selby, D. (2008) 'Introduction' in J. Gray-Donald and D. Selby (eds.) *Green frontiers: environmental educators dancing away from mechanism*. Rotterdam: Senso Publishers, pp.1–10.

Greig, S., Pike, G. and Selby, D. (1987) *Earthrights: education as if the planet really mattered*. London: Kogan Page/WWF-UK.

Hall, D. (1976) *Geography and the geography teacher*. London: Allen & Unwin.

Hanlon, B., Short, J.R. and Vicino, T. (2010) *Cities and suburbs: new metropolitan realities in the United States*. London: Routledge.

Hannigan, J. (2006) *Environmental sociology*, 2nd edn. London: Routledge.

Hargreaves, D. (1999) 'The knowledge-creating school', *British Journal of Educational Studies* 47(2): 122–44.

Harrison, B. (2009) *Seeking a role: the United Kingdom 1951–70*. Oxford: Oxford University Press.

Hartshorne (1939) *The Nature of Geography*. Lancaster, PA. Association of American Geographers.

Harvey, D. (1974) 'What kind of geography for what kind of public policy?' *Transactions of the Institute of British Geographers*, 63, pp.18–24.

Harvey, D. (1996) *Justice, Nature and the geography of difference*. Oxford: Blackwell.

Harvey, D. (2005) *A brief history of neoliberalism*. Edinburgh: Edinburgh University Press.

Harvey, D. (2010) *The enigma of capital (and the crises of capitalism)*. London: Profile Books.

Hawken, P., Lovins, A. and Hunter Lovins, L. (2010) *Natural capitalism; the next industrial revolution*, 2nd edn. London: Earthscan.

Henderson, G. and Waterstone, M. (eds) (2009) *Geographic thought: a praxis perspective*. London: Routledge.

Herbert, D. (1972) *Urban geography: a social perspective*. Newton Abbot, UK: David & Charles.

Herbertson, A.J. and Herbertson, F.D. (1899/1963) *Man and his work: an introduction to human geography*, 8th edn. London: A. & C. Black.

Herod, A. (2009) *Geographies of globalization: a critical introduction*. Chichester: Wiley.

Hewitt, K. (ed.) (1983) *Interpretations of calamity from the viewpoint of human ecology*. Boston, MA: Allen & Unwin.

Heynen, N., Kaika, M. and Swyngedouw, E. (eds) (2006) *In the nature of cities: urban political ecology and the politics of urban metabolism*. London: Routledge.

Hickman, G., Reynolds, J. and Tolley, H. (1973) *A new professionalism for a changing geography*. London: Schools Council.

Holloway, J. (2010) *Crack capitalism*. London: Pluto Press.

Hoskins, W.G. (1955) *The making of the English landscape*. London: Hodder & Stoughton.

Hough, G. (1984) *City form and natural process*. London: Croom Helm.

Howard, E. (1898/1985) *Garden cities of to-morrow: a peaceful path to real reform*. Eastbourne, UK: Attic Press.

Huckle, J. (ed.) (1983) *Geographical education: reflection and action*. Oxford: Oxford University Press.

Huckle, J. (1985) 'Geography and schooling', in R. Johnston (ed.) *The future of geography*. London: Methuen, 291–306.

Huckle, J. (1986) 'Ecological crisis: some implications for geographical education', *Contemporary Issues in Geography and Education* 2 (2): 2–13.

Huckle, J. (1988–93) *What we consume: The teachers' handbook* and eight curriculum units. A module of WWF's Global Environmental Education Programme. Godalming and Oxford: WWF and Richmond Publishing.

Huckle, J. and Martin, A. (2001) *Environments in a changing world*. London: Pearson.

Hudson, R. (2000) *Producing places*. New York: Guilford Press.

Hudson, R. and Williams, A. (1986) *The United Kingdom*. London: Harper and Row.

Hulme, M. (2009) *Why we disagree about climate change*. Cambridge: Cambridge University Press.

Humble, N. (2005) *Culinary pleasures: cookbooks and the transformation of British cuisine*. London: Faber & Faber.

Humphery, K. (2008) *Excess*. Cambridge: Polity Press.

Ilbery, B. and Bowler, I. (1998) 'From agricultural productivism to post-productivism' in B. Ilbery (ed.) pp.54–84, *The geography of rural change*. Harlow: Longman.

Inglis, F. (1975) *Ideology and imagination*. Cambridge: Cambridge University Press.

Inness, S. (2006) *Secret ingredients: race, gender and class at the dinner table*. New York and Basingstoke: Palgrave Macmillan.

Irwin, A. and Michael, M. (2003) *Science, social theory and public knowledge*. Maidenhead, UK: Open University Press.

Jackson, P. (1989) *Maps of meaning: an introduction to cultural geography*. London: Unwin Hyman.

James, O. (2007) *Affluenza*. London: Vermillion.

James, O. (2008) *The selfish capitalist: origins of affluenza*. London: Vermillion.

James, O. (2010) *Britain on the couch: how keeping up with the Joneses has depressed us since 1950* (first published 1998). London: Vermillion.

Jarvis, H. (2005) *Work/life city limits; comparative household perspectives*. Basingstoke: Palgrave Macmillan.

Jarvis, H., Pratt, A. and Cheng-Chang Wu (2001) *The secret life of cities: the social reproduction of everyday life*. London: Prentice Hall.

Joad, C.E.M. (1935) *The book of Joad*: a belligerant autobiography. London: Faber & Faber.

Johnston, J. and Baumann, S. (2010) *Foodies: democracy and distinction in the gourmet foodscape*. London: Routledge.

Johnston, R. (1989) *Environmental problems: nature, economy and state*. London: Belhaven Press.

Johnston, R. and Taylor, P. (eds) (1986) *A world in crisis? Geographical perspectives*. Oxford: Blackwell.

Kaika, M. (2005) *City of flows: modernity, nature and the city*. London: Routledge.

Keil, R. and Graham, J. (1998) 'Reasserting nature: constructing urban environments after Fordism', in B. Braun and N. Castree (eds) *Remaking reality: nature at the millennium*. London: Routledge, 100–25.

Klingle, M. (2007) *Emerald City: an environmental history of Seattle*. New Haven: Yale University Press.

Knox, P. (2011) *Cities and design*. London: Routledge.

Knox, P. and Mayer, H. (2009) *Small town sustainability*. Basel: Birkhäuser Verlay AG.

Kovel, J. (2007) *The enemy of nature: the end of capitalism or the end of the world?*, 2nd edn. London: Zed Books.

Kunstler, J.H. (2005) *The long emergency: surviving the converging catastrophes of the twenty-first century*. London: Atlantic Books.

Lang, T., Barling, D. and Caraher, M. (2009) *Food policy: integrating health, environment and society*. Oxford: Oxford University Press.

Lappé, F.M. (1971) *Diet for a small planet*. New York: Ballantine Books.

Lash, S. and Urry, J. (1987) *The end of organized capitalism*. Madison, WI: University of Wisconsin Press.

Lash, S. and Urry, J. (1994) *Economies of signs and space*. London: Sage.

Lawson, N. (2009) *All consuming*. London: Penguin.

Levitt, S. and Dubner, S. (2006) *Freakonomics: a rogue economist explores the hidden side of everything*. London: Penguin.

Lewis, and Potter (eds) (2010) *Ethical consumption*. London: Routledge.

Leyshon, A., Lee, R. and Williams, C. (eds) (2003) *Alternative economic spaces*. London: Sage.

Littler, J. (2008) *Radical consumption*. Buckingham: Open University Press.

Lowe, P. *et al.* (1986) *Countryside conflicts*. Aldershot: Cower.

Lowe, R. (2007) *The death of progressive education: how teachers lost control of the classroom*. London: Routledge.

McGuigan, J. (2010) *Cool capitalism*. London: Pluto Press.

Machon, P. (1987) 'Teaching controversial issues: some observations and reflections', in P. Bailey and T. Binns (eds) *A case for geography*. Sheffield, UK: Geographical Association.

Macnaghten, P. and Urry, J. (1998) *Contested natures*. London: Sage.

Marr, A. (2007) *A history of modern Britain*. London: Macmillan.

Marsden, W. (1976) *Evaluating the geography curriculum*. London: Oliver & Boyd.

Marsden, W.E. (1996) *Geography 11–16: re-kindling good practice*. London: David Fulton.

Marston, S., Jones, J.P. III and Woodward, K. (2005) 'Human geography without scale', *Transactions of the Institute of British Geographers* 30(4): 416–32.

Martin, R. (1999) 'The new geographical turn in economics: some critical reflections', *Cambridge Journal of Economics*, 23 (1): 65–91.

Massey, D. (1984) Spatial divisions of labour. Basingstoke: Macmillan.

Massey, D. (2009) 'Invention and hardwork', in J. Pugh (ed.) *What is radical politics today?* Basingstoke: Palgrave Macmillan, 136–42.

Matthews, J. and Herbert, D. (eds) (2004) *Unifying geography: common heritage, shared future*. London: Routledge.

May, J. (1996) 'A little taste of something more exotic: the imaginative geographies of everyday life'. *Geography*, 81(1), 57–64.

Meadows, D.H., Meadows, D.L., Randers, J. and Behrens, W.W. III (1972) *The limits to growth*. London: Earth Island.

Mercer, C. (1975) *Living in cities*. London: Penguin.

Milanokis, D. and Fine, B. (2009) *From political economy to economics*. London: Routledge.

Miller, D. (ed.) (1995) *Acknowledging consumption*. London: Routledge.

Miller, D. and Dinan, W. (2008) *A century of spin: how public relations became the cutting edge of corporate power*. London: Pluto Press.

Milonakis, D. and Fine, B. (2009) *From political economy to economics: method, the social and the historical in the evolution of economic theory*. London: Routledge.

Monk, J. and Hanson, S. (1982) 'On not excluding half of the human in human geography', *Professional Geographer*, 34 (1): 11–23.

Moore, A. (2004) *The 'good' teacher: dominant discourses in teaching and teacher education*. London: RoutledgeFalmer.

Moore, P., Chaloner, B. and Stott, P. (1996) *Global environmental change*. Oxford: Blackwell.

Moran, J. (2007) 'Subtopias of everyday life'. *Cultural and Social History* 4(3) pp.401–421.

Mort, F. (1996) *Cultures of consumption*. London: Routledge.

Nairn, I. (1964) *Your England revisited*. London: Hutchinson.

Neill, J.R. (2000) *Something new under the sun: an environmental history of the twentieth century*. London: Penguin.

Newby, H. (1979) *A green and pleasant land? Social change in rural England*. London: Penguin.

Newell, P. and Paterson, M. (2010) *Climate capitalism: global warming and the transformation of the global economy*. Cambridge: Cambridge University Press.

O'Connor, J. (1996) '*The Second Contradiction in Capitalism*', in T. Benton (ed.) *The Greening of Marxism*. New York: Guilford Press, 197–221.

O'Keefe, P., Westgate, K. and Wisner, B. (1976) 'Taking the naturalness out of natural disasters', *Nature* 260: 566–67.

O'Riordan, T. (1976) *Environmentalism*. London: Pion.

Oliver, J. (2001) *Happy days with the naked chef*. London: Michael Joseph.

Outka, E. (2009) *Consuming tradition: modernity, modernism and the commodified authentic*. New York: Oxford University Press.

Page, M. (2008) *The city's end*. New Haven, CT and London: Yale University Press.

Panayi, P. (2008) *Spicing up Britain: the multicultural history of British food*. London: Reaktion Books.

Park, R.E. and Burgess, E.N. (1967) *The city*. Chicago, IL: Phoenix Books.

Patel, R. (2008) *Stuffed and starved: the hidden battle for world food*. London: Portabello.

Peet, R. (2008) *Geography power: the making of global economic policy*. London: Zed Books.

Pepper, D. (1984) *The roots of modern environmentalism*. London: Routledge.

Pepper, D. (1986) 'Why teach physical geography?' *Contemporary Issues in Geography and Education*, 2(2), pp.62–71.

Phillips, M. and Mignall, T. (2000) *Society and exploitation through nature*. London: Pearson.

Pickles, J. (1986) 'Geographic theory and educating for democracy', *Antipode* 18: 136–54.

Pike, G. and Selby, D. (1988) *Global teacher, global learner*. London: Hodder and Stoughton.

Pollan, M. (2004) *The omnivore's dilemma*. London: Bloomsbury.

Pollan, M. (2008) *In defence of food: the myth of nutrition and the pleasures of eating*. London: Allen Lane.

Porritt, J. (1984) *Seeing green*. Oxford: Basil Blackwell.

Porritt, J. (2005) *Capitalism as if the world matters*. London: Earthscan.

Preston, W.C. (1883) *The bitter cry of outcast London: an inquiry into the condition of the abject poor*. London: James Clarke & Co. www.archive.org/details/bittercryofoutca00pres

Project Environment (1975) *Ethics and environment*. London: Schools Council/Longman.

Pye-Smith, C. and Rose, C. (1984) *Conservation in crisis*. London: Penguin.

QCDA (2009) *Sustainable development in action – a curriculum planning guide for schools*. Coventry: Qualifications and Curriculum Development Agency.

Rawling, E. (2000) *Changing the subject: the impact of national policy on school geography 1980-2000*. Sheffield, UK: Geographical Association.

Relph, E. (1976) *Place and placelessness*. London: Pion.

Robbins, P. (2004) *Political ecology: a critical introduction*. Chichester: Wiley.

Robbins, P., Hintz, J. and Moore, S. (2010) *Environment and society: a critical introduction*. Chichester: Wiley.

Roberts, P. (2009) *The end of food: the coming crisis in the world food industry*. London: Bloomsbury.

Roberts, P., Ravetz, J. and George, C. (2009) *Environment and the city*. London: Routledge.

Sack, R. (1992) *Place, modernity and the consumer's world*. Baltimore: John Hopkins Press.

Sandbrook, D. (2005) *Never had it so good: a history of Britain from Suez to the Beatles*. London: Abacus.

Sandlin, J. and McLaren, P. (eds) (2010) *Critical pedagogies of consumption: living and learning in the shadow of the shopocalypse*. London: Routledge.

Sayer, A. (1986) 'Systematic mystification: the 16–19 project', *Contemporary Issues in Geography and Education*, 2(2), pp.86–93.

Schaefer, F.K. (1953) 'Exceptionalism in geography: a methodological examination', *Annals of the Association of American Geographers* 43: 226–45.

Schlosser, E. (2002) *Fast food nation: what the all-American meal is doing to the world*. London: Penguin.

Schlosser, E. and Wilson, C. (2006) *Chew on this: everything you don't want to know about fast food*. New York: Houghton Mifflin.

Schumacher, E.F. (1973) *Small is beautiful: economics as if the planet mattered*. London: Harper and Row.

Seager, J. (1993) *Earth follies: coming to feminist terms with the global environmental crisis*. New York: Routledge.

Selby, D. (2008) 'The need for climate change in education', in J. Gray-Donald and D. Selby (eds) *Green frontiers: environmental educators dancing away from mechanism*. Rotterdam: Sense, 252–62.

Shields, R. (1991) *Places on the margins: alternative geographies of modernity*. London: Routledge.

Shields, R. (ed.) (1994) *Liefstyle shopping*. London: Routledge.

Shoard, M. (1980) *The theft of the countryside*. London: Temple Smith

Short, J.R. (2008) *Urban theory: a critical appraisal*. Basingstoke: Macmillan.

Shurmer-Smith, P. (2002) *Doing cultural geography*. London: Sage.

Sim, S. (2010) *The end of modernity: what the financial and environmental crisis is really telling us*. Edinburgh: Edinburgh University Press.

Simms, A. (2008) *Ecological debt: global warming and the wealth of nations*, 2nd edn. London: Pluto Press.

Sims, P. (2003) 'Previous actors and current influences: trends and fashions in physical geography', in S. Trudgill and A. Roy (eds) *Contemporary meanings in physical geography: from what to why?* London: Arnold, 3–23.

Skelton, T. and Valentine, G. (eds) (1998) *Cool places: geographies of youth cultures*. London: Routledge.

Sklair, L. (2009) 'Commentary from the Consumerist/Oppressive City to the Functional/ Emancipatory City'. *Urban Studies* 46 (12), 2703–2711.

Slater, C. (2003) *Entangled Edens: visions of the Amazon*. Berkeley, CA: University of California Press.

Smart, B. (2010) *The consumer society*. London: Sage.

Smith, D. (1971) *Industrial location*. London: Wiley.

Smith, D.M. (1974) 'Who gets what, where, and how: a welfare focus for geography', *Geography: An International Journal* 59: 289–97.

Smith, N. (1984) *Uneven development: nature, capital and the production of space*. Athens, GA: University of Georgia Press.

Smith, N. (1993) 'Homeless/global: scaling places', in J. Bird (ed.) *Mapping the futures*. London: Routledge, 87–119

Smith, N. (2007) 'Nature as accumulation strategy', in L. Panitch and C. Leys (eds), pp.16–36, *Coming to terms with nature*. London: Verso.

Soper, K. (2007) 'Paper from Kate Soper to Sustainable Development Commission Meeting on "Living well (within limits) – exploring the relationship between growth and wellbeing"', www.sd-commission.org.uk/publications/downloads/kate_soper_thinkpiece.pdf

Soper, K. (2009) 'The fulfilments of post-consumerism and the politics of renewal', in P. Devine, A. Pearmain and D. Purdy (eds) *Feelbad Britain: how to make it better*. London: Lawrence & Wishart, 130–40.

Speth, J.G. (2008) *The bridge at the end of the world: capitalism, the environment and crossing from crisis to sustainability*. Newhaven, CT: Yale University Press.

Stamp, D. and Beaver, S. (1954) *The British Isles: a geographic and economic survey*, 4th edn. London: Longman.

Standish, A. (2009) *Global perspectives in the geography curriculum: reviewing the moral case for geography*. London: Routledge.

Stanford, J. (2008) *Economics for everyone: a short guide to the economics of capitalism*. London: Pluto Press.

Steel, C. (2008) *Hungry city: how food shapes our lives*. London: Chatto and Windus

Steffen, W., Crutzen, P. and McNeill, J.R. (2007) 'The Anthropocene: are humans now overwhelming the great forces of nature?', *Ambio* 36 (8): 614–21.

Storm, M. (1973) 'Schools and the community: an issues-based approach' in J. Bale, N. Graves and R. Wilford (eds.) *Perspectives in Geographical Education*. London: Oliver and Boyd, pp.289–303.

Stott, P. (2001) 'Jungles of the mind: the invention of the "Tropical Rain Forest"', *History Today* 51 (5): 38–44.

Stott, P. and Sullivan, S. (eds) (2003) *Political ecology: science, myth and power*. London: Arnold.

Stretton, H. (1976) *Capitalism, socialism and the environment*. Cambridge: Cambridge University Press.

Susman, P., O'Keefe, P. and Wisner, B. (1983) 'Global disasters, a radical interpretation', in K. Hewitt (ed.) *Interpretations of calamity from the viewpoint of human ecology*. Boston, MA: Allen & Unwin, pp.263–283.

Svensen, H. (2009) *The end is nigh: a history of natural disasters*. London: Reaktion Books.

Swyngedouw, E. (2007) 'Impossible "sustainability" and the postpolitical condition', in R. Krueger and D. Gibbs (eds) pp.13–40, *The sustainable development paradox: urban political economy in the United States and Europe*. New York: Guilford Press.

Szerszynski, B. (2005) *Nature, technology and the sacred*. Oxford: Blackwell.

Tainter, J. (1988) *The collapse of complex societies*. Cambridge: Cambridge University Press.

Taverne, R. (2005) *The march of unreason: science, democracy and the new fundamentalism*. Oxford: Oxford University Press.

Tester, K. (1991) *Animals and society: the humanity of animal rights*. London: Routledge.

Thompson, D. (1952) 'Your England – and how to defend it', The Use of English Pamphlet No. 1.

Timberlake, L. (1985) *Africa in crisis*. London: Earthscan.

Tomlinson, A. (1990) 'Introduction: consumer culture and the aura of the commodity', in A. Tomlinson (ed.) p.1–40, *Consumption, identity and style: marketing, meanings, and the packaging of pleasure*. London: Routledge.

Tomlinson, A. (ed.) (1990) *Consumption, identity and style*. London: Routledge.

Townsend, A. (1993) *Uneven regional change in Britain*. Cambridge: Cambridge University Press.

Tudge, C. (2004) *So shall we reap: what's gone wring with the world's food – and how to fix it*. London: Penguin.

Urry, J. (2000) *Sociology beyond societies: mobilities for the twenty-first century*. London and New York: Routledge.

Urry, J. (2007) *Mobilities*. Cambridge: Polity Press.

Urry, J. (2010) 'Consuming the planet to excess', *Theory, Culture and Society*, 27(2–3), 191–212.

Ward, C. (1978) *The child in the city*. London: Penguin.

Weeks, J. (2007) *The world we have won*. London: Routledge.

Weight, R. (2002) *Patriots: national identity in Britain 1940–2000*. London: Macmillan.

von Weizsacker, E., Lovins, A. and Hunter Lovins, L. (1997) *Factor four: doubling wealth, halving resources use*. London: Earthscan.

von Weizsacker, E., Hargroves, K., Smith, M., Desha, C. and Stasiniopoulos, P. (2009) *Factor five: transforming the global economy through 80% improvements in resource productivity*. London: Earthscan.

Wheeler, K. (1975) 'The genesis of environmental education' in G. Martin and K. Wheeler (eds.) *Insights into environment education*. Edinburgh: Oliver and Boyd.

Wheeler, K. and Waites, B. (eds) (1976) *Environmental geography: a handbook for teachers*. St. Albans: Hart-Davis Educational.

White, D. and Wilbert, C. (eds) (2009) *Technonatures: environments, technologies, spaces and places in the twenty-first century*. Waterloo, ON, Canada: Wilfrid Laurier University Press.

Whitehead, M. (2007) *Spaces of sustainability*. London: Routledge.

Whitehead, P. (1985) *The writing on the wall: Britain in the seventies*. London: Michael Joseph.

Wilkinson, R. and Pickett, K. (2009) *The spirit level: why equality is better for everyone*. London: Penguin.

Williams, A. (2008) *The enemies of progress: dangers of sustainability*. London: Societas.

Williams, C. (2005) *A commodified world? Mapping the limits of capitalism*. London: Zed Books.

Williams, R. (1976) *Keywords*. London: Fontana.

Williams-Ellis, C. (1928) *England and the octopus*. Penrhyndeudraeth, Wales, UK: Portmeiron.

Williams-Ellis, C. (ed.) (1937) *Britain and the beast*. London: Dent.

Wolch, J. (2007) 'Green urban worlds', *Annals of the Association of American Geographers* 97: 373–84.

Wolch, J. and Emel, J. (eds) (1998) *Animal geographies: place, politics and identity in the nature–culture borderlands*. London: Verso.

Work Foundation (2006). *Ideopolis: Bristol Case Study*. London: Work Foundation. Available at: http://www.theworkfoundation.com/research/publications/publicationdetail.aspx?oItemId=130&parentPageID+102&PubTypre= (last accessed 6 June 2011).

World Commission on Environment and Development (1987) *Our common future*. Oxford: Oxford University Press.

Worldwrite (2002) *Time to ditch the sustainababble: a critical memorandum*. London: Worldwrite. www.worldwrite.org.uk/criticalcharter.pdf

Wright, W. and Middendorf, G. (eds) (2007) *The fight over food: producers, consumers and activists challenge the global food system*. University Park, PA: Penn State University Press.

Young, M.F.D. (ed.) (1971) *Knowledge and control: new directions for the sociology of education*. London: Collier Macmillan.

Zalasiewicz, J. *et al* (2008) 'Are we now living in the anthropocene?' *GSA Today*. 18(2): 4–8.

Index

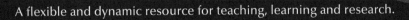